THE NORTHEAST
1861

0   50   100   200   300
SCALE OF MILES

81°   78°   75°

MAINE

Bangor
Freedom
45°

CANADA

Malone
Potsdam

NEW YORK

VT.

N.H.
CONCORD

Yarmouth
Saco

Auburn   Syracuse
Richfield Springs
Cooperstown   ALBANY
Ithaca
Corning

LAKE ONTARIO
Buffalo

RIE

Lowell   Haverhill
Stoneham
BOSTON   FORT WARREN
42°

HARTFORD
CONN.
New Haven

PROVIDENCE
New Bedford
R.I.

HUDSON R.

DELAWARE R.

PENNSYLVANIA

New York
Easton   N.J.
Brooklyn
FORT LAFAYETTE

OCEAN

Pittsburgh
HARRISBURG   Philadelphia   TRENTON
Steubenville   West Chester   Burlington
Chambersburg   Wilmington
Baltimore
ANNAPOLIS
WASHINGTON   FORT
BULL RUN   McHENRY   DEL.
39°

VIRGINIA   MD.

RICHMOND

RALEIGH

Big Bethel   FORTRESS
MONROE

ATLANTIC

36°

Elizabeth
City   ROANOKE
ISLAND

NORTH CAROLINA

New Bern   CAPE
HATTERAS

·········· Approximate extent
of control by Union
forces, Sept. 1861

FREEDOM UNDER LINCOLN

Dean Sprague

As the Civil War began, the Lincoln Administration faced in its most acute form the timeless problem of how to govern free men in the midst of overwhelming crisis. How far should the need for a strong government yield to the rights of states and people? To what degree do the imperatives of crisis justify the suspension of constitutional liberties?

Freedom Under Lincoln tells us the dramatic story of how Lincoln and his administration handled this problem. It is a little-known chapter of history, never before so skillfully told.

The story starts with the rioting of the Baltimore mobs as Northern troops cross the city on the way to defend Washington. Although the soldiers are temporarily prevented from getting through, we see the full power of the federal government slowly swung into the balance against Maryland, as the necessary steps are taken to force the state to remain in the Union. During the ensuing weeks, with the war becoming more desperate, the growing power of Washington is brought to bear against subversion and anti-war propaganda, not only in the border slave states but also in the free states of the North. When the climax is reached, with arbitrary imprisonment of citizens and suppression of newspapers occurring

FREEDOM

UNDER LINCOLN

throughout the entire country, a fundamental change in the American political
system takes place. The federal government replaces the states as the center of
power. The North makes the transformation that is necessary if the great
struggle with the South is to be won.

Whether these ends justified the sometimes ruthless means employed will continue to be debated. Here are the facts.
Whatever one's opinion, the events of
1861 and early 1862 perhaps decided
once and for all that the balance of
political power should be with the federal government and that it would take
what steps it must to preserve the nation.
But resistance to this decision persists
to our own day and this book implies
much about contemporary political problems. Dean Sprague has written a lively,
authoritative and important book.

FREEDOM
UNDER LINCOLN

BY DEAN SPRAGUE

*illustrated with
photographs and maps*

HOUGHTON MIFFLIN COMPANY BOSTON
The Riverside Press Cambridge
1965

For my wife, Edna, without whose help
this book could never have been written

CONTENTS

ILLUSTRATIONS

All of the illustrations in this book, which appear following page 164, are reproduced from photographs in the collections of the Library of Congress.

MAPS

FREEDOM
UNDER LINCOLN

CHAPTER 1

INSURRECTION IN BALTIMORE

A LOW HUM of excitement possessed the city of Baltimore as the dawn of April 19, 1861, broke. The city was a tinderbox, ready to burst into flame the moment anyone struck a spark. At 11 A.M. that morning the spark was provided by 850 Massachusetts volunteers rushing to the defense of Washington. This regiment of militia, rounded up and sent on its triumphant way just seven days after the Battle of Fort Sumter, was really not much more than an unorganized crowd of abolitionists. Some of the troops had neither uniforms nor rifles. Yet the progress through Baltimore of this group of unmilitary volunteers in April, 1861, was the occasion for the shedding of the first blood of the Civil War.

Lincoln's call for 75,000 troops after Fort Sumter had started these men toward Washington from their homes in northern Massachusetts. As the regiment moved southward, it was cheered in Boston, New York and Philadelphia. But the southern city of Baltimore was another matter. Secessionist mobs had controlled the streets of Baltimore for several days and officials had carefully worked out a plan to slip the regiment through the city without starting a war. One and a half miles separated the railroad station where the troops would arrive from Philadelphia and the station where they would board another train for Washington. Getting the volunteers through this one and a half miles would not be easy because it led through the tough, Democratic heart of Baltimore. It was therefore decided that the troops would not march through the city, they would ride through on the street railway.

And so, as the train pulled into the city from Philadelphia, crews quickly went to work. They detached all the cars and harnessed horses to them. Ten cars with over half the troops were started toward the Washington depot over the tracks along Pratt Street. A mob had begun to gather as the cars started up Pratt Strect. It jeered, shouted, hallooed, and screamed in the most vile language against the "damn black Republicans," from Massachusetts.

The volunteers took it, looking neither left nor right. About half way to the Washington depot, the little caravan came to the corner of Gay Street where several hundred of the Baltimore mob stood in a knot waiting in defiance. As the cars approached, they shook their fists and shouted in hatred. But they were not organized, and eight of the cars got by them. The ninth car, however, stopped momentarily and suddenly a cobblestone crashed through a window. The car started with a jerk but before it had gone twenty yards every window was broken. Like wildfire, the excitement spread and other cars were assaulted. The volunteers inside the cars dove to the floor and pulled down the blinds. But not before the Baltimore mob had caught a glimpse of blood gushing from their faces badly lacerated by flying glass. This was the first blood shed in the Civil War, for in the Battle of Fort Sumter, where the two sides were miles apart, no one had been killed or wounded. In the Battle of Baltimore, where they were just a few feet apart, blood flowed freely from the first moment.

These nine cars fought their way grimly toward the Washington depot, suffering the insults, the derision, the vituperation, and the stones of the mob. When they got there, most of the glass windows were broken and the sides of some of the cars were badly battered in. As the volunteers made the transfer to the Washington train, the scene was fearful. Taunts, clothed in the most obscene language, were hurled at them as men pressed up to the car windows, threatening with knives and revolvers. The city police were there in force and formed a physical barrier to try to keep the crowd away from the cars. As the volunteers changed cars, many of them cocked their muskets to have them in readiness. But no shots were fired and no one was killed. Nine carloads of men had gotten through the city.

But the tenth car didn't make it. When the stoning began on Pratt Street this car was in the rear, and the mob was in no mood to let another carload of abolitionists through. The cry went out to stop the car, and rocks and anchors were quickly laid on the track. Even a nearby sand wagon was requisitioned and its contents dumped on the track. The men in the tenth car saw there was no way through and beat a hasty retreat back to the Philadelphia depot where several companies were still waiting.

At this point, the Massachusetts forces in Baltimore were split in two. About five hundred men, including all the ranking officers, were ahead at the Washington depot, ready to leave. And another 350 men in four companies were a mile and a half to the rear. Between these two forces were 20,000 secessionists. After a half hour of milling around, the four company captains in the rear decided to fight their way through the city on foot, the one thing the officials had sought to avoid. Captain Follansbee was selected to take command and they moved out of the station. Just as they started, a group of young Baltimore rowdies charged them, led by a man bearing a Confederate flag in one hand and swinging a long iron chain in the other. The rowdies broke into the ranks of the troops and forced them back a few paces. But the volunteers recovered and thrust forward along the street, finally breaking clear.

As they did, the mob closed in behind them and started heaving rocks at the rear troops. Two soldiers fell in the street and were immediately set on by the citizens. The police succeeded in rescuing the soldiers and took them into a nearby drugstore for treatment. The rest of the troops started running,

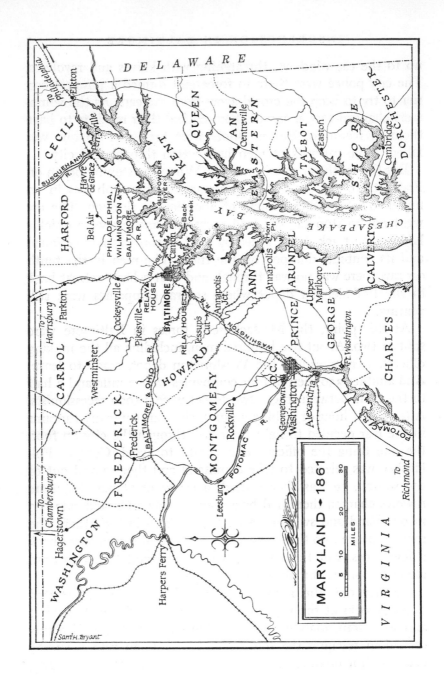

MARYLAND → 1861

MILES

0 5 10 20 30

and the last semblance of discipline broke down. They became a mob of abolitionists trying to fight their way through a much larger mob of secessionists. The odds were heavily against them.

That they got through at all was due to the determination of the volunteers and the feverish efforts of Mayor Brown, Marshal Kane and the city police. The police tried to form a cordon behind the volunteers as they ran up Pratt Street but the mob at Gay Street managed to get between them and let loose a new volley of paving stones at the soldiers. At this point the soldiers, tormented beyond endurance, wheeled and fired on the mob in the rear. The fire was returned by the mob and six people fell dead — two Union soldiers and four Baltimore civilians. These six were the first to die in battle in the Civil War.

As the troops continued up the street, Mayor Brown of Baltimore suddenly appeared beside them. He ran up to Captain Follansbee, shook hands with him and said, "I am the mayor of Baltimore. For God's sake, don't shoot!" Then he fell in step beside the captain and marched with him at the head of the column for a few minutes, trying to prevent bloodshed and calm the mob. But it only grew bolder and more violent. He saw several injured persons fall to the ground, finally decided he was helpless to stem the tide, and withdrew.

The worst trouble, however, was in the rear of the column. With the front ranks moving rapidly forward, the rear troops had to defend themselves from rocks, turn and fire their rifles, and try to keep up. It was not an easy job. Finally, the volunteers reached the corner by the Washington station and rounded it at a fast pace, letting out a final volley of shots at the mob and receiving rocks, paving stones, and bullets in exchange. They came up against the angry crowd waiting at the station and dashed for the waiting cars. A new cascade of bricks and stones hurtled down on them and many of the windows in the Washington cars were smashed. The train pulled out of the station immediately.

As the train left, John Davis, a prominent Baltimore merchant, was standing talking with some friends beside the track. Most of the blinds of the train were drawn, but there was one car with five rifles sticking out of its windows. As a last gesture of defiance, the group by the track gave a hurrah for Jeff Davis and the rifles, in the hands of green troops on the verge of panic, fired. Mr. Davis dropped with a bullet through his heart. To Baltimore, his death was the crowning blow.

As the train pulled out of the city, the people of Baltimore realized that they had declared war on the North. Almost immediately the leaders of the city began to take steps to defend themselves against Northern vengeance. The political chief of Baltimore was Mayor George Brown, a man of great charm, kindly, thoughtful and dignified, whom even the Union men found it hard to hate. He was a Democrat who had been elected in 1860 as mayor in a wave of reaction against the lawless tactics of the Know-Nothing Party which had controlled the state for eight years. His enemies accused him of being a secessionist, which he denied, but there was no doubt that he was 100 per cent against the war. Mayor Brown had tried to stem the bloodshed during the riot and his act of walking in front of the troops in the midst of the battle excited the admiration of not only the city of Baltimore but the entire country. It impressed even Massachusetts, whose hatred of Baltimore knew no bounds. But Mayor Brown was absolutely convinced that no more northern troops should be allowed through Baltimore.

In this belief, he was joined by Police Marshal George Kane. Kane was the real leader of Baltimore and of the Civil War in Maryland during the "week of terror" that was just beginning. Marshal Kane was a big, cocky, and highly respected secessionist, who had been appointed to his job largely because it was felt that he could handle the city toughs. In the election of November, 1859, Baltimore had suffered mob rule and widespread interference with the election by gangs of Know-Nothings roaming the streets. This caused the state legislature to pass a law removing all police authority from the city of Baltimore and placing it in the hands of Marshal Kane and four police commissioners under the direct control of the state legislature. Marshal Kane owed his job to that law and his personal reputation was therefore at stake in preventing this riot, regardless of his political sympathies.

But this riot turned out to be much worse than any of the earlier outbreaks that had brought about his appointment. At one point during the riot, the marshal turned in exasperation to the milling crowd and yelled: "Do you want to ruin my reputation?" They replied, "No, Marshal," and then went right on ruining it. For this was one riot that Marshal Kane could not stop.

Among the men actually leading the rioting was George Konig, a young, brawling secessionist living in Baltimore. Two nights before the riot he had been temporarily arrested for drunken and disorderly conduct while driving up Balitmore Street with four companions shouting and bellowing for South Carolina and the Southern Confederacy. During the riot, he had led a mob of rowdies into the marching troops holding a Confederate flag in one hand and an iron chain in the other. He tossed paving stones at the soldiers and helped build a barricade across the bridge on Pratt Street to try to stop the troops. Everything considered, he had a full day, and of all the citizens later brought to trial for rioting in the Baltimore County Court, he was the only one convicted.

William P. Smith was one of the few Union men on the streets that day. When the troops arrived at the Philadelphia depot he watched the crowd cheer for the South and Jeff Davis. He listened as they cursed the soldiers, calling them Negroes, spitting tobacco quids and throwing mud in their faces. He stood it as long as he could and finally let go with a cheer for the Union. He was immediately arrested for inciting a riot.

Andrew Robbins was a volunteer from Stoneham, Massachusetts. He was shot in the back of the neck four blocks from the Washington depot and fell in the street. He was left there by his company, but some citizens took him into a drugstore and treated his wound. In a few days he recovered and was sent back home to Massachusetts. Another soldier, Samuel Needham, was struck by a brick and suffered a fractured skull. He dropped senseless and was left by the troops. Some citizens took him into a book store on Pratt Street and after the riot he was moved to a hospital. He lingered on for a week without regaining consciousness and finally died. His body was returned to Massachusetts.

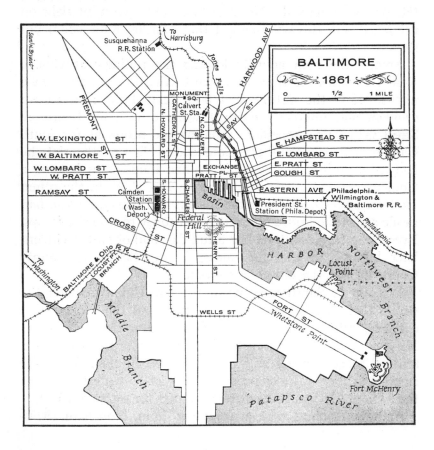

James Myers, one of the rioters, was shot in the right side of his back by a Minié ball which passed through his body and lodged among his ribs. He died before nightfall. A boy named William Reed was at work on an oyster sloop docked at Pratt Street, when the troops passed. He climbed up on the dock and stood watching the riot. A Minié ball caught him in the abdomen and that evening he died in the hold of the schooner.

The total number killed was sixteen, including twelve civilians and four military. As many more were seriously wounded. These numbers, however, were greatly magnified by early reports that had hundreds of soldiers and civilians dead on the streets of the city. The day before the riot, opinion on the war in Baltimore had been fairly evenly split. But the battle of April 19 delivered the city firmly into the hands of the secessionists and they immediately began a series of moves designed to deny the city permanently to the North.

A mass meeting was called for four o'clock in the afternoon at Monument Square and when the meeting got under way, the square was packed. Dr. A. C. Robinson of Baltimore, a leading secessionist, rose to address the people, but he had uttered only a few words when Mayor Brown walked into the square and pandemonium broke loose. The Mayor stepped to the rostrum and said that he and Governor Hicks had requested that no more troops be sent through Baltimore. He said he did not believe in the right of secession but he did believe in the right of revolution on the part of the oppressed people of the South. He added that Governor Hicks thought it was folly and madness for one portion of this great nation to subjugate another portion.

He was followed by S. Teackle Wallis, dean of the Baltimore bar and a brilliant lawyer. Wallis gave a short speech, well designed to stir the mob:

I have not come to speak. If the blood of citizens on the stones in the streets do not speak, it is useless for man to speak.

I assure you my heart is with the South and I am ready to defend Baltimore. I hope that the blood of the citizens, shed by an invading foe, will obliterate all past differences, and seal the covenant of brotherhood among the people.

Pandemonium broke loose once again.

A special escort was sent to invite Governor Hicks to speak. This was a crucial moment for secession in Maryland. Governor Hicks was a member of the Know-Nothings, a party that had become very strong in Maryland in the 1850's as a nativist reaction against the Catholic foreigners, particularly from Ireland and Germany, who had poured into the state following 1848. Hicks, from the Eastern Shore, embraced the Know-Nothing creed, and under the state constitution which rotated governors between the sparsely settled Eastern Shore and the rest of the state, he was elected governor in 1857. Three uneventful years had confirmed his career as a minor governor of a modest state, when suddenly he was catapulted by the secession movement into a critical position. In his heart he was a Union man and when the secessionists had tried early in the year to get him to call a special convention of the state legislature as the first step toward secession, he had refused. Now, four months later, he still refused, the only border state governor to stand so firm.

But the secessionists hated him and in this moment of triumph following the riot, they "invited" him in full public view to go to Monument Square and address a riotous mob which had just killed Union soldiers in the streets of the city. Would he stand firm for the Union, and perhaps be lynched, or would he bend with the mood of the people and perhaps lead Maryland into secession? The threatening, deafening roar that went up from the mob as he was brought to Monument Square was too much for him and he gave in, saying, "I coincide with what your worthy mayor has said. . . . I bow in submission to the people." Then he concluded with a stirring sentence that perfectly fitted the mood of the people: "I am a Marylander, and I love my State, and I love the Union, but I will suffer my right arm to be torn from my body before I will raise it to strike a sister state."

That was all it took. As the mob in Monument Square went wild with joy, Baltimore seceded from the Union. No vote had to be taken to sense the mood of the people. The city was now completely under the control of the secessionists.

Plans were immediately put into motion to arm the city against invasion. No telegraphic dispatches could leave the city without authority of the marshal. Pro-Southern mass meetings were held throughout the city. A telegram was sent to President Lincoln by Mayor Brown, informing him that "it is not possible for more soldiers to pass through Baltimore unless they fight their way at every step." Governor Hicks added at the bottom of this dispatch that he concurred fully.

The Baltimore militia was ordered out and immediately began drilling. Mayor Brown and Governor Hicks wired the presidents of the railroads coming into Baltimore not to bring any more troops to the city. Marshal Kane wired to Bradley Johnson, the militia leader in Frederick, Maryland, that the streets of Baltimore were running with Maryland blood:

> Send expresses over the mountains and valleys of Maryland and Virginia for the riflemen to come down without delay. . . . Fresh hordes will be down on us to-morrow. We will fight them and whip them or die.

Virginia, of course, had seceded from the Union two days before. A half hour after receiving the telegram, the militia in Frederick was ordered to Baltimore to help repulse the invader.

That night the Baltimore mob set out to wreak its vengeance on one of its favorite Republican enemies, the German-language newspaper, The Baltimore *Wecker*. Its office was completely demolished and the proprietor and his editors were driven from the city.

The most drastic step of all, however, was taken late in the evening of the 19th. A report began to spread in the city that new troops from Philadelphia had crossed the Susquehanna River at Perryville and were on their way to the city by train. At midnight, Marshal Kane received a telegram with information that another regiment was on its way south from Harrisburg. He immediately went to see Mayor Brown, Governor Hicks and the Board of Police. In view of the crisis, the Marshal proposed that troops be sent at once to destroy all the railroad bridges leading into Baltimore from the north. After some discussion it was agreed to destroy the bridges and the orders were issued.

At 2 A.M. a squad of Maryland Guard and forty police officers started eastward along the Philadelphia line. First they burned the Canton bridge near the city. Then they proceeded about fifteen miles out to the large bridge over the Gunpowder River and burned out the center span of the bridge. Originally, they had intended to go to Havre de Grace and burn the ferry that brought the railroad cars across the Susquehanna River. But they decided the ferry could be replaced too easily so they abandoned the scheme. They returned nearer the city and burned the Back River bridge.

About 3 A.M. another group of Maryland Guardsmen and police officers proceeded out the other railroad to the north toward Harrisburg. They went about five miles and destroyed the Melville Bridge. A detachment was sent further on to the Relay House where they destroyed another bridge. They also cut the telegraph wires along the railroad. All in all, it had been a full night and when the work was done, Baltimore was completely cut off from the north.

In the city itself, few slept soundly that night. The decision for secession had been made. Fighting in the streets was expected the next day as "hordes" of Northerners descended on the city and took their revenge. Throughout the North there was a great clamor for an assault on the city, as one New York editor wrote, "through breaches in the walls, by doors or windows, by sappers and miners with crowbars, with sledge hammers, with picks, with gunpowder in small bags, armed with hand grenades, revolvers and cutlasses, or other weapons as shall be best adapted to the storming party and hand-to-hand conflict." Baltimore had good reason for fear.

Early the next morning the streets became filled with people. Rumors were everywhere. Troops were reported to be on their way into the city in overwhelming numbers, marching over the roads and through the fields of Maryland to get at Baltimore. "Civil War in Baltimore," cried the headlines of both the Union and secessionist newspapers in the city. The local militia drilled in every park. Horses for the artillery were procured from the stables of the city passenger railroad. Additional military companies were rapidly organized and drilled and the Mayor asked for donations of arms and ammunition "for the defense of the city." Rifles were obtained from outlying counties and even from Virginia. It was ordered that no flags should be displayed, and no provisions should leave the city. The people were greatly excited but were determined to defend the city with their lives.

Before noon the City Council met and unanimously authorized the Mayor to raise $500,000 for the defense of the city. In view of the critical state of affairs, a group of bankers, led by Johns Hopkins, called on the Mayor and offered to advance the money to him immediately. Mayor Brown accepted the offer as an act of "great patriotism."

Toward evening, rumors began to circulate that Fort McHenry, a federal fort in Baltimore harbor, was to be attacked. Fort McHenry was not on an island, like Fort Sumter, and could have been assaulted by the local militia. It had only one hundred recruits and most of its guns were out of commission. Shortly before midnight the militia were ordered to proceed to the vicinity of the Fort and a strong police force accompanied them. The mob followed in full strength. The troops remained near the Fort during the night, but the guns of the Fort looked very formidable and the militia didn't know they were useless.

So no assault was made and the next morning the Maryland militia retired.

The news of the collision between the citizens of Baltimore and the Northern invaders fired the energies of the entire state. Maryland had given less than three thousand votes to Lincoln in the November election, and it was Breckinridge, the Southern Democratic candidate who had actually won the state's electoral vote. Some counties had not delivered a single vote to Lincoln. These people wanted nothing of Lincoln's war and when they heard the news from Baltimore, they flocked to its defense.

First to arrive were the Frederick Rifles, who came in from the west on Saturday afternoon and were quartered in a building opposite the old city hall. The Patapsco Light Dragoons, from Anne Arundel County to the south, arrived later in the afternoon. Their captain reported to Mayor Brown that when the emergency came, his dragoons "would be found with stout hearts and strong arms in the defense of Maryland." The next morning, the steamer *Pioneer* reached Baltimore, having on board the Home Guard of Easton, with 60 fully armed men. Two hours after hearing of the conflict they had chartered the steamer and hastened to the city. They reported that the citizens of the Eastern Shore stood "as a unit in defense of the South." The Howard Dragoons, from Howard County to the west, thirty-five strong, reached the city later. By this time Baltimore was as well prepared to resist invasion as it would ever be.

And suddenly, at 10 A.M. on Sunday morning, just two days after the riot, the crisis came. A man mounted on horseback dashed through the streets of the city and stopped at the City Hall. He ran inside to Marshal Kane and said there were between 5,000 and 10,000 Northern troops just a few miles to the north and they were marching directly for the city.

In a few moments, the entire city was in an uproar. Bells started ringing and drums began to roll. Church services were dismissed as the worshippers rushed out to join their units. Within a few minutes after the call to arms the recruiting stations were thronged with people anxious to join in the defense of Baltimore. Large quantities of grape and canister shot, together with heavy balls, were issued to the artillery for the coming battle. The militia units began deploying to meet the invader, determined to resist to the death.

While this activity was going on, about 2,500 untrained Pennsylvania troops were unloading themselves and what little equipment they had from a railroad train a dozen miles north of Baltimore at the village of Cockeysville. They had just arrived under General Wynkoop from Harrisburg and were unable to go any further because the bridges had been destroyed. They had no tents, no food, and very few arms. Many did not have uniforms. General Wynkoop didn't know whether he should advance against Baltimore, or whether the mob at Baltimore was advancing against him. So he and his troops just sat in a wheat field at Cockeysville and waited.

At this point, an armed conflict of considerable proportions was in the offing. The two camps were just twelve miles apart and in the minds of both contestants, it was the North against the South. Had the Pennsylvania volunteers advanced against the city, it would have caused a bloody battle. The North would have lost heavily in this battle, not only because the Pennsylvania militia would never have gotten through Baltimore, but also because the battle would have solidified the position of Maryland as part of the South. Had Maryland found itself engaged in a large-scale action against Northern troops, and had Virginia rushed troops into the state to help, the course of the war could have been profoundly affected.

Nobody understood this fact more fully than the man in the White House. President Lincoln had watched the events in Baltimore very closely. He had been relieved that Pennsylvania had slipped a regiment through Baltimore on the day before the riot. But the news of April 19 was black and when the Sixth Massachusetts arrived in Washington that afternoon it showed the scars of battle.

The most serious word, however, came the next morning, when Washington awoke to find itself completely cut off from the North. The railroad bridges had been burned, the telegraph wires cut and Washington, which depended on the railroad for almost everything, including its food, was helpless. The two convoys that had gotten through Baltimore were a very small part of the 75,000 troops Lincoln had asked for and, as he put it, "Those Carolinians are now crossing Virginia to come here and hang me, and what am I to do?"

He decided to do what he could. At 3 A.M. on Sunday morning, April 21, Mayor Brown and Governor Hicks received messages asking them to confer with the President. Hicks did not go but Mayor Brown, United States Senator Anthony Kennedy, and several others from Baltimore spent a good part of Sunday with Lincoln, Secretary of War Cameron and General Winfield Scott. Out of these discussions, it was finally agreed that the Union troops would abandon the route through Baltimore and use another route. This alternate route was to run by train from Philadelphia to Perryville at the mouth of the Susquehanna River, by boat from Perryville to Annapolis, some forty miles from Washington, and then by rail to Washington. The President agreed to the route and Mayor Brown and Senator Kennedy were authorized to inform the citizens of Baltimore of the agreement.

While these meetings were going on, Baltimore had been in its panic over the troops at Cockeysville. At 4 P.M., after six hours of unholy tension and fervid preparation, word came to the city that the troops had been ordered back to Pennsylvania. A wave of relief swept over the city but the militia remained alert, ready to answer at an instant's notice should the bells peal forth once again.

Out at Cockeysville, the Pennsylvania troops were being kept under surveillance by a detail of cavalry under the command of Lieutenant John Merryman of the Baltimore County Horse Guards. He and his men watched from the surrounding hills as word was brought to the troops that they had been ordered back to Pennsylvania. The troops, however, did not trust the Baltimore citizenry any more than the latter trusted them. After nightfall wild rumors began to spread in the camp that an armed force of 6,000 men was on the way from Baltimore to attack them. The guard was doubled as tension began to build up. Suddenly, pounding hoofs were heard in the distance and the entire camp was called to arms. In the excitement, a young private from Easton, Pennsylvania, dropped dead in the ranks from a burst blood vessel and the remainder of the camp kept alert throughout the night. Morning finally came without any attack and at 8 A.M. the troops climbed aboard their train and withdrew. As the train moved northward, it was followed by Lieutenant Merryman and his cavalry. He burned one more bridge, at Parkton, just ten miles south of the Pennsylvania border, to make sure that no more Pennsylvania troops could get to Baltimore. His efforts this day were to make his name a legal landmark in habeas corpus.

Washington had now been cut off completely from the North by the secession of the city of Baltimore. But at this same moment, another route to the capital was about to be tested as a Breckinridge Democrat from Massachusetts named Ben Butler prepared to invade the sovereign state of Maryland from the sea.

CHAPTER 2

THE OCCUPATION OF MARYLAND

MASSACHUSETTS lay at the very heart of the abolitionist movement in the North. It was hated by the South for having spawned such anti-slavery men as William Lloyd Garrison and Wendell Phillips, who worked together to beat implacably upon the conscience of the North to rid the country of slavery. And Massachusetts' Senator Charles Sumner was yet another focal point of Southern hatred. The savage beating which Preston Brooks of South Carolina gave him in the Senate following a particularly bitter speech denouncing the South served greatly to increase the hatred that led to the Civil War.

But among the Massachusetts politicians was another man, Benjamin Franklin Butler, who was not hated at all. Butler was brigadier general of the Massachusetts militia, prominent lawyer and wealthy citizen of Lowell. Born in poverty, Butler had worked his way to a position of modest eminence by the time war came. He had served in both houses of the Massachusetts legislature and was no Johnny-come-lately to the militia. Back in 1839, he had joined the Lowell City Guard, served in the ranks and had been promoted up the ladder until he became colonel of his regiment. In 1856 he was appointed brigadier general at the age of 37. When he met old General Winfield Scott shortly after his appointment, Scott told him he was "very glad that the oldest general in the United States has the pleasure of receiving the youngest general in the United States." Butler took great interest in his military responsibilities and camped regularly with his brigade in summer training. He even claimed that he had "commanded a larger body of troops, duly uniformed and equipped, than any general in the United States army then living except General Scott."

The fact that Southerners had no hatred for Butler (something that he changed before the end of the war) arose, however, from quite another facet of his enigmatic character. He was a dyed-in-the-wool Democrat who had voted for the nomination of Jefferson Davis at the 1860 convention. When the Southerners, infuriated at the nomination of Stephen Douglas, withdrew and formed a splinter convention at Charleston, Butler went with them. He worked hard for the election of the Southern Democratic candidate, but when Breckinridge was defeated and secession swept the South, Butler parted company with his friends. As events moved rapidly toward war in early 1861, Butler encouraged Governor Andrew of Massachusetts to prepare his militia for a possible call to national duty. As a result, after Fort Sumter Butler's brigade was the first in the state to be called up and one of the first in the country to be mobilized. At this point, Butler represented a rare quantity, a Breckinridge Democrat who was a staunch Union man, and a general as well. The Republicans hoped to get a lot of mileage out of him.

These first regiments that responded to President Lincoln's call liked to think of themselves as "Minute Men of '61" and some of the accounts of their call-up resembled those of the Revolutionary War. Butler himself was trying a case before a Boston court when he received an order at 4:45 in the afternoon of April 15th that his Sixth Regiment should report to Faneuil Hall the next morning. The regiment was spread over four counties and Butler knew that getting the men away from their jobs and assembled in Boston by the next morning would be a difficult task. He rose dramatically in court (Butler was always dramatic) and said he was "called to prepare troops to be sent to Washington, and I must ask the court to postpone this case." The case was immediately postponed and he left for Lowell and the organization of his troops. Butler wrote years later that the case he was trying "remains unfinished to this day." Butler was to have a busy war.

Throughout Massachusetts, the President's call for militia created intense excitement. The people poured into the streets, waving flags, ringing bells and firing cannon. The excitement "has not been equalled since the war of 1812" said the Boston *Post*, and the idols of the moment were the militia men. Some of them were awakened in their sleep during the night of the 15th and told to report immediately to their units. As the companies fell in in the center of various towns and prepared to go to Boston they were surrounded by cheering citizens. In New Bedford, during the morning of the 16th, a company formed in the square in front of the City Hall with several thousand looking on. They were prayed over by a preacher, given a patriotic speech by an ex-governor, and told by the mayor that their families would be taken care of. The New Bedford Brass Band volunteered to accompany the troops to Boston and at every station along the way they were wildly cheered. The enthusiasm in Boston was as great as in the smaller towns.

As soon as he had gotten the troops organized, Butler sent Colonel Jones on his way to Washington with his Sixth Regiment and arranged to follow the next day with his Eighth. As a result, he missed the famous march through Baltimore on the 19th. However, he was in an enviable position. Poised to move on Washington, he could be the first to bring relief to the beleaguered city. When he reached Philadelphia, he heard the details of the attack on the Sixth Regiment by the Baltimore mob. He decided to go on to Perryville, seize the ferryboat *Maryland* and use it to get his regiment to Annapolis. This bold plan worked because the Baltimore militia, who had been ordered to burn the ferry, had decided not to do it. Butler deployed his troops, captured the ferryboat and its captain and set sail for Annapolis.

Just before dawn on Sunday morning, two days after the Baltimore riots, this ferryboat sailed into the harbor at Annapolis with troops drawn up in full battle array, prepared to fight their way ashore and conquer Maryland inch by inch. But to their great surprise they were greeted as brothers-in-arms by the officers in charge of the Naval Academy when they came to the dock. By quick action, Butler could have had his regiment in Washington by nightfall and saved that city and its worried government a week of suspense.

But the easy way was never chosen by Ben Butler. He was by nature a contentious man who was the center of dispute in everything he did. His great ego required constant nourishment and the eyes of the nation were on him at this moment. He therefore decided upon a plan which he thought would dramatically avenge the honor of Massachusetts. The famous "Old Ironsides," the U.S.S. *Constitution*, was being used at the Naval Academy as a training ship when Butler arrived. He lashed his ferryboat to the side of "Old Ironsides" and towed it through the mud of the harbor out into the Chesapeake Bay. Then he issued the first of his many famous orders, just to make sure that everybody understood the significance of this strange act. The *Constitution*, he said, was intimately associated with the history of Massachusetts. But it "has lain for a long time at this port substantially at the mercy of the armed mob." He then went on:

> It was given to Massachusetts and Essex county first to man her; it was reserved for Massachusetts to have the honor to retain her for the service of the Union and the laws.
>
> This is a sufficient triumph of right, and a sufficient triumph for us. By this the blood of our friends shed by the Baltimore mob is in so far avenged. The Eighth Regiment may hereafter cheer lustily on all proper occasions, but never without orders.

Having pulled off this rather questionable coup, he started back to Annapolis with his regiment. But Ben Butler was no sailor and his ferry ran aground on the mud outside Horn Point. And there it stayed for thirty long hours, while his regiment grew thirstier and the Union cause in Maryland languished. To add insult to injury, before he got his boat free the New York Seventh Regiment came sailing up in another steamer and landed at Annapolis ahead of him.

The Seventh Regiment was one of the best New York had. Drawn from some of the upper classes of the city, it lacked the mechanical competence of the Massachusetts regiments but made up for it in the literary abilities of one of its privates, Theodore Winthrop. Winthrop was to die just two months later at Big Bethel. But before his death he wrote the story of the campaign while quartered with the rest of his regiment in the Chamber of the House of Representatives. There, he told of the excitement and exhilaration of the city of New York as his regiment marched out to the war that would, indeed, very soon cost him his life:

> It was worth a life, that march. Only one who passed, as we did, through the tempest of cheers, two miles long, can know the terrible enthusiasm of the occasion. I could hardly hear the rattle of our own gun-carriages, and only once or twice the music of our band came to me muffled and quelled by the uproar. . . .
>
> My fellow-citizens smote me on the knapsack. . . . "Bully for you!" alternated with benedictions, in the proportion of two "bullies" to one blessing.

Across the river in New Jersey, the same reception awaited them. "Jersey City turned out and filled up the railroad station, like an opera house, to give God-speed to us. . . . At every station the Jerseymen were there, uproarious as Jerseymen, to shake our hands and wish us a happy dispatch. I think I did not see a rod of ground without its man, from dusk till dawn, from the Hudson to the Delaware." Winthrop's regiment, which was commanded by Colonel Marshall Lefferts of New York, was in Philadelphia the same time as the Massachusetts Eighth. Lefferts and Butler clashed over plans for reaching the capital with

Lefferts finally chartering a boat to take around the Virginia Capes to Annapolis, and Butler following his plan to seize the ferry at Perryville, which would get him to Annapolis sooner than Lefferts. One can imagine the feelings of the two men when Lefferts sailed up while Butler was stuck in the mud outside Annapolis. Though Lefferts tried to get the Massachusetts Eighth off the mud bank, the effort was in vain. The New York troops, however, did catch a glimpse of the Massachusetts troops, who had spent thirty hours on the mud bank, tired, hungry and black, their "uniforms all grimy with their lodgings in the coal dust. They could not have been blacker," said Winthrop.

And so the New York Seventh went ashore, and took Annapolis. "It was a parade, not a battle," wrote Winthrop. "At sunset our band played strains sweet enough to pacify all Secession." The ferry was sent back to bring the stranded Massachusetts troops ashore.

While Butler had been stuck in the mud Governor Hicks, who had returned to the state capital at Annapolis after the riots in Baltimore, was vacillating once again. The terror in Baltimore had shaken him greatly and he begged Mayor Brown to keep the mob away from Annapolis: "Do not let them come," he wired. "The troops will not land." Then he sent messages to Washington and to Butler imploring them not to bring the troops ashore. But the landing on Monday afternoon was made despite his protests and encountered no opposition whatsoever. As the troops were landing, the shaken Hicks signed a proclamation calling for a special session of the state legislature in Annapolis the following Friday, the one act the secessionists had tried for months to get him to do. Hicks "has turned traitor," wrote Horace Greeley when he heard the news. Ben Butler felt the same way and he decided to make this session of the legislature his personal responsibility. He told the governor that if Hicks recommended any discussion of secession in his message to the legislature, he would arrest him and if the legislature discussed it he would disperse the body, or better still, lock them all up. Hicks assured him that he had no intention of bringing up the subject and said he would never permit the great seal of Maryland to be affixed to any ordinance of secession. As proof of his intention he turned the great seal over to Butler and the latter held it during the entire session. Yet Butler's overbearing attitude convinced Hicks that an explosion would occur if the legislature met at Annapolis and he transferred the meeting place to Frederick, a town some fifty miles west of Baltimore and fairly well up in Union country. The enraged Butler was unable to do anything about it.

He did, however, issue a number of orders which caught the imagination of the North and served to anchor his position as the leading Democratic general in the early days of the war. One order said that it was his intention to push on to Washington "peaceably, quickly and civilly, unless opposed by some mob. . . . If opposed we shall march steadily forward." By the time he got around to moving out of the Naval Academy grounds, however, some Southern-minded men had torn up sections of the railroad track leading to Washington and rumors were afloat that the countryside was swarming with Maryland militia waiting to attack the volunteers.

So Butler waited for two days as reinforcements poured in by sea and then started moving his troops toward Washington along the railroad line. The Civil War was the first great conflict ever fought using railroads and in this first Northern offensive maneuver, the railroad dominated the action. Butler put out pickets ahead and on both sides as he marched his main body of men up the railroad track. No resistance was encountered and twenty-four hours of marching and repairing track finally brought them to the main Baltimore-Washington line at Annapolis Junction, some twenty miles from Annapolis. The trains were running between the Junction and Washington and by noon on the 25th, just six days after the Battle of Baltimore, the first trainload of troops reached Washington. The road from the north had been reopened.

Although Baltimore remained untamed, troops continued landing every day at Annapolis and the sheer numbers of volunteers rushing to Washington began to overawe the little state of Maryland. Within a week, nearly 20,000 Union troops passed through Annapolis, a far cry from the few hundred who had gotten into trouble in Baltimore. The Union was beginning to show some muscle in Maryland.

On the day the road to Washington was reopened, the first arbitrary arrests of the war were carried out. A Maryland lad came rushing into the camp at Annapolis Junction on the 25th and said he knew who had torn up the railroad track near Annapolis. The volunteers were extremely interested and when he named three residents of Annapolis Junction, Robert Bruce, Benjamin Biggs, and Jeremiah Kuen, they were immediately arrested. But as soon as the arrests were made, a large number of indignant citizens came into the camp and protested. There resulted a long parley between the local citizens and the military and the men were finally released.

Two days later, however, President Lincoln formally suspended the privilege of the writ of habeas corpus along "the military line . . . used between the city of Philadelphia and the city of Washington." By this action he declared war on his enemies in the North just as completely as he had, by calling up the militia after Fort Sumter, declared war on his enemies in the South. Although the Constitution provided that the privilege of the writ of habeas corpus could be suspended when "in Cases of Rebellion or Invasion the public safety may require it," it was silent as to exactly where the power of suspension resided. When Lincoln clothed himself with this power a great many people were shocked. But the explosion was slow in building up and the first issuance of the suspension aroused little comment.

No rash of arbitrary arrests followed his order. The Union occupation of Maryland continued as troops poured into the little state from the great population centers of the North.

Slowly the tension and fear in Washington eased as more and more military camps appeared in the city. With his new strength, General Winfield Scott's thoughts began to turn back to Baltimore, the vital rail center to the north which he must have if he were to fight the South. He planned to use the Massachusetts Sixth Regiment in his attack on the city and early in May he ordered this regiment out of Washington to Relay House, a rail center just nine miles south of Baltimore on the main line of the Baltimore and Ohio Railroad. The troops arrived there on May 5, took control of the buildings and set up camp in the various estates in the area. Cannon were put into position overlooking the bridge over the Patapsco River.

When word got to Baltimore that the Massachusetts Sixth was at Relay House, the camp was soon flooded with a crowd of curiosity seekers and enterprising merchants intent on selling beer and cake to the soldiers. A rather festive spirit of friendliness developed between soldiers and civilians but Ben Butler soon put an end to it. A soldier who had eaten too much pie and beer had a stomach ache during the first night at Relay House and the next day Butler issued a special order covering the situation. He said that he had found well-authenticated evidence that the soldier had been poisoned by means of strychnine administered in the food brought into the camp. And he sent a thrill of horror throughout the North and made headlines everywhere by adding:

> Are our few insane enemies among the loyal men of Maryland prepared to wage war upon us in this manner? Do they know the terrible lesson they are teaching us? Can it be that they realize the fact that we can put an agent, with a word, into every household, armed with this terrible weapon?

His questions went unanswered, but the soldier recovered. By this time even the Union men in Baltimore were beginning to worry about Ben Butler. One newspaper gave Butler the sobriquet "Poisoner General" for this incident.

As soon as the federal forces were established in Relay House, they began intercepting shipments on the Baltimore and Ohio Railroad coming in from Virginia and points west. One of the Baltimore businessmen who came out from the city to see about his goods was a talkative fellow named Joseph Spencer. Spencer bragged loudly that the Baltimore mob which had stoned the troops on April 19th "had done right" and that when the Sixth Massachusetts returned to the city they would "get a worse reception." He was immediately arrested by two soldiers and Butler issued a general order later in the day saying that "for these treasonable speeches . . . Spencer had been arrested and sent to Annapolis, where he will be properly dealt with."

Spencer spent a week in the county jail at Annapolis, but he was not properly dealt with. In fact, nobody had the slightest idea what to do with him. So he sat in jail while his friends besieged Butler with pleas that he be released and allowed to return to his family in Baltimore. After a week, Butler gave in and ordered his release "to show that his arrest was a measure of precaution merely." Joseph Spencer was the first man arrested in the Civil War for making "treasonable speeches," sent to prison, and released, without reference to any laws of the land. He was not to be the last.

As the noose tightened on Baltimore, General Scott worked out a plan for the capture of the city. He gave orders for a four-pronged offensive with one column coming west from Perryville, another south from Harrisburg, another north by sea from Annapolis, and the fourth directly north by rail from Relay House. But in the three weeks since the Battle of Baltimore, something had happened to the mood of that city. It was no longer the ferocious tiger that had deliberately baited the Union, and then defiantly prepared to resist to the death. For Baltimore, in cutting the rail line to Washington, had really succeeded only in cutting its own jugular vein, and it came very near to destroying itself in the process.

CHAPTER 3

BALTIMORE REJOINS THE UNION

EXCITEMENT had remained intense in Baltimore during the week after the riots. Every morning crowds gathered in the streets to discuss the latest events and rumors. The city was an armed camp, with troops marching in the streets and drilling in the parks. Pickets watched the approaches to Baltimore and an alarm system was set up by which any word of troops from the north could be relayed immediately to the command center at the Central Police Station. All regular work stopped and every day was a vast holiday.

It was on Monday, three days after the riots, that Governor Hicks finally gave in to the pressure from the secessionists and called a special session of the legislature. Ten Baltimore seats in the house of delegates had previously been declared vacant by the Maryland General Assembly as a result of election-day violence, and the secessionists in Baltimore determined to fill these seats with their own men. A States Rights convention was immediately called together on Monday night and candidates were nominated for a special election to be held just two days later.

The convention nominated a blue ribbon slate that, for respectability, could hardly have been improved upon. The ten men nominated were:

– John C. Brune, President of the Baltimore Board of Trade, President of the Maryland Sugar Refinery and one of the leading merchants of the city.
– Ross Winans, a very wealthy industrialist and a tireless

inventor, whose factory was turning out pikes at top speed
for the defense of Baltimore.

– Henry M. Warfield, President of the Baltimore Corn Exchange.
– Dr. J. Hanson Thomas, leading physician in Baltimore,
director of the Farmers and Merchants Bank of Baltimore
and a man of considerable wealth.
– T. Parkin Scott, leading lawyer of the city, a man later
destined to become Chief Judge of the Supreme Court of
Baltimore.
– S. Teackle Wallis, brilliant lawyer, dean of the Baltimore
bar and author of two books.
– Lawrence Sangston, owner of a large drygoods store in the
city.
– H. M. Morfit, Charles H. Pitts and William G. Harrison,
leading citizens of Baltimore.

None of these men was a politician and in the midst of all
the secessionist excitement no Union slate was even nominated.
For this was destined to be perhaps the only election in American history in which every man who was nominated was elected
and every man who was elected went to prison or into exile
shortly afterward.

As the election approached, a new afternoon penny newspaper called *The South* appeared on the streets of Baltimore
"devoted to the South, Southern Rights, and Secession." It
flourished. All mail communication and travel were cut off
from the north, and no steamboat was permitted to leave the
harbor without permission of the authorities. No provisions of
any kind could be taken from the city. But this did not stop a
general exodus of families from Baltimore, joined by thousands
more pouring out of Washington. The road north to Harrisburg
was choked with wagons and carriages. The price of a twelve-mile trip from Baltimore to Cockeysville rose to $10 and the
price of a thirty-five-mile trip to the railroad at Perryville
was $20.

Within Baltimore, new volunteer companies were formed

every day and named after the new heroes of the city. The Jeff Davis Rifles and the Southern Guerrilla Guards were organized and began drilling to defend the city against the North. In the 11th ward, the Howard Guards were organized, using as a nucleus the Southern Rights organization of the ward. The Winans Guard, named in honor of the munitions manufacturer Thomas Winans, was also formed. Some 2,000 stand of arms were received from the seceded state of Virginia for use in the defense of Baltimore. In Charles County, $25,000 was appropriated to arm and equip volunteers to defend themselves against invasion and a public meeting called for immediate secession of the state. Talbot County on the Eastern Shore voted $20,000 to arm its citizens and Prince George's County, on the Western Shore, appropriated $25,000. The march toward secession seemed irresistible.

Then, all at once, the great secessionist streamroller began to run out of steam. A combination of political, economic and military factors very quickly wrenched control of Maryland from the secessionists and turned the state back into the arms of the Union.

The first cloud on the horizon occurred in the Baltimore election just five days after the riots. When the votes were counted, the city was astonished to discover that the ten blue ribbon States Rights candidates for the house of delegates had polled only 9,200 votes, compared with 30,000 polled by all candidates in the Presidential election the previous November. Although there was no opposition, the city was a political cauldron, on a permanent holiday, and they should have done better. The secessionists were reminded of the situation in Missouri, where earlier that year not a single secessionist candidate had been elected to a state convention called for the purpose of seceding from the Union. Some began to wonder if perhaps the sentiment in Baltimore was not quite as wholeheartedly against the Union as had been supposed.

But this was nothing compared with the shock that confronted the secessionists when the general assembly met in Frederick two days later. Except for the ten States Rights delegates who had just been elected in Baltimore, it was exactly the same legislature which had passed a resolution in 1860 stating that "should the hour ever arrive when the Union must be dissolved, Maryland will cast her lot with her sister states of the South and abide their fortune to the fullest extent." Now, as the legislature prepared to meet again, the probability that it would secede was so great that President Lincoln and the cabinet considered suppressing it. But opinion in the cabinet was divided on the question and Lincoln was reluctant to take such drastic action. "I think it would *not* be justifiable," he wrote, and cited two factors:

First, they have a clearly legal right to assemble; and we can not know in advance, that their action will not be lawful, and peaceful. . . .

Secondly, we can not permanently prevent their action — If we arrest them, we can not long hold them as prisoners; and when liberated, they will immediately re-assemble, and take their action. . . .

I therefore conclude that it is only left to the Commanding General to watch, and await their action, which, if it shall be to arm their people against the United States, he is to adopt the most prompt, and efficient measures to counteract, even, if necessary, to the bombardment of their cities, and in the extremest necessity, the suspension of the writ of habeas corpus.

While Lincoln was considering this question, Hicks settled the whole matter by moving the session to Frederick where there were no federal troops. The legislature which many thought would align Maryland with the South therefore met on schedule on the 26th of April, just one week after the riot in Baltimore.

From the first, the legislators talked as though they were determined to do the Union harm. They solemnly protested against the war "which the Federal Government has declared on the Confederate States of the South, and our sister and neighbor Virginia, and [we] . . . announce . . . [Maryland's] resolute determination to have no part or lot, directly or indirectly, in its prosecution." They gave Maryland's "cordial assent" to the independence of the Confederate states, because "the willing return of the Southern people . . . is a thing beyond hope, and . . . the attempt to coerce them will only add slaughter and hate to impossibility." They appointed four commissioners to see President Lincoln and four to see President Davis to try to reconcile the two, thus recognizing the independence of the Confederacy.

But it soon became apparent that this legislature would never pass an ordinance of secession. Shortly after convening, the senate unanimously voted a resolution stating that although a large proportion of the citizens of Maryland expected them to pass a secession ordinance, "we know we have no constitutional authority to take such action. You need not fear that there is a possibility that we will do so." The house of delegates passed a similar resolution the next day, adding that its only power was to call a state convention to consider the question. But when T. Parkin Scott, one of the Baltimore delegates, introduced a bill to call such a Sovereign Convention, it was sent to a committee and buried. And when Coleman Yellott, the radical secessionist leader in the senate introduced his "Safety Bill" which would have provided for the legislature to take over control of the state militia from the governor, it was also sent to committee and never heard from again. This monumental inactivity proved a body blow to the secessionists from which they never recovered. By the time the legislature adjourned on May 14, secession in Maryland was dead. Not even the first step in that direction had been taken while the state was armed to prevent passage of federal troops.

The problem with the secessionists was that they failed to understand the economic facts of life in Maryland. In 1800,

Maryland had some 100,000 slaves out of a population of 350,-
000. But by 1860 the number of slaves had dropped to 87,000
while the total population had grown to 680,000. Slavery had
become only a small part of the economy of Maryland and psychologically the state had moved northward as a result. When
the final test came, it found it could not join its beloved sister
state, Virginia, in secession.

But for the average citizen of Baltimore, the worst blow to
secession came from another source. Amidst all the excitement
and gaiety immediately after the Battle of Baltimore, nobody
had worried about Baltimore's trade. But by the end of the first
week, the city began to realize what a crippling blow it had
dealt itself in burning the bridges. Baltimore was a trading
center and its trade was gone. Not only were there no trains, but
the ships had left the harbor right after the rioting and had not
returned. The Pratt Street wharf, which had always been
crowded with vessels, was almost empty now. Business was
utterly prostrated and for a time the markets of the city were
almost destitute of food, as the farmers feared to bring their
produce to town. The wharves were silent, the warehouses deserted, the workshops closed and the people were starving.

Prices climbed rapidly as coal sold for $15 a ton, and the cost
of flour went up 50 cents a barrel. Unemployment mounted,
and soup kitchens were established to feed the starving people.
To add salt to this wound, reports came back from Annapolis
of the great buzz of activity and prosperity in that town "where
no less than $1 million will be left by the troops." Not only
were the avenues of transportation and trade gone, but Union
troops soon formed a blockading ring around the city by land
and by sea. Washington was getting supplies while Baltimore
starved. Baltimore, in its agony, began to regret its defiance of
the North. Instead of plotting to keep the federal troops out,
the people of Baltimore began to wonder how they could en-
tice them back into the city. The militia, which had been organized to stop an invasion, was useless under such conditions.

So a full dress parade was held in which the military might of Baltimore was put on display for the last time and the companies began disbanding. By the third of May, the last of the militia were discharged from their duty. Baltimore was now defenseless.

As the secessionist ferment subsided, Union men became more bold. The Stars and Stripes appeared on the streets and Union meetings were held in several of the wards. One day a crowded boat sailed past Fort McHenry covered from stem to stern with Union flags and the passengers cheered and saluted as they passed the Fort. A Union Army recruiting office opened in Baltimore and accepted eighty-one enlistments on the first day of business. The Baltimore *Wecker*, the Republican German-language newspaper which had been demolished by the mob on April 19, reappeared on the streets of the city and was not disturbed. The city authorities lifted the restrictions on trade and the Baltimore Corn Exchange addressed a memorial to the state legislature requesting that it repair the bridges leading into the city. Although the legislature refused to act, the authorities in Baltimore fully realized by this time that instead of blockading Washington from the North, they had only succeeded in blockading themselves. On May 7, just two and a half weeks after the riots, Mayor Brown sent a message to the city council in which he pointed out that "the authorities of the city fully recognize and admit their obligations to submit to the lawful authority of the government of the United States."

As the mood in Baltimore changed, the federal government began repairing the bridges. It was found that their foundations had not been damaged and before the middle of May, the railroads from Philadelphia and Harrisburg were both ready for use. General Scott ordered a simultaneous descent on the city by troops from Philadelphia, Harrisburg, Annapolis, and Relay House, but delayed carrying out the plan until troops at all four points were in readiness. Above all, he wanted to show such strength that any secessionist elements in Baltimore would be overawed. Baltimore, however, had learned its lesson and during the afternoon of May 9, some 2,500 Pennsylvania troops were actually passed through the city without opposition, arriving by ferry at Locust Point and continuing by rail to Washington. Delay was no longer necessary.

Ben Butler realized this from his strategic position at Relay House and decided to do something about it. Without giving any advance notice of his intentions either to Washington or to Baltimore, he quietly loaded the Massachusetts Sixth aboard a train on the cold, dreary, wet night of May 13. Then, disobeying direct orders from General Scott, he set out to tame the city of secession all by himself and avenge the dead of April 19.

For several days Baltimore had been caught in the ebb and flow of wild rumors announcing the arrival of Northern troops in the city. Each rumor had sent crowds of people dashing to the railroad stations and the Mayor had warned that no attempt should be made to interfere with the troops lest the city suffer as a battleground. Toward evening on May 13 the story spread that the Sixth Massachusetts was on its way to the city from Relay House and a crowd hurried to the Washington station to see them. When Butler arrived there at 7 P.M. with his troops, he was met by cheers instead of bullets, and the men of the Sixth were relieved not to have to fight their way back into the station from which they had been driven three weeks before. A large, friendly crowd was on hand as they moved out into the streets and started marching to their camp. Many civilians appeared in front of their houses with lamps and candles, helping to light the way.

The troops marched a mile from the station to Federal Hill, a height south of the harbor which commanded the entire city. Although Butler made no immediate attempt to occupy the center of the city, he began fortifying the hill and issuing proclamations. His first stated that he was there "in order to testify the acceptance by the federal government of the fact that the

. . . inhabitants are loyal to the Union and the Constitution."
He added that he intended to enforce "respect and obedience
to laws." He prohibited assembly of people, forbade all drilling
of troops except those loyal to the governor, prohibited the
display of Confederate flags, and directed the seizure of all
property in aid of the rebellion. He then summoned Mayor
Brown to his headquarters and informed the mayor personally
of these orders.

With less than 1,000 soldiers, Butler had avenged the honor
of Massachusetts. But the next day, he displayed to the world
the meekness of Baltimore's 200,000 inhabitants by sending 35
troops into the heart of the city to seize the city's supply of
arms. The troops marched along the same Pratt Street
on which the attack of April 19 had occurred, without arousing
any excitement. They demanded surrender of the weapons at a
downtown warehouse but the policeman on guard said they
could not do so without orders from Marshal Kane. Kane was
summoned but he said he couldn't surrender the arms without
approval of the police commissioners. Word was sent to the
police commissioners as an unfriendly crowd began to gather
around the troops. Three cheers were given for Marshal Kane
whereupon the marshal asked the crowd to remain quiet and
nothing further was attempted. Finally a note arrived from the
commissioners authorizing Marshal Kane to surrender the arms
under protest. The doors were opened and thirty-five furniture
wagons were filled with weapons. Included in the seizure were
2,200 muskets, many of which had come from Virginia. When
the loading was completed the wagons started for Federal Hill.
A few shouts went up from the crowd to "wade in at them,"
and "kill them," but the little party was not molested.

The next day was Butler's last day in Baltimore. Not only
was he severely reprimanded by General Scott for taking the
city without orders but his proclamations were considered in-
flammatory. Still, as a Breckinridge Democrat who supported
the Union cause, Butler was immune from punishment. He
was assigned to command of Fortress Monroe and promoted

to Major General. By the time he left the city, Northern troops were pouring through Baltimore at a rate of several thousand a day, on their way to Washington. He was replaced by another Democrat, General George Cadwalader of the Pennsylvania militia.

As General Butler was being eased out of Baltimore, the fate of another man was under consideration by the authorities in Washington. He was Ross Winans, the Baltimore manufacturer reputed to be worth $15,000,000, who had been elected to the Maryland house of delegates during the insurrection. Winans was sixty-five years old, a thick-set, brawny old gentleman whose heart was with the South. Some years earlier Winans had helped Peter Cooper design the "Tom Thumb" and just before the war had tried to build a cigar-shaped submarine in which he dreamed of crossing the Atlantic Ocean in four days. His latest contraption was a steam-gun, a weapon which was reported to have the capacity to discharge three hundred bullets a minute. How well the gun worked was not established but it impressed everyone as a particularly formidable weapon during the semi-military days of May 1861. Winans sold it to the city of Baltimore during the insurrection and as the military ardor of Baltimore began to wane, the city fathers put it on a train for Harpers' Ferry as a gift to Virginia. It was captured by Union troops at Relay House and because it had Winans' name on it, orders were issued by the War Department for his arrest.

On May 14, when the special session of the legislature ended, Winans dutifully sent a telegram to his family in Baltimore that he would arrive by train that afternoon. The telegram was intercepted at Relay House and when his train arrived there a Union officer boarded it, went up to Mr. Winans, and told him to consider himself a prisoner. The governor and other legislators on the train protested vehemently but were only told he was being arrested for treason. Winans was held at Relay House until midnight and then forwarded to Annapolis. The next day he was sent to Fort McHenry in Baltimore.

Major Morris, Commander of the Fort, received Winans, his first important prisoner, with great courtesy. He walked aboard the boat when it docked, ordered the guard to keep at a respectful distance, and taking Mr. Winans' arm, escorted him into the interior of the Fort. Winans was accorded every privilege while he was there and was visited by his wife and friends. His arrest stirred up a hornet's nest of criticism, even among the Union men in Baltimore. His lawyer and friend, Reverdy Johnson, brought great pressure for his release. In twenty-four hours he was released on special orders from the War Department after giving his parole not to commit any act of hostility against the Government of the United States.

Butler later claimed that his removal from Baltimore was caused by the severe treatment he meted out to Winans. He said that he planned to bring Winans before a military commission composed of officers from the Sixth Massachusetts, with the idea that they would recommend that he be hanged. "I also thought that if such a man, worth $15,000,000, were hanged for treason, it would convince the people of Maryland, at least, that the expedition we were on was no picnic excursion," Butler wrote.

However, in reality, this incident had nothing to do with his removal. He was removed because he had disobeyed General Scott. The day after Butler occupied Baltimore, General Scott sent him a dispatch:

> Sir: Your hazardous occupation of Baltimore was made without my knowledge, and, of course, without my approbation. It is a godsend that it is without conflict of arms. It is also reported that you have sent a detachment to Frederick; but this is impossible. Not a word have I received from you as to either movement. Let me hear from you.

Butler did not reply to this message and was relieved the next day and reassigned to the quiet post at Fort Monroe. He immediately went to Washington to see Scott. During the interview Scott gave him a dressing down and a lecture on obeying orders. He told Butler that he could not be trusted again with anything in the army. And so Butler came out second best in his fight with Scott. Nevertheless, he was entrusted with several important posts during the war although he continued to cause difficulty wherever he went. Butler was destined to be relieved of many posts before the war was over.

Ross Winans had been fortunate enough to get in and out of prison so fast that the judicial hierarchy did not become involved. But the case of John Merryman was different. The Pennsylvania militia had a special distaste for Merryman. As a lieutenant in the Maryland militia, Merryman had reconnoitered them during their brief stay at Cockeysville during the insurrection, and with his Baltimore County Horse Guards he had followed them when they retreated to the north. Later, when Pennsylvania troops had occupied the entire railroad line from Harrisburg to Baltimore, Major General William Keim, their commanding officer, decided the time had come to strike at treason. He called in Lieutenant Abel and told him to take some troops, arrest Merryman, and send him to Fort McHenry.

At 2 A.M. on the morning of May 25, Lieutenant Abel and his troops arrived at Hayfields, the Merryman family estate just outside Cockeysville. The mansion was located at the top of a hill, with extensive, well-groomed grounds. Merryman was a very wealthy man, a leader in his community, and President of the Maryland Agricultural Society. Lieutenant Abel aroused Merryman from his bed and told him he was under arrest. The prisoner dressed and was escorted to the railroad station in Cockeysville, where the party waited for the 7 A.M. train for Baltimore. When it arrived, Merryman and his escort boarded the train and by 9 A.M. he was safely in Fort McHenry.

The entire city of Baltimore started to buzz when it learned of the Merryman arrest. Although he had many friends who might have interceded with the authorities, Merryman decided to seek legal relief. A petition for a writ of habeas corpus was sent to the United States district court in Baltimore. As it happened, this court was in the circuit of Roger B. Taney, Chief Justice of the Supreme Court of the United States. Taney was eighty-four years old, having been appointed to the Supreme Court by Andrew Jackson a quarter of a century earlier as a reward for helping Jackson break up the national bank. A Marylander by birth, he had lived many years in Baltimore, and was a strong believer in States Rights. He had written the Dred Scott decision in 1857 which held it unconstitutional for Congress to outlaw slavery in the territories. He was, above all, not a man to be cowed by military authority.

Taney issued the writ of habeas corpus, commanding General Cadwalader to appear before him at 11 o'clock on May 27, bringing "the body of John Merryman . . . now in your custody." But Cadwalader refused, and said he had been authorized to suspend the writ of habeas corpus by the President of the United States. He added, "This is a high and delicate trust and it has been enjoined upon him that it should be executed with judgment and discretion. . . . He [Cadwalader] most respectfully submits for your consideration that those who should co-operate in the present trying and painful position in which our country is placed should not by reason of unnecessary want of confidence in each other increase our embarrassments. He therefore respectfully requests that you will postpone further action upon this case until he can receive instructions from the President of the United States when you shall hear further from him." At the same time, Cadwalader sent a message to Washington outlining his problem and asking for instructions. But Taney would countenance no delay. He immediately ordered the United States marshal to bring General Cadwalader to court "to answer for his contempt." The marshal was denied admission to Fort McHenry and returned to inform Taney that he could not execute the writ. The executive had defied the judiciary and Taney resolved to demand redress.

In one of the supreme moments of drama in American judicial history, Justice Taney appeared in court on May 28, 1861, to hurl his defiance at President Lincoln. He was greatly admired in Baltimore and as he approached the crowded courthouse, leaning on the arm of his grandson, the citizens silently lifted their hats and opened a path for him. With great dignity, this veteran of innumerable legal battles took his seat on the bench and slowly began reading an opinion to be known ever afterward as *Ex parte Merryman*. As elaborated in greater detail shortly afterward, it was to serve as the basic source document for all who opposed the policy of repression throughout the war. The President, he said, had usurped the power to suspend the writ of habeas corpus from Congress, and he cited many precedents in support of this belief. He said that the Constitution had been drawn up after a war against the tyranny of the British sovereign and it did not give the President "more regal and absolute power over the liberty of the citizens than the people of England would have thought it safe to intrust to the Crown." And even if the privilege of the writ of habeas corpus was suspended by act of Congress, there would still be no authority to hold a man indefinitely without trial. The Constitution provides that "in all criminal prosecutions the accused shall enjoy the right to a speedy and public trial by an impartial jury of the state and district wherein the crime shall have been committed, . . . and to be informed of the nature and cause of the accusation; to be confronted with witnesses against him; to have compulsory process for obtaining witnesses in his favor and to have the assistance of counsel for his defense." The basic intent of the Constitution, according to Taney, was being subverted when President Lincoln authorized the arbitrary arrest of persons such as Merryman.

But even more flagrant, in his opinion, was the manner in which the action was carried out. For the military authorities had gone far beyond the mere suspension of the privilege of the writ of habeas corpus. This military force "has by force of arms thrust aside the judicial authorities and officers to whom the Constitution has confided the power and duty of interpreting and administering the laws and substituted a military government in its place to be administered and executed by military officers, for at the time these proceedings were held against John Merryman the district judge of Maryland — the commissioner appointed under the act of Congress — the district attorney and the marshal all reside in the city of Baltimore a few miles only from the home of the prisoner. . . . And yet under these circumstances a military officer stationed in Pennsylvania without giving any information to the district attorney and without any application to the judicial authorities assumes to himself the judicial power in the district of Maryland; undertakes to decide what constitutes the crime of treason or rebellion; what evidence (if indeed he required any) is sufficient to support the accusation and justify the commitment; and commits the party without having a hearing even before himself to close custody in a strongly-garrisoned fort to be there held it would seem during the pleasure of those who committed him."

The President, he said, "does not faithfully execute the laws if he takes upon himself the legislative power by suspending the writ of habeas corpus — and the judicial power also by arresting and imprisoning a person without due process of law." He concluded that in such a case his duty was too plain to be mistaken. "I have exercised all the power which the Constitution and laws confer on me but that power has been resisted by a force too strong for me to overcome." He therefore ordered that his opinion be filed and a copy of it transmitted under seal to the President of the United States, where it would remain "with that officer in fulfillment of his constitutional obligation to 'take care that the laws be faithfully executed.' "

After Taney had finished reading the opinion, Mayor Brown went up to the bench and thanked him for upholding the integrity of the writ of habeas corpus.

"Mayor Brown," said Taney. "I am an old man, a very old man, but perhaps I was preserved for this occasion."

"Sir, I thank God that you were," Brown replied.

Taney said that he knew his own imprisonment had been under consideration by the Lincoln Administration. In this he was probably correct. The newspapers were filled with stories of the imminent arrest of Taney. Horace Greeley's New York *Tribune* reported that Taney might "suddenly find himself in the embraces of the strong arm of that same military power which he is so defiant of. It may be necessary to teach him . . . that a Judge of the Supreme Court of the United States can be just as obnoxious to the laws against treason as John Merryman can be." But the danger passed and Taney was not arrested.

On May 30, the district attorney in Maryland consulted with President Lincoln about the Merryman case. The pros and cons of giving up the prisoner were weighed but it was finally decided that he should be held. Even the personal friendship of the Secretary of War, Simon Cameron, was not enough to bring Merryman's release. The matter had gone too far. Taney's opinion had been headlined in many newspapers, especially in the border states, and many printed it verbatim. President Lincoln did not feel that he could give in to the old Chief Justice at this point. And so Merryman was held. It was to prove a fateful decision. The fabric of American society had already been torn geographically by the secession movement. Now it was to be wrenched once again as the theory of balance of power so carefully written into the Constitution to safeguard individual liberty was cast aside and judicial restraint ignored.

Merryman's niche in history was carved by his petition and he was forced to pay the penalty. He remained in Fort McHenry throughout June and into July. On July 10, the grand jury of the United States district court found an indictment for treason against him, charging that he had burned six bridges on the Harrisburg railroad, cut the telegraph lines and "with a great multitude of persons . . . to the number of five hundred persons and upwards, armed . . . with guns, pistols, dirks, clubs and stones, and other warlike weapons . . . [did] traitorously join and assemble" against the United States of America. Finally, on July 13, just seven weeks after his arrest, he was surrendered to the civil authorities, and admitted to bail in the amount of $40,000. He was charged to appear for trial at the November term of the United States circuit court in Baltimore and released to receive the cordial greetings of his many friends. He then returned to his home at Hayfields where he resumed his duties as a gentleman farmer.

Merryman was never brought to trial. When the November term convened, so many others persons had been sent to prison that neither he nor the district attorney could get the necessary witnesses. So they agreed to postpone the case till the May term. But in May they had precisely the same problem and the trial was postponed once again. By then the district attorney realized the folly of bringing Merryman to trial among his friends in Baltimore, and the case was dropped.

CHAPTER 4

A CITY ON TRIAL

By THE MIDDLE of May, Maryland was firmly on the Union side. The insurrection in Baltimore had run out of power and the legislature had met without making the slightest move toward seccession. The state was in the hands of Union troops and the road to Washington was wide open. In the month since Fort Sumter, insurrection had been tried in Maryland and failed. The South had not seized the tremendous opportunity presented by this slave state which was on the frontier of the new Confederacy. The insurrection was allowed to languish and die without help. A bold stroke by Virginia immediately after the insurrection might have altered the history of a continent.

But no help came from the South and Baltimore, back in the United States, could only hope that its punishment would not be too great. Its position was precarious. As long as men who had close ties of friendship with the city, such as General Cadwalader, remained in command, the punishment would be light. But should the tide turn against Baltimore, it would find that it had forfeited its right to a fair hearing. Any argument in favor of dealing lightly with the city could be overhwelmed by a passionate reference to the blood of the Massachusetts Sixth. Baltimore was therefore treading a fine line, with full knowledge that any incident against the federal troops would be magnified many times.

It was Baltimore's misfortune that the correspondent of the

New York *Tribune* in Baltimore was a man named Worthington G. Snethen. He was a politician whose father, Nicholas Snethen, had been one of the best-known and most eloquent preachers in Maryland. His own talents, however, were more in the direction of writing and he had edited the Baltimore *Patriot* in 1860. After the election of Lincoln, he sought the ministry to Russia, but was refused and took a job as Baltimore correspondent of Mr. Greeley's *Tribune*. During May and June he carried out an increasingly bitter campaign against the police commissioners and Marshal Kane which was read by people all over the North. For the power of the New York press was tremendous and went far beyond the confines of New York City. The *Tribune*, particularly, was read avidly all over the North. Snethen's influence as editor of a Union Baltimore newspaper would have been negligible, but as the Baltimore correspondent of the *Tribune*, he could wield enormous power. This he proceeded to do.

Playing on the hatred of the North for the city, he built up a case against the secessionists in Baltimore that grew with every passing day. In the columns of the *Tribune*, he criticized the release of Ross Winans and the failure to displace the police commissioners and Marshal Kane, which, he said, had "only served to madden enemies of the Republic." He reported that the Board of Police were busy displacing every man suspected of Unionism. "Not less than a dozen have bitten the dust in the last ten days."

Criticism of the conditions in Baltimore was linked with criticism of General Cadwalader, the Union commander there. Cadwalader was from Pennsylvania, and had been a brigadier general of the militia during the Mexican War. He was a Democrat, owned property in Baltimore and was generally sympathetic with the agonizing position of the people who lived in the border slave states. He did not initiate any repressive measures when he succeeded Butler. The more radical Union elements in the city, including Snethen, hated him for this and appealed continually for his removal.

The campaign against Cadwalader succeeded by the 10th of June, just before the special Congressional election in Maryland. Cadwalader was replaced by General Nathaniel P. Banks of Massachusetts, a man of entirely different attitudes. He came from the hated state of Massachusetts, home of the Sixth Regiment that had been mauled on the streets of the city. Banks was a driving, dynamic man who had been speaker of the national House of Representatives and governor of Massachusetts. The radical elements among the Union men expected great things from him, and they were not to be disappointed.

There were dire predictions that the secessionists planned a riot in Baltimore during the Congressional election. The day before the election Snethen's article in the New York *Tribune* stated that "there is a decided purpose on the part of the Rebels here to create a disturbance on election day. They have been holding secret meetings and a riot was in contemplation. Yesterday, there were boys offering for sale Secession flags, printed on cards — the same as were sold the day before bloody Friday." But when the voters went to the polls, they cast their ballots without interference from either the secessionist mobs or the Union troops. They were able to choose between three parties, the Unconditional Unionists who pledged unquestioned loyalty to the Union, the States Rights party which was secessionist-minded, and the Conditional Union party standing about halfway between them. This was the last free election to be held in Maryland during the war and the result proved once again Maryland's basic loyalty. Of the six Congressmen elected, five were Unconditional Union men, and one was a Conditional Union candidate. Not a single States Rights candidate was elected. The one Conditional Union man elected was Henry May, who won mainly because of antipathy in Baltimore for his Unconditional Union opponent, Henry Winter Davis, a brilliant but contentious former Know-Nothing. Any lurking questions about the possibility of secession in Maryland was settled by this election.

After the election, Snethen's articles in the *Tribune* and stories appearing in other New York papers became even more vehement against the secessionists in Baltimore. Of course, the raw materials that Snethen had to work with were considerable. Treasonable talk was still common on the streets as small groups of secessionists frequently gathered in defiant groups for discussion. Furthermore, the men running the city were exactly the same ones who had led the insurrection. The mayor, police marshal, police commissioners and the members of the police force were nearly all opposed to the war and many were outright secessionists. This was a highly unstable situation for a city as vital to the Northern cause as Baltimore.

As it happened, however, not a single incident occurred in the passage of the tens of thousands of troops through the city during June. Not a shot was fired against them, not a single demonstration occurred. But to read Snethen's articles, one would think the troops were forced to fight their way through the city daily. One day, for instance, he reported that there had been rumors of an attack, so a troop train was stopped, and the soldiers were ordered to load their muskets and "fight to the death." As they marched through the city, Snethen reported, "a brick was thrown at a private," "a shot came from behind a fence," and "firing was heard from one of our picket guards." But they got through all right.

Among the many stories that Snethen wrote to stir the emotions of loyal men everywhere, was one about the Baltimore *Sun*:

> I must tell you also about *The Sun* newspaper corner. Here it is that the last fragment of the Rebels daily congregate, and, when a U.S. soldier passes, remarks are indulged in of the most offensive character; such as "you will make good manure for the soil of Virginia." The police take no notice of this, but laugh after the soldier has passed.

Each day had its own story. Another day it was:

I learned through a lady who was sitting at a window, and saw
the transaction, that while the 3d Maine Regiment was passing
the corner of Hanover and Pratt streets, yesterday, a man drew
his revolver and pointed it at the soldiers, as though he was going
to shoot, when a police officer seized him and quietly carried
him off.

Secession songs are hawked about the streets to-day with unusual activity and by droves of boys. Secession flags are paraded
in the windows and doors of shops on Lexington street, and the
boys, too, in their mock marches, display them more boldly.

With every new story, the bombardment became more effective. By June 21, Snethen was reporting that Union troops were
being "grossly insulted by bodies of Secessionists who used
their foul tongues without restraint, accompanying their abuse
with displays of the Jeff. Davis pirate flag. The insolence of
these rebels was insufferable, and their boldness unusual. . . .
Just remove the 5,000 bayonets now bristling around Baltimore, and a second St. Bartholomew would instantly ensue."
The next day, he reported that "according to the best Secession authority, there are not less than 10,000 arms of the best
kinds in the hands of the disaffected in this city, distributed
separately among the Secessionists, and ready to be turned
upon the loyal population at the first signal. The Secession
leaders of the State are in daily communication with the leaders
of the rebellion in Virginia, and are kept constantly advised of
the designs of Jeff. Davis, which look steadily to the invasion of
Maryland."

These stories were just what Greeley wanted for his paper.
New York's great riot, which was destined to be 100 times more
destructive than Baltimore's, was still two years away. Baltimore had the misfortune of being the first and it was helpless
in the hands of men like Snethen and Greeley. Although some
other New York papers echoed his sentiments, it was the *Tribune* which was leading the pack against Baltimore.

And so, after building up national sentiment against Baltimore, Snethen finally decided that the time had come for direct action. He went to Washington and had a conference with his friend, Simon Cameron, and old General Scott. He persuaded them that Marshal Kane and the police commissioners should be arrested. Scott issued a secret order to General Banks to "seize at once and securely hold the four members of the Baltimore police board . . . together with their chief of the police." He gave the order to Snethen to deliver to Banks.

Although Baltimore was a hotbed of rumors during this period, not the slightest hint of this order got out. The orders were hand carried to Baltimore and General Banks laid his plans carefully. He knew that the key to success lay in arresting Marshal Kane first. The mighty Kane had become almost a legend in the city. Tough, cocky, intelligent, he was the kind of man who instantly commanded any situation in which he found himself. It was decided that the arrest of such a man would require a major effort.

Banks sent 1,000 men in the middle of the night to do the job. About 1:30 in the morning of June 27, the troops moved quietly out from the dark recesses of Fort McHenry. They marched past Federal Hill, turned north and crossed the center of the dark city. Each policeman who was passed along the route was picked up and taken along with the troops, lest he give the alarm. At 3 A.M. this small army reached Kane's house in the northern part of the city and surrounded it. Men were placed on all the adjacent streets, in case of an attempted escape, and when all was in readiness, an officer stepped up to the door of the house and rang the bell.

Marshal Kane was asleep when the troops arrived. When the bell rang, he stuck his head out of the upstairs window and asked what was the matter. He was told to come down to the front door. He came downstairs, opened the door and was told by the officer that he should consider himself under arrest. Kane took a look at the mass of men sent to arrest him and said that if General Banks had wanted to see him he "need only have sent a note." Kane was placed in a hack and escorted

to Fort McHenry by the 1,000 troops. He was given a room
to share with John Merryman.

The next morning, the city awoke and did not believe. The
first salutation between friends was, "I hear Marshal Kane has
been arrested. Is it so?" Such a thing as arresting "*the* Marshal
Kane" seemed utterly impossible. Citizens congregated on the
street corners and the excitement grew amid cheers for
Jeff Davis. A Union soldier named James Manley made a loud
remark that now that they had Marshal Kane at the Fort they
would hang him. The crowd immediately threatened to hang
Manley and the police were forced to rescue him. On Federal
Hill, cannon were placed to command each street leading to
the camp and orders were issued to all military units in the city
to hold themselves in readiness for attack.

Later in the morning, General Banks issued a proclamation
in which he said that groups of men in the city were organizing
against the federal government and Marshal Kane had been
"by direction or indirection, both witness and protector" of
such groups. He said that he had therefore arrested Kane and
had appointed Colonel Kenly, of his staff, as provost marshal
of Baltimore. Thus he placed the city of Baltimore under martial law.

Colonel Kenly was a good choice for a difficult job. He had
been called to duty when Governor Hicks had summoned four
regiments of militia to the colors in his delayed response to
President Lincoln's call for troops after Fort Sumter. Kenly
was a Baltimore lawyer and politician whose services on active
duty in the Mexican War had earned him the official thanks
of the state "for distinguished gallantry." On the morning that
Banks appointed him provost marshal, he went to see the
mayor and police commissioners and told them he was taking
over the police power. The commissioners protested the move
but decided to allow Kenly to exercise authority until they
had had time to consider the matter. Then the commissioners
went into secret session to work out their own strategy.

It took them just three hours to decide on a dramatic

counter-move. At 2 o'clock that afternoon they passed a resolution suspending the police law in Baltimore. The city's
four hundred policemen were called to their station houses
and notified that they were "off duty for the present." The
police captains were ordered to leave the station houses immediately and take with them all movable effects. Within a
few minutes all portable property had been carried off,
including all the official records, dockets, blank warrants, revolvers, muskets, rattles, and sticks. The station houses were
left completely empty and by mid-afternoon the 200,000 inhabitants of Baltimore were without police protection.

This bold move to seize the initiative from the federal forces,
however, was defeated by the energy of Colonel Kenly. He
asked Deputy Marshal Gifford to assume charge, but when
Gifford said there wasn't "enough money in the federal
treasury" to persuade him to do that, Kenly began swearing
in new policemen. With a vast army of unemployed in the
city, he had no difficulty in finding men and by nightfall there
was a fairly sizable force at his command. All the saloons were
closed and no disturbances occurred during the night. The
lack of police uniforms was met temporarily by having each
man wear a pink ribbon in the buttonhole of his coat. This
makeshift police force was backed up, of course, by some 7,000
federal troops in the city.

The next day, word reached General Banks that a vast quantity of war material intended for the secessionists was concealed in the old City Hall. An inspection of the rafters and
closets uncovered 200-300 assorted rifles and muskets, some
six-pound guns, a half keg of shot for Winans' famous steam-
gun, about 12,000 cartridges of various types and a ten-pound
cannon ball from Fort Sumter which had been presented to
Marshal Kane. Some of the weapons had come from the baggage train of the Sixth Massachusetts, seized on April 19.
General Banks had this "concealed arsenal" seized and cited
it as proof of a secessionist plot in Baltimore.

Snethen was fearful that the police commissioners would not be arrested and sent a letter to Scott that "there is no telling how soon they may rally their old police, and precipitate the city into convulsion." And so more arrests were ordered by General Banks. He laid his plans very carefully for the arrest of the four police commissioners. It was decided that some 1,200 troops would be necessary to do the job in the middle of the night. He mustered them into four commands of 300 men each, and they set out at 2 A.M. on the morning of July 1 in a drizzling rain. Each of the commands was given the name of one police commissioner to arrest. To Colonel Jones, who had led the Sixth Massachusetts through the city on April 19, went the honor of arresting the President of the Police Board, Charles Howard, in his fine home on Cathedral Street. Colonel Jones proceeded there with his troops, arriving about 3 A.M. He rang the bell and Mr. Howard, who had three sons in the Confederate Army, appeared at the upper window, asking what the matter was. Colonel Jones answered that he desired to see him forthwith. When Mr. Howard appeared at the door, he was told that he was under arrest. Howard said he would be ready in a moment, dressed and said goodbye to his wife. Then he was escorted by the 300 troops to Fort McHenry.

About the same time, another group of 300 soldiers visited the home of Mr. Charles D. Hinks, a member of the Police Board. When he came to the door, the officer making the arrest read his "warrant," in the form of an order from General Banks. Hinks was in very delicate health but went readily with the troops to Fort McHenry. The two other police commissioners, William Gatchell and John W. Davis were also arrested that night in similar manner and taken to the Fort.

Banks, probably at the bidding of Snethen, took action to prevent an uprising in the city after the arrest of the commissioners. Federal troops, which had previously been stationed on the outskirts of the city, were ordered to occupy the entire city before dawn on July 1. In the early hours of the morning, infantry and artillery troops quietly marched to the center of the city and occupied the principal streets. A contingent of Massachusetts artillery, with four field pieces, was stationed in Monument Square and a number of men were quartered in the courthouse. All the gates leading to the post office were guarded and some thirty men took up positions inside the building. The guard at Exchange Place, the commercial heart of the city, was stronger than anywhere else, and two brass pieces were planted there, ranging east and west, covering all approaches to the front door of the custom house. Guards controlled the railroad stations and the troops bivouacked in the streets.

When the city awakened that morning it was greeted by a proclamation from General Banks stating that he had arrested the commissioners because of the "concealed arsenal" he had found in the old City Hall, plus the fact that they had discharged the police force and still held them "subject to their orders." He said that he had placed part of his command in the city to prevent incidents but he had no intention of interfering with the ordinary municipal affairs. During the day, no one showed any interest in starting another insurrection and there was not even the threat of a riot. Several additional persons were arrested but most were released within twenty-four hours. William McKewen, clerk of the commissioners, was arrested when the office of the Police Board was seized. Colonel Kenly, however, ordered his immediate release. Two others were arrested near the post office for using disrespectful language about the federal government. They were confined for a short time in the custom house and then released.

Searches and seizures were carried on throughout the city. The home of Charles Howard, President of the Police Board, was searched by a squad of five federal policemen while he was in prison. His wife protested when the soldiers arrived and she refused to give them keys to the locked rooms and cabinets in the house. Her son, Frank Key Howard, editor of one of Baltimore's pro-Southern newspapers, was called in and he

demanded that the soldiers stop their search. Despite these
protests, a locksmith was obtained and the house ransacked
from top to bottom. Three muskets were found. Many other
homes of secessionist sympathizers in the city were visited
during the next few days and similarly searched. As this activity continued the military forces remained in the center of the
city, camping in the streets, on private lots and in parks. After
about a week, they were withdrawn and the city returned more
nearly to normal.

Police Commissioner Charles Hinks was released only four
days after his arrest. A man already in the advanced stages of
consumption, he had been living in the South due to his illness.
His return to Baltimore after the insurrection had plunged
him into the midst of political events in which he had played
no part. It was felt by Union officials that "his death in prison
would make an unpleasant impression," and when General
Banks recommended his release on parole the authorities in
Washington were agreeable. Marshal Kane and the other three
police commissioners remained in prison however.

The city was completely quiet now. General Banks reported
that "there is no fear of an outbreak." But Reverdy Johnson
and some other men in the city were proposing that Charles
Howard be released from Fort McHenry. During consideration
of the case, Banks expressed his opinion of the need for holding these men in prison. "I think the government must make
these men feel its power, just as a matter of argument. They
do not comprehend the condition of things at all. They read
nothing but their own papers. They talk only with each other.
They live and move in small coteries into which no ideas can
penetrate except their own. . . . They have as little idea of
national sentiment or power as a man corked up in a phial
would have of a natural atmosphere — and thus though they
are pestilent traitors, they are innocent as babes. If the government makes them feel its power they will immediately understand the condition of things, and think and talk and act as

the rest of the world does. The arrest did them good. Those that are not to be tried . . . should be sent to Fort Delaware for a few weeks and then released." And so Howard remained in prison.

The arrest of the marshal and police commissioners was greeted with unrestrained glee in the North. The New York *Tribune* which had labored so untiringly to bring about the arrests reported that "General Banks has struck a blow at the heart of treason in Baltimore by the arrest and imprisonment of George P. Kane." It added that Baltimore "is virtually placed under martial law, as it should have been long since. All know that it is a focus of conspiracy and treason; all know that it is liable at any critical moment to break out into open and violent rebellion."

Everybody connected with the event received commendations and it was considered one of the great victories of the war. General Scott was quoted as saying that "its bloodlessness does not detract from its brilliance, but rather adds to its glory."

For the Union had few enough victories in Maryland to boast of, and none that the Marylanders themselves had won. But some eight hundred miles to the west lay another slave state, Missouri, where the same testing of wills was taking place as in Maryland. In this state, however, the stronger will lay on the side of the Union. While Maryland was being won by troops from the North, Missouri was being won by troops from St. Louis, led by a fanatical Army captain and a politician whose brother was in Lincoln's cabinet. These two men set the stage for an explosion in the West that began just a few weeks after Fort Sumter and resulted in the first Southern military defeat of the war.

CHAPTER 5

THE BATTLE OF ST. LOUIS

BEFORE DAWN on the morning of May 10, 1861, a lone horse-man could be heard galloping southward from the city of St. Louis to the military post at Jefferson Barracks, just eight miles away. In his tunic he carried special orders from the Union commander at St. Louis to the First Regiment of Missouri Volunteers stationed at the Barracks. The orders were delivered to the commanding officer of the post and they spoke dramatically. Every man in the regiment was to be given forty rounds of ammunition and the entire regiment was to march immediately. At 8 A.M., the gates of the Barracks opened wide and the regiment began moving out exactly as ordered, toward a field in St. Louis called Lindell's Grove. As they were marching northward, the gates of another military post, the great United States Arsenal in St. Louis, swung open and two more regiments began filing out. Every man had forty rounds of ammunition and every rifle was loaded. The troops turned north on Broadway and headed toward the heart of Democratic St. Louis. Their destination was the same, Lindell's Grove.

At precisely the same time still another regiment moved out of the Marine Hospital in St. Louis and turned northward with the steady tread of marching feet toward Lindell's Grove. At other points in the southern wards of St. Louis, smaller companies of armed men were forming up and marching toward the Grove. By noon all southern St. Louis was astir. But the troops moved quietly, without announcement, and without

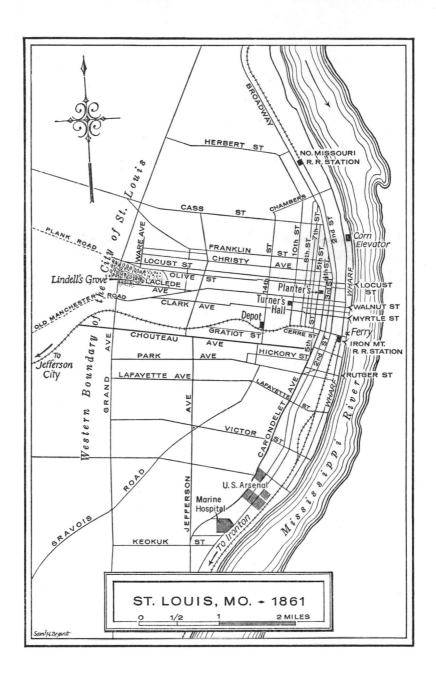

ST. LOUIS, MO. - 1861

0   1/2   1   2 MILES

drums or bugles. Their foremost weapon was surprise. Most of them were Germans who had been given military training in Europe. They were now marching against an enemy whose ancestry in America could be traced back many generations.

As regiment after regiment of Germans moved toward the heart of St. Louis, the excitement began to rise. The people of the city slowly became aware that their Civil War was beginning this day. Down Broadway the troops marched into the center of the business district, where they wheeled to the west and moved onto the long streets leading to Lindell's Grove. In command was Brigadier General Nathaniel Lyon, who had been a captain in the Regular Army just two weeks before. A thin-faced man of impetuous temperament, he hated slavery, loved the Union, and believed in offensive action. He had conceived and planned this attack on the state militia and was now launched into the greatest day in his short but meteoric career.

Out in Lindell's Grove, some 800 Missouri State Militia were camped, most of them without blankets, guns or uniforms. Their commander, Brigadier General D. M. Frost, heard about 10 A.M. the incredible report that Lyon was marching toward him. Even more incredible was the fact that Lyon had at his back some 5,000 troops, which gave wings to the thought that Lyon might be planning to capture the entire camp. In desperation, Frost decided to ask Lyon himself what his plans were. "I am constantly in receipt of information that you contemplate an attack on my camp," he wrote in a note to Lyon. "I would be glad to know from you personally whether there is any truth in the statements." General Frost gave the note to a colonel in his command who dashed off on horseback and reached Lyon in full march at the head of a column of troops. He tried to hand the message to Lyon but the General refused even to look at it and brushed the colonel aside without uttering a word. His troops continued marching forward without losing a step.

Frost was still waiting for a reply when Lyon's men suddenly reached the camp and surrounded it from the dominating heights. As the Union troops appeared, a few of the state militia dropped their arms and ran. The remaining men looked up and found themselves staring at the barrels of several thousand rifles and a number of artillery pieces.

General Lyon reached into his pocket and pulled out a letter he had prepared for the occasion, demanding from Frost the "immediate surrender of your command, with no other conditions than that all persons surrendering under this demand shall be humanely and kindly treated." He sent it off to Frost and gave him a half hour for compliance. When Frost sent back a request for more time, Lyon scribbled on the back of his note that unless Frost surrendered within ten minutes he would open fire.

At this moment, the Civil War in Missouri hung in the balance. It was less than a month after Fort Sumter, and Union and secession men in Missouri were facing each other behind rifle sights and artillery pieces. War had come quickly in the West but pressure had been building up for a long time. Through the long, dreary years of the repeal of the Missouri Compromise, the Dred Scott case, and the Kansas wars, Missouri had been the breeding ground of the "irrepressible conflict." When 1861 dawned on the nation, with secession an actuality rather than a remote possibility, Missouri was thrown into a convulsion. Early in the year, the secessionist state legislature under the leadership of its new Governor, Claiborne Jackson, had overwhelmingly passed a bill calling for a Sovereign Convention, in the expectation that Missouri would secede from the Union. But ten years of open conflict had developed the kind of Union leadership in Missouri that was absent in Maryland. The leader of this Union group was the dominant, driving Frank P. Blair, Jr., brother of Montgomery Blair, soon to become Postmaster General in the Lincoln cabinet. In early 1861, Frank Blair organized the Unconditional

Union party and this group, together with the Conditional Union party, delivered a stunning defeat to the secessionists. When the votes were counted on election day, it was discovered that not a single Secessionist Party candidate had been elected to the state convention, although the party had numbered among its leaders the governor, lieutenant governor, a majority of the state legislature, and both United States Senators. This was the blackest day for secession in Missouri and one of the blackest for the South in the entire war. For without the border slave states the South was hopelessly outnumbered and this election, coming on February 18, 1861, served notice on the Southern Confederacy that the border states were slipping from them.

While the election was being contested, the secessionists formed a military group they called the Minutemen, composed of Southern-minded citizens of St. Louis, who were hopeful that they could seize the United States arsenal in the city. The St. Louis arsenal was the key to Missouri, with the largest cache of military weapons west of the Mississippi River. It was garrisoned by a handful of regular troops and could easily have been taken by a determined attack. As early as February, the Minutemen had several hundred men drilling in the city and on March 4, when Lincoln was inaugurated, they nearly precipitated a riot in downtown St. Louis by hoisting a Confederate flag over their headquarters. In April, when President Lincoln made his call after Fort Sumter for troops to help put down the insurrection, Governor Jackson replied that such a request was "inhuman and diabolical" and said that Missouri would furnish "not one man" for such an "unholy crusade." At the same time, Jackson was writing to the Confederate Secretary of War that he had plenty of men "ready, willing and anxious to march at any moment to the defense of the South." The gathering strength of the secessionists looked ominous to the Union cause in St. Louis.

But the Union men were not sleeping. Union sentiment

had long been active and well led. Its main source of power in St. Louis lay in the German wards south of the business district. Many of these Germans had fled the tyranny of Europe after the failure of the revolutionary movement of 1848 and had personal reasons for hating slavery. As the strength of the Minutemen began to threaten the arsenal, the Union men, under the leadership of the politician Frank Blair, the general Nathaniel Lyon, and a self-appointed Committee of Safety, began to enlist the Germans at the arsenal. As luck would have it, the arsenal was located in the German section and as the priceless rifles and ammunition found their way into the hands of German Unionists, the danger of attack by the Minutemen passed. By early May, there were several thousand Union men under arms.

Now it was the secessionists who were being threatened. With the state government firmly under their control, they formed a militia camp on the western edge of St. Louis and called it Camp Jackson, after their secessionist governor. Lindell's Grove, where the camp was located, had been a militia summer training ground for years and it formed a kind of amphitheater, lying in a gully between two roads from which there was a perfect view of the entire camp. With many well-to-do young men drilling there, the camp within a few days became a fashionable resort, as General Frost wrote, for "all sexes, ages, classes and conditions of citizens, who thronged its shady avenues all day and into night." Among the visitors in early May was General Lyon, who drove through the camp in disguise to reconnoiter. He soon realized that although the camp was fine for watching the soldiers drill, its location in a gully made it impossible to defend. With his imagination fired, Lyon asked the Union Committee on Safety to let him attack the camp and rid the city of this threat. After some debate, it was finally agreed and Lyon sent out his carefully scheduled orders, designed to have regiments from all parts of St. Louis arrive simultaneously on all four sides of the camp. He succeeded to a remarkable degree and so he and General Frost faced each other in mid-afternoon on May 10, with one army demanding the complete surrender of the other within ten minutes.

Frost's position was completely hopeless. He was vastly outnumbered by well-armed troops which occupied the high spots surrounding his camp. He had ten minutes to decide whether to fight and die gloriously with his command, or surrender and spend the rest of his life under the shadow of his failure. Frost took the full ten minutes allotted him and then surrendered his entire camp, saying that he was "wholly unprepared" to defend himself from this "unwarranted attack." All of his troops were immediately ordered to lay down their arms and the Union troops moved into the camp and took charge. They seized the artillery and mortars and the prisoners were lined up in the center of the road with a single file of Union soldiers on each side. The state militia were offered their freedom if they would take the oath, but few agreed. Soon everything was ready for the long march back to the arsenal.

But around the Union troops, an ominous wave of hatred was building up. Camp Jackson had deliberately been located in a secessionist area, and a large unfriendly mob had followed Lyon out from the city. The crowds had grown rapidly around the camp and soon the area was jammed with people who hated the Germans and were humiliated by the surrender of their troops. While the mob was getting more exasperated, the order was given to the volunteers to march. They had gone only a few feet, however, when the line stopped and there was another long, unexplained delay. They continued to wait for two whole hours while the mob surrounding the troops became angrier and angrier. Insults and abuse were heaped on the German troops as the crowd called out the names of individual prisoners and cheered them. "Damn the Dutch" went up along the line and repeated cheers were given for Jeff Davis.

Just at sunset the order was finally given to the volunteers to march. As they started forward, "this clapped the demon on the fury of the mob," one correspondent wrote. All along the line fighting suddenly broke out. William T. Sherman, later the famous Union general, was president of the St. Louis Railroad Company on May 10th and along with many other citizens he went out to Camp Jackson to see the spectacle. As the column started moving forward about sunset he saw a drunken civilian try to cross the road along which the troops were moving. A sergeant ordered him back, and he tried to seize the sergeant's rifle. There was a short scuffle and the civilian fell into a ditch beside the road. Sherman said that when he got up, he "had in his hand a small pistol, which he fired." This started the fighting in Sherman's area, and as the soldiers began firing, a general stampede developed. Several soldiers dropped dead in the road and the volunteers began firing wildly at the mob. The confusion was terrible. With the ununiformed volunteers and citizens bumping against each other it was difficult to tell who was shooting whom. Some of the soldiers were killed by Minié balls from the rifles of their comrades. General Lyon ordered the firing to cease, but it did no good.

The troops by now were marching forward and the mob fell in at their rear and started throwing rocks and firing revolvers at them. One infuriated man took three shots at the lieutenant in charge of the rear and missed him three times. As he was leveling his revolver on his arm to fire the fourth time, a soldier rushed up to him and thrust him through with a bayonet. Women and children were caught in the cross-fire and fled screaming from the scene. Some were hit by bullets as they ran.

A gardener who lived just across the street from Lindell's Grove had come out of his house to see the excitement. He was hit by a bullet and killed instantly. One of the bartenders from Barnum's Hotel in downtown St. Louis had followed the troops out from the center of the city. He was shot through the head and killed instantly. A carpenter who had built up quite a business in the city with his partner was killed in the fighting.

But it was the prisoners who were in the worst position of all. Not able either to run or to defend themselves, they were forced to stay where they were and several who had surrendered without firing a shot at Camp Jackson were killed during the rioting. William T. Sherman, who had his son with him, was able to jump into a small gully and thus gain shelter. The war would certainly have been much different had he not been so fortunate. The wounded and dying were scattered all along the road and in the fields.

One wealthy resident of St. Louis had heard about the attack on Camp Jackson and had ridden out there on his horse. In the fighting that followed the surrender, he became a prime target. One Minié ball shattered his arm and another killed his horse under him, but he survived to tell the story. The conductor of the streetcar that ran out to the camp started running away from the scene when the firing began. But he was picked off by a stray bullet and severely wounded. The reporter of a St. Louis newspaper wrote that night:

> We went over the grove immediately after the occurrence, and a more fearful and ghastly sight is seldom seen. Men lay gasping in the agony of death and staining the green grass with their blood as it flowed from their wounds. Children of 8 or 10 years of age were pale and motionless as if asleep under the trees, and women cried in pain as they lay upon the ground. One, a girl of 14, presented a mournful picture, as she reclined against a stump, her face cold and white from the sudden touch of death. We found fifteen dead persons, and half as many wounded, lying around.

Others died later from that most dread of all Civil War diseases, infection. An eighteen-year-old son of a well-known St. Louis family started running away when the firing began. In the confusion one of the soldiers pierced his back with a bayonet, causing a small wound about an inch deep. He walked to his home three miles away after the riot and his parents called the doctors to look at the wound. They thought it was not serious. But the next day it became inflamed and internal hemorrhaging began. By nightfall he was dead. Another man, a boot and shoe merchant in the city, was struck by a Minié ball and his left leg shattered. The leg was amputated but a week later he died from gangrene.

The most famous of all the injured was Captain Blandovski. He was a Polish officer serving with the Union troops. A man of striking appearance and easy manner, he was fond of recounting his exploits in the revolutionary movements of Poland and Hungary and the story of how he had drifted over America and traveled the Rocky Mountains. A skilled fencing master, he had been employed by the wealthy people in the city to give fencing lessons to their children. He was on his horse with the Union troops when the riot began and his leg was shattered by a Minié ball from the misdirected rifle of a comrade. The next day his leg was amputated but infection had set in and the doctors could not stop it. Each day the newspapers reported his progress and his increasingly hopeless condition. Finally, after lingering for two weeks, he died and a funeral with full military honors was given him.

It was estimated that about fifteen or twenty people were killed in the riot. The firing did not last long. As soon as the troops had proceeded a few blocks away from Camp Jackson it was over. By now it was dark and as the column passed down the long street into the city, the doors and shutters were slammed shut on them and the street became very quiet and gloomy. The volunteers had not eaten since morning, but their victory was complete and they were in good spirits. About halfway into the city, they wheeled to the right and started marching south. Here they were beginning to get into some of the German wards and a few people were gathered in the streets to cheer them on. Union flags appeared along the way and ladies waved their handkerchiefs.

As block followed block the scene became more animated and by the time they reached the heavily German wards, there were thousands of people on the sidewalks, at the windows, and on the porches. Cheer after cheer was given to them and the whole avenue looked like a living sea as the big stream of glistening bayonets flowed southward. The leading prisoner was General Frost who had been humiliated and whose military career was ruined by the events of this day. He later said he would have "preferred total annihilation to being dragged like convicts through our native city, scouted at and derided by men who could scarcely speak our language, and finally to be penned up like slaves upon the middle passage." He and the rest of the militia were locked up in the arsenal that night and news was sent to Washington of the first Union success of the Civil War. Coming at just this time, after the fall of Sumter and while Baltimore was still closed to Northern troops, this decisive victory elated the Government in Washington. St. Louis had been won for the Union.

But elation was scarcely the word to describe the reaction in the Missouri State Capital at Jefferson City when news of Camp Jackson arrived. Here the secession legislature was still in session, plagued with the same indecision that infected the legislatures of the other border slave states. It had failed for months to confront the primary issues of the day, hoping to be able to avoid any decision as to war or peace by simply doing nothing. Suddenly, in the midst of this monumental inactivity, the bolt of lightning struck on May 10, when news arrived of the capture of Camp Jackson by the Union forces. Anger, fear and panic took hold of the legislature as it began to mobilize for war against the Union. It immediately started passing a set of laws designed to gather the entire state in arms against the aggressive Unionists in St. Louis.

CHAPTER 6

MISSOURI IN TURMOIL

AFTER Fort Sumter, the secessionists in the Missouri legislature had set out to pass a military bill designed to arm the
governor, Claiborne Jackson, with all the money and power he
needed to organize an effective army. They felt that if the North
and South came to blows, they would remain aloof from the
battle, request both sides to keep troops out of the state, and
use the state militia to enforce the decision. This armed neutrality was the goal of the secessionists in Missouri and they were
determined to bring it about.

The Union men, on the other hand, knew that armed neutrality was the equivalent of secession and they were determined to prevent passage of the Military Bill. There was
a moderately large Union minority in the state legislature and
this minority used all kinds of parliamentary maneuvering to
bring the legislative machinery to a halt on the Military Bill
and prevent its passage. This effort had proven quite successful.
Not only had the bill not yet been passed, but it appeared that
it probably would not be passed. And that was where matters
stood on the morning of May 10, 1861.

About mid-day the word was received in Jefferson City that
Frank Blair and the Germans were moving on Camp Jackson.
And then a few hours later came the dramatic news that the
entire camp had surrendered without a shot. The message was
rushed from the telegraph office to Governor Jackson who
hurried into the house of representatives while it was in session

and announced that the camp had fallen. The news created a frenzy of excitement and the Military Bill was passed in just fifteen minutes. It was sent to the senate where it was passed immediately. The Governor signed it that night. Lyon's attack on Camp Jackson had accomplished something in a few hours that all the secessionists in the state had been unable to accomplish in the month since Fort Sumter.

While this was happening, a kind of hysteria developed in Jefferson City, and the legislators had visions of Union troops descending upon the capital and taking them all prisoner. A special train was ordered by Jackson and at 10:30 that night forty men were sent eastward toward St. Louis to see if any Union troops were advancing. The men were ordered to burn the bridges over the Gasconade and Osage Rivers if Union forces were moving toward the capital. Many of the legislators sent their families across the river to be safe from the fighting and the funds in the state treasury were removed from the city. Dispatches and messengers were hurriedly sent all over the state ordering up troops to defend the capital against Blair and his Germans.

Suddenly at midnight the entire community was aroused once again by the ringing of the church bells. Legislators hurried to the capitol building, carrying pistols, rifles, shotguns, swords, and anything else they thought might be useful for a fight. The legislature looked like a council of war when it met, with guns, pistols, and swords lying about on desks and chairs, and leaning against the walls and tables.

Governor Jackson dramatically entered the chamber shortly after midnight and announced that two Union regiments were on their way to the capital. He told them that they must stand by him or else they "would all be prisoners in 24 hours." Then the panic-ridden legislature proceeded to pass a series of laws such as Missouri had never seen before. In this midnight session, the Governor was voted almost dictatorial powers and $1 million was appropriated for use as he determined. The en-

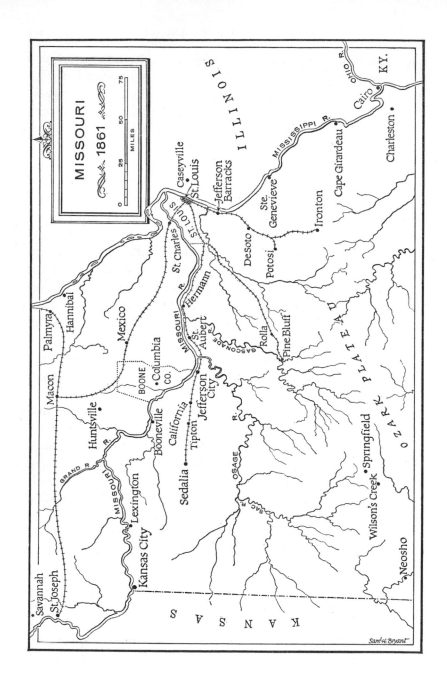

MISSOURI
1861

MILES
0   25   50   75

ILLINOIS

KY.

OHIO R.

Cairo

Charleston

MISSISSIPPI R.

Cape Girardeau

Caseyville
St. Louis
Jefferson
Barracks

Ste.
Genevieve

Ironton

ST. CHARLES R.

ST. LOUIS R.

St. Charles

St. Hermann

DeSoto

Potosi

Rolla

Pine Bluff

GASCONADE R.

OZARK   PLATEAU

Palmyra

Hannibal

Mexico

Macon

Columbia
CO.

BOONE
CO.

MISSOURI R.

St.
Aubert R.

Jefferson
City

Springfield

Wilson's Creek

Huntsville

GRAND R.

MISSOURI R.

Lexington

Booneville

California

Tipton

Sedalia

OSAGE R.

SAC R.

Neosho

Kansas City

Savannah
St. Joseph

KANSAS

Sam'l H. Bryant

tire state School Fund was seized to support military costs, a measure which was very quickly to close the schools in St. Louis. After an exhausting session the members were allowed to go home and get some sleep, subject to reconvening at 7 o'clock in the morning.

Meanwhile, the train which had been sent eastward to reconnoiter proceeded to the limits of St. Louis County but found no evidence of any attack on the capital. So the men returned to Jefferson City. In an excess of zeal the crew burned part of the Osage River Bridge, just eight miles from Jefferson City, doing enough damage to prevent trains from using it. The next morning at 7 A.M. the legislature met once again and finished the business of the night before. Jefferson City was put under strict military control, all drinking saloons were closed and all business was temporarily suspended. By mid-morning state militia were arriving at the capital to defend it against an attack from St. Louis.

In St. Louis itself, after the capture of Camp Jackson, the anger and humiliation of the secessionists knew no bounds. The streets in the center of the city were filled with people, and everyone was seeking the latest news of dead and wounded. A meeting which was addressed by leading secessionists was held in front of Planters' House during the evening. In the noise and confusion, it was almost impossible to hear the speakers. A large angry knot of men formed near the Health Office, where the dead from Camp Jackson had been taken. Slowly the anger in the city began to take the form of action as the mob broke into a gun store and secured fifteen or twenty guns. "To Hell with the Black Republicans" went up the cry and the mob started moving toward the leading Union newspaper in the city, the Missouri *Democrat*, waving a secession flag. Just before they got to the office of the *Democrat*, they were met by some twenty-five policemen, lined up shoulder to shoulder from one side of the street to the other. The leaders of the mob charged the police and pelted them with stones, all the time howling at them "like wild beasts," as the *Democrat* later reported. But the police sergeant gave the order to charge and in a very short time had cleared the street and driven the mob back from the newspaper office. The mob eventually dispersed with some parting cheers for Jeff Davis. Later during the night several lone Germans met their death in the side streets of the city, as they were seized and killed in reprisal for the Camp Jackson dead. At 4:30 A.M., a company of volunteers was called out in a drenching rain to go to one of the railroad stations when it was reported some state troops were planning to attack the city. But this report proved to be a false alarm and the troops returned to their quarters.

Although St. Louis was under Union control, the enormous State of Missouri remained to be conquered. Missouri, which anchored the western end of the frontier between North and South, was an empire by itself, with 70,000 square miles of land, almost as large as England, Scotland and Wales together. Outside St. Louis there were a million people within the borders of the state. Events in St. Louis could be nothing but a prelude to the drama that must unfold soon as the Union forces in St. Louis clashed with the state forces of Governor Jackson. With the Union volunteers well armed and confident, and the state forces demoralized and scattered, the Union cause had everything to gain by prompt, decisive action. Under the aggressive leadership of Frank Blair and Nathaniel Lyon, this clash could not be far off.

But in the midst of all the excitement the day after Camp Jackson, there arrived in St. Louis a man who was to put a complete stop to further aggressive moves. He was Brigadier General William S. Harney, on his way back from Washington to take command of the Union forces in the city. Harney was a Regular Army officer who had been in command at the St. Louis Arsenal earlier in the year. He was a Southerner and a slaveowner from Louisiana, and as he had watched his friends in the Army desert their government in early 1861, he was forced to consider whether he should follow their example. But Harney had once hanged 60 men in Mexico for deserting the flag and it was not easy for him to contemplate such action. So Harney did not "go South." He had no stomach, however, for the aggressive proposals of Blair and Lyon. As Union commander at the arsenal early in 1861, he had refused to enlist Union volunteers when Blair and Lyon had urged him to do so. After Lincoln's inauguration, Frank Blair had arranged Harney's removal from command. However, old General Scott and Missouri's representative in Lincoln's cabinet, Attorney General Edward Bates, were worried about turning over affairs in the state completely to the two young firebrands, Blair and Lyon, and Harney was soon reinstated in command. He arrived back in the city the day after the capture of Camp Jackson, ready to take charge once again.

On the day of Harney's return, St. Louis awoke to find itself utterly divided in war and politics. Business was at a standstill as the entire population argued the events of the previous day. Fights broke out between Union and secession men and even in the august halls of the Exchange, the financial mart of St. Louis, there was a fight in which one of the oldest and richest merchants traded blows with a secessionist.

In the midst of this maelstrom, General Harney arrived in the city. He could hardly believe the conditions he found. Three weeks before, when he had left St. Louis, there had been only 500 troops at the arsenal and they were outnumbered by the secessionist-minded Minutemen in the city. When he returned the Union troops numbered 10,000 and all the secessionists were prisoners. Such was the energy of Blair and Lyon.

Harney's first move was to try to get rid of the German volunteers whom he felt had been the source of all the trouble. He called a meeting to consider the move, but the German colonels refused to go, one of them remarking, "I know the stinker." Harney soon realized that any attempt to disarm these troops would be regarded as treason and gave up. However, he issued a proclamation citing "the deplorable state of things existing here" and made it clear that he wished he could send the Germans out of the city by adding, "upon careful review of instructions, I find that I have no authority to change the location of the 'Home Guards.'" To soothe the ruffled feelings of his secessionist friends, he said that he would use only "the regular army" if called upon to preserve public order. The Germans were disgusted with him and considered him completely disloyal at heart.

The day Harney arrived back in St. Louis, enlistment of volunteers was being pushed vigorously by General Lyon. Late in the afternoon, several companies which had been sworn in at the arsenal started out the gates and headed for their homes in the northern part of the city. On the way they marched straight through the Democratic heart of the city where large crowds of secessionists gathered to hiss and hoot at them. As they marched past a Presbyterian Church at the corner of Fifth and Walnut Streets, a mob on the church porch started throwing rocks at them, calling them "white-livered cowards" and daring them to fire.

But the troops kept on marching. They were almost past the corner when suddenly a shot rang out from the porch of the church. A soldier dropped in the ranks. Then another shot followed and another soldier dropped. Immediately, tremendous confusion enveloped the troops as a hasty order was shouted by an officer to turn about and fire. The rear troops stopped, leveled their rifles and fired point-blank toward the mob behind them. Several citizens dropped in the street. As the bullets hit the sides of buildings, they threw up puffs of dust that looked much like pistols firing. The troops began shooting at the puffs of dust in all directions. Two more soldiers were killed by the rifles of their own comrades and several others injured. The mob quickly dispersed but not until several citizens lay dead in the streets.

As rapidly as the incident had started, it ended. A German cabinetmaker who was a member of the volunteers had been caught in the right side of the head with a Minié ball and killed. Another volunteer, a collector for a German singing society, was struck in the left temple and killed. A book peddler from Louisiana who had been mocking the troops was killed in the street. A young German wine dealer whose shop happened to be located near the scene was killed as he stood watching. The dead-carts, which were becoming such familiar sights during these days in St. Louis, were soon at work removing the corpses and carrying them to the Health Office. There were eight dead in all.

The incident, which soon became known as the "Walnut Street Tragedy," cast a further pall over the city. It also gave a shocking demonstration of the power of the Minié balls. Something of the slaughter they would bring during the ensuing four years was written on the walls of Walnut Street after the incident. "The force of these leaden messengers was truly astonishing," wrote one correspondent. "Notches large enough to hold a man's fist were made in solid stone. In many spots whole bricks were crumbled to fragments." The surrounding buildings were pitted with gunshot, and doors, windows and casements were shattered.

But the biggest scare that hit St. Louis occurred the next day. Early Sunday morning rumors began spreading that the "Dutch" soldiers were in revolt against General Harney and threatening their vengeance against the secessionists. As each rumor was repeated it became more and more vivid, and by noon people in the center of St. Louis were running from house to house saying that Harney and Blair had lost all control of the "Dutch" and the soldiers were on their way to burn the city.

Suddenly a complete panic seized the city. Thousands of people began fleeing for safety. Carriages were frantically harnessed and men, women and children hurried away from the city. Hackmen demanded exorbitant prices, as high as $25 a trip, just to take a load of people to the outskirts of St. Louis. Hundreds more rushed to the wharves to get across the river, and soon every boat was filled. Those who could not leave sought out Republicans and tried to obtain protection from them. General Harney, whose headquarters was in the center of the city, where the panic was worst, ordered up some Regular troops with artillery to protect his headquarters.

There was no basis for the rumors, however, as the Germans were completely quiet. About 5 P.M. General Harney issued a statement that the Germans were entirely disciplined and there was not the slightest foundation for the rumors. Slowly the panic subsided. By next morning, the city had returned to its normal state, and people began returning.

During this same weekend, the state militiamen who had been captured at Camp Jackson, paraded through the city in ignominy, and locked up in the arsenal for the night, were released on parole. All but one of them returned home to be warmly welcomed by secessionist friends. There was one prisoner, however, who refused to give his parole. He was Captain Emmet McDonald, an unreconstructed Irishman who had just returned from military duty on the southwest frontier, where he had helped promote the cause of slavery. McDonald refused to give his parole and took his fight to the federal courts. He sued out a writ of habeas corpus and late one night word was received at the arsenal that the writ was about to be served for him. A hasty conference was held by the Union officials in the arsenal and it was decided to smuggle him out of St. Louis across the river into Illinois. He was marched out of the arsenal under guard of a squad of soldiers, down to the river bank where a skiff was waiting to take him across the Mississippi. As the little band was preparing to launch the skiff some of McDonald's secessionist friends made a rush to rescue him.

But McDonald would have no rescue. He told his friends not to interfere and they finally let the party through. The prisoner was placed in the frail boat with his military guard and they started on their perilous journey. The soldiers began rowing for the opposite shore but the river current was so strong that they drifted rapidly southward. Everybody was becoming worn out when the boat sprung a leak and started sinking. All hands went to work bailing and rowing and they finally reached an island in the middle of the river. Here another boat was obtained and they eventually reached the Illinois shore.

At this point, another adventure began. Two Illinois regiments were camped near Caseyville, just eight miles across the river. Now McDonald's escort set out in the dark to find the camp where they hoped to deposit their charge. All night long they marched and searched for the camp. They finally found it just as dawn was breaking and delivered their prisoner to Colonel McArthur of the Illinois regiment. Then they returned to St. Louis.

When they got back, the judicial processes in St. Louis were in full swing to bring about the release of McDonald. Judge Treat, of the United States district court, issued the writ of habeas corpus in the McDonald case and served it on General Harney. Harney replied that he was not holding McDonald, which was true enough. The sufficiency of this return was argued before the court for several days and finally a new writ of habeas corpus was issued on General Lyon. Lyon replied that he did not have the prisoner.

The McDonald case was the first of the habeas corpus cases to come up in the Civil War. The writ of habeas corpus was served some two weeks before the famous Merryman case arose in Baltimore. But the argument pro and con before Judge Treat consumed these two weeks. Long before this case was settled, John Merryman had become a national figure and Justice Taney had become the leading authority on habeas corpus. And so McDonald's name was never enshrined in the judicial lore of habeas corpus.

In the meantime, however, Emmet McDonald was enjoying himself immensely at Caseyville. He was a very handsome young man, with pleasing manners and an air of confidence about himself. He was made the personal guest of Colonel McArthur of the Illinois volunteers, and given full privileges of the camp. He was permitted to see his many visitors and soon became the general favorite of the camp. A full dress parade was held when the camp was visited by some wealthy St. Louis citizens. Emmet McDonald, who by now was a famous man in St. Louis, stole the show, was the favorite dancing partner for the ladies and withal acted like anything except a downtrodden prisoner.

Another writ of habeas corpus was issued in Illinois for the prisoner and Colonel McArthur made a return to the effect that McDonald had been arrested for treason and that he was in command of rebel troops when taken at Camp Jackson. Shortly after he sent the return to the court, General George B. McClellan, his superior officer, ordered that McDonald be delivered to the jurisdiction of the civil authorities. And so, after spending four weeks as a prisoner, McDonald was taken to the district court in Illinois by Colonel McArthur. The handsome McDonald appeared in full uniform and made a little speech asking to be released.

The court held that the return was obviously insufficient and ordered the prisoner discharged. McDonald hastily left the courtroom, followed by the crowd that had come to hear the case. That evening he appeared at the Planters' House in St. Louis, a hotel noted for its Southern patronage. He was received with joy by his friends who hoisted him on their shoulders and carried him in triumph up the steps of the hotel.

The entire West had followed the day-to-day events of the McDonald case and in the end legal process had been vindicated. In the handling of such cases, it was one of the few times during the Civil War that this was to happen.

CHAPTER 7

THE HARNEY-PRICE AGREEMENT

I N ST. LOUIS itself, events had returned pretty much to normal
after the excitement of the Camp Jackson weekend. In fact,
the city returned to a state far quieter than normal. St. Louis
had been suffering for months from a general drying up of trade
with the South. Now, with war actually at hand, the markets
in St. Louis did almost no business at all. As a newspaper said
in reporting one day's activity: "The market was so insignificant
that extended remarks would destroy the sublime beauty of its
nothingness." Relief for the unemployed became a major question for the City Council. The schools were closed by the action
of the state government in seizing the school funds and some
two hundred St. Louis teachers joined the growing ranks of the
unemployed.

Slowly, General Harney was prodded into taking some action against the secessionists in the city. He issued a proclamation saying that upon his return to St. Louis he had found,
to his "astonishment and mortification, a most extraordinary
state of things existing in this state." He added that the destiny of Missouri lay with the Union for "her geographical
position — their soil — productions, and in short, all her material interests point to this result." He went on to point out
that he would "deem it my duty to suppress all unlawful
combinations of men, whether formed under pretext of
military organizations or otherwise."

The Minutemen's Headquarters in St. Louis was abolished

and Confederate flags were ordered down. Harney laid plans for the complete occupation of St. Louis and at 4 o'clock one morning a regiment of troops moved out and occupied three strategic points in the northern part of the city. Later in the morning, Lindell's Grove was occupied by Union volunteers and another group went a mile out to the south and set up a camp. Soon, a network of forts stretched in an arc from the river south of the city, across the western areas and back to the river north of the city. They were designed to prevent any uprising from within St. Louis and any attack by the state militia from without.

Harney also made the first moves toward control of individual secessionists. A man named John Dean was the owner of a lead manufacturing plant in the town of Potosi, south of St. Louis. He had been very active in the secessionist cause and was believed to be filling orders from the state forces. He was on his way home from Jefferson City by train on May 16, when he was arrested by the military and lodged in the arsenal. At the same time, a general search of the city of St. Louis was undertaken to find hidden arms belonging to secessionists. Search warrants were carefully sworn out and provided to the United States marshal, who found several hundred rifles in the State Tobacco Warehouse and the Central Police Station.

But General Harney was missing a great opportunity. The secessionists in the state were only then beginning to get organized, whereas Union troops in large numbers were trained and equipped with arms. Frank Blair and his friends felt that an attack should be made immediately out into the state and had been working hard to get Harney relieved of his command once again. Lincoln finally agreed and on May 18th, just seven days after Harney had arrived in St. Louis, Lincoln wrote a note to Frank Blair indicating the difficult time he was having making up his mind about Harney:

I understand an order has gone from the War Department to you to be delivered or withheld in your discretion relieving

General Harney from his command. . . . I do not write now to countermand it, but to say, I wish you would withhold it, unless in your judgment, the necessity to the contrary is very urgent. . . . We first relieve him, then restore him and, now if we relieve him again, the public will ask, "Why all this vacillation?"

Frank Blair, a colonel in one of General Harney's regiments, now had the power to discharge Harney if he saw fit. He would undoubtedly have done so immediately had not Harney already arranged a peace agreement with the secession forces in Missouri. On the 21st of May, the General got together with Sterling Price, the new commander of the state militia, and signed an agreement to bring peace to the state. In dealing with Price, Harney was working with a man who enjoyed the confidence of all secessionists in Missouri. Price had served in the Mexican War and had proved to be a soldier of great ability and vigor. After that war, he entered politics, was elected to Congress and later became governor of Missouri for one term. He was a Douglas Democrat, holding the post of Bank Commissioner when the Civil War broke out. Although elected to the Missouri State Convention as a Conditional Union man and named Convention Chairman, he was decidedly lukewarm in his support of the Union cause. Many men still hoped, however, that when the final choice had to be made, he would be found on the side of the Union.

Price's final decision for secession came after the capture of Camp Jackson. He went to the Governor and told him that the "slaughter of the people" at Camp Jackson had been too much for him. General Frost now being in disrepute, Price was immediately offered command of the state militia. He was a big man, six feet two inches high, a superb horseman, with a kindly face and snow-white hair and beard. The choice of Price thrilled the secessionists in the state.

The agreement between Harney and Price had its genesis in a problem that was to plague Missouri during four years of civil war. Union refugees were flooding into St. Louis from outlying areas where secessionists were driving the Union men from their homes. A few days after Camp Jackson, thirteen families arrived who had been forced to abandon their homes in Tipton and Sedalia, small towns to the west of Jefferson City. One man in this group who arrived with his wife and six children said that his life had been threatened by armed secessionists if he did not leave his home and he had been given twenty-four hours to get out. He said a reign of terror existed in that part of the state and that to declare for the Union was to put one's life in danger. In St. Joseph, in the northwest part of the state, the Union flag was torn down from the post office building and the States Rights flag hoisted. The postmaster was threatened and all Union men were considered unsafe.

To the south of St. Louis, the situation was even worse. Union men were being driven from their homes in such towns as De Soto and Potosi within seventy-five miles of St. Louis and militia companies were being formed to fight under General Price. General Lyon decided to do something about this problem. The Iron Mountain Railroad ran right through this section of the state and at 10 o'clock one night, just four days after Camp Jackson, Lyon put 150 men aboard a special train headed south for Potosi. They arrived there at three the next morning and threw a chain of sentinels around the entire town. Guards were stationed at the dwellings of the most prominent secessionists, and shortly after daylight, some 150 men in the town found themselves prisoners. Later in the day, nearly all the prisoners were released on their taking the oath and giving parole.

The remaining men, numbering eleven in all, who were the leaders of the secession sentiment in the town, were marched off and locked up in a railroad car. Among them was the editor of the Potosi *Miner*, a newspaper of strong Southern proclivities. The troops then descended upon the lead manufactory of John Dean and seized a quantity of lead. Various pistols, rifles, shotguns and a number of secession uniforms were also found in the town and taken to St. Louis.

On their way back to the city, the train stopped at De Soto, where a secession meeting was planned for the day. When they arrived a company of secession cavalry was drilling for the occasion, but took to its heels as soon as the Union troops came into view. The troops raised the Union flag on the 100-foot flag pole and then searched the town for a rebel flag that was rumored to have been made for the celebration. They finally found it peeping underneath the hoops of one of the grand ladies of the town. She was delivered of her burden and the flag proved to be 30 feet long. The Jefferson County *Herald*, a secession sheet printed in De Soto, was raided. The editor had fled but Union troops took possession of the office, changed the title of the paper to *The U.S. American Volunteer*, called the printers in the ranks and turned out the new paper in a hurry.

It was to end this sort of episode that the Harney-Price agreement was signed. Under the terms of the agreement, General Price directed the state officers to maintain order among the people of the state, and General Harney agreed not to make any military movements out of his base in St. Louis. The agreement further stated:

> We mutually recommend to all persons to respect each other's rights throughout the State, making no attempt to exercise unauthorized powers, as it is the determination of the proper authorities to suppress all unlawful proceedings, which can only disturb the peace.

The agreement was signed in St. Louis on May 21, just eleven days after Camp Jackson. After it was signed, most Union men applauded it, thinking that it might stop the attacks on Union men throughout the state. This caused Frank Blair to pause. He had the order removing General Harney in his pocket, but it was difficult to remove the general just at the moment when he was bringing new heart to Union men, and possibly saving many of them from dispossession. Blair decided to wait.

After the agreement was signed, Price began dismissing the militia that had flocked to Jefferson City. He knew that simply keeping them at the capital with nothing to do would demoralize them. Planting time had arrived so he sent them back home and told them to drill and continue to keep themselves organized as companies. In St. Louis, the Potosi prisoners were released along with John Dean as a result of the agreement.

It soon became clear, however, that the agreement was having no effect on the atrocities being committed in the state. Twenty-five families which had come from Pennsylvania and settled in central Missouri the previous spring were threatened with their lives and ordered to leave immediately. They went to St. Louis and appealed to General Harney, to whom they made a full statement of the circumstances without getting any action. Then they saw Sterling Price who told them to "return with your friends to your usual avocations, and I will see that you are protected." But they did not dare to return since their homes were fifty miles from the capital, too far away for Price to exert any real authority. The refugees continued to flock into St. Louis.

On May 30, Frank Blair delivered the order to Harney relieving him of his command. At the same time, Blair wrote to President Lincoln that Harney had prevented any attempt at clearing the state of secessionists. The Harney-Price agreement was protecting only the secessionists, he said, and he had therefore relieved the General. It was a bitter end to Harney's brilliant military career.

Harney left St. Louis immediately. The train on which he was traveling was captured at Harper's Ferry by the Confederate forces, and he was taken to Richmond, where the Confederate authorities ordered his release. Harney returned north but was not used any more during the war. He was retired in 1863 as a brigadier general, and after the war ended he was breveted a major-general. He died many years later at his home in Pass Christian, Mississippi, one of the few Southern generals who had not deserted the Union during the Civil War.

CHAPTER 8

WAR COMES TO MISSOURI

THE DECISION to remove Harney was the decision to conquer Missouri. Both sides began frantic preparations for the war that seemed inevitable. By the time Harney was dismissed, nearly all the state militia which had gathered at Jefferson City had been sent back home and General Price found himself without an army. Five days after Harney's removal, Price issued a proclamation stating that he had entered into agreement with Harney to preserve the peace in Missouri. But, he added, the federal government "has thought proper to remove General Harney from command." He cited "rumors in circulation" that Lyon was planning to move out into the state and said that such a movement "would be resisted to the last extremity." At the same time, Price issued secret orders to his brigadiers to hasten the organization of troops in their districts.

In Jefferson City, Governor Jackson began moving his state government westward. The capital was too near St. Louis, and too much in Union territory to be defensible. Vehicles of every description could be seen moving out of the city, headed toward Boonville, some forty miles to the west. Preparations were going forward in St. Louis at top speed to recruit and organize additional regiments and get them ready for the campaign into the state.

In the midst of all this military activity, one last effort was made to avert war in Missouri. It was, after all, early June, 1861, and many men were still hopeful that the differences between North and South could be reconciled. A meeting was therefore arranged between the Union and secession leaders in a last attempt to prevent bloodshed. Governor Jackson and General Price were given a safe conduct pass to come to St. Louis to see Blair and Lyon. A special train was sent to Jefferson City for them and when they arrived at the Planters' House in St. Louis, General Lyon offered them a special escort to the arsenal. But they sent word that since they had come all the way from Jefferson City, they felt that General Lyon could come downtown to Planters' House. He agreed and so it was in the Planters' House that the fate of Missouri was decided.

Governor Jackson and Frank Blair were the leading politicians in the state, and they were both in the conference. Yet it was not long before it developed into a verbal dueling match between General Lyon, the fiery, disputatious, well-informed leader of the Union troops, and General Price, the benign, paternal and inflexible leader of the state troops. These two men argued for hours, while Jackson and Blair remained largely silent. General Price argued that Union troops should remain within St. Louis and that Union volunteer companies should not be formed throughout the state. In this way, he said, peace could be maintained in Missouri. Lyon argued that, on the contrary, Missouri was federal territory and that no state leader could ever forbid Union forces from acting for the federal government. He said that the federal government could never agree to being restrained from asserting its authority or sending its troops wherever they were needed.

After four long hours of conversation and debate, it was clear that the two sides could never reach agreement. Suddenly Lyon, in the midst of a heated exchange, dramatically turned to his adversaries and shouted:

> Rather than concede to the State of Missouri the right to demand that my government shall not enlist troops within her limits, or bring troops into the State whenever it pleases. . . . I would (rising as he said this, and pointing in turn to every one in

the room), see you, and you, and you, and you, and you, and every man, woman, and child in this State, dead and buried.

Without another word, and without another look, he turned on his heel and strode out of the room. This meant war.

And war was not long in coming. The special train took Jackson and Price back to Jefferson City where they arrived at 2 o'clock the next morning. As the train was coming to a stop in the capital, Governor Jackson jumped down on the depot platform, and called to the engineer in charge, "We want two passenger cars and an engine." General Price then proceeded with his own hand to cut the telegraph wire out of the city. Captain Kelly, in command of the few state troops left in Jefferson City, was ordered to procure drills, crowbars and powder, and take a train to destroy all the bridges east of the capital. They left hurriedly and went as far as the Gasconade bridge, some thirty miles to the east. There they put seven kegs of powder under the bridge and set a match to it. But the explosion did not damage the bridge, so they set fire to the wooden turntable, and watched it burn until the draw fell into the river. Then they proceeded back toward Jefferson City and burned the span over the Osage River, which had previously been burned and repaired after the capture of Camp Jackson. By morning, St. Louis had been cut off entirely from the state capital.

During the day Governor Jackson issued a proclamation formally declaring war on the Union forces. He told of his trip to St. Louis and of General Lyon's intention to occupy the entire state and to reduce it "to the exact condition of Maryland." He called up 50,000 militia to repel the federal invasion and said that although Missouri was still one of the united states, the first allegiance of its citizens was to the state rather than to "the military despotism which has enthroned itself in Washington" and "its wicked minions in this State."

Final evacuation of the state capital was immediately

ordered. The few remaining militia troops were told to retreat westward along the Missouri Pacific railroad some thirty miles to Tipton, and to burn all the bridges behind them. Messengers were sent to all parts of the state ordering mobilization of units. Governor Jackson and the few state officers in Jefferson City then boarded a steamer and left for Boonville to the west.

While the evacuation of Jefferson City was taking place, Lyon was planning his campaign against the capital. All the railroad bridges having been burned, he decided that the fastest way to get to Jefferson City was by boat up the Missouri River. He obtained two river steamers and loaded 1,500 men aboard them, with horses, wagons, and ammunition. At 11 A.M., on the 13th of June, just two days after the conference in Planters' House, they started up the river, amid wild cheering and great enthusiasm from the crowds in St. Louis. The advance up the Missouri was an exhilarating experience for the soldiers. They were cheered from the banks as they went by the towns and villages bordering the river. They reached Hermann, about 45 miles from the state capital, without any trouble, but from that point on, progress was slow. The river was shallow, and twice it was necessary to disembark the men in order to get the steamer over sand bars. Lyon also stopped to take a look at the damage to the railroad bridge over the Gasconade River. Here as in Maryland, it was found that the basic structure of the bridge had not been damaged by the burning. Railroad men were already at work repairing it.

At night the steamers laid up a few miles below St. Aubert, some twenty-five miles from Jefferson City. The next morning they continued on their way and by 2 P.M. the troops began unloading near Jefferson City. They went ashore just below the town, occupied some heights in the area, and with General Lyon at their head, moved in to take the city. There was no resistance. The townspeople cheered the federal troops as they occupied the capitol building, and a delegation from the city assured them of its loyalty. The Jefferson City band was out for the occasion and as the Stars and Stripes were raised over the cupola of the capitol, it played The Star-Spangled Banner. There were no secession demonstrations of any kind.

From the state capital, General Lyon issued a proclamation to the people of Missouri in which he said that Governor Jackson had "set at defiance the authority of the United States, and urged you to make war upon them." He said that his duty was to suppress treason and that he would look to "all good citizens" to support the federal government.

Then Lyon set out to hunt down the secessionists and drive them out of the state. Lyon and Blair never gave the state of Missouri a chance to move slowly by easy steps over to the Union side, as Kentucky did. And so Missouri found itself fighting a civil war all by itself within two months after Fort Sumter. Such was the legacy of hatred that had been building up in the state for more than a decade.

While Blair and Lyon were chasing the secessionists out of the rest of the state, several suspected traitors were arrested in St. Louis. One of the most vociferous secessionist newspapers in the city was the State Journal, edited by Joseph Tucker. On June 14, a federal warrant for his arrest was obtained upon an affidavit accusing Tucker of writing and publishing treasonable articles. Tucker was arrested by the United States Marshal in his office in downtown St. Louis. The marshal also searched the office, and confiscated some manuscripts, correspondence, and back copies of the State Journal. This being in the center of the heavily Democratic wards of the city, a large and unfriendly crowd gathered around the marshal. But Mr. Tucker offered no resistance and no disturbance occurred. A writ of habeas corpus was obtained from Judge Treat, and Tucker was released on a bond of $10,000 to appear before a grand jury assembling the following month. He continued to run his newspaper in much the same manner as he had in the past.

Mr. Overton Barrett, a lawyer in the city and brother of a former Congressman from Missouri, was another man in the habit of speaking out forcibly for Southern rights. A federal warrant for his arrest was obtained, sworn out by the United States Marshal and he was brought in for a hearing, only to be released on $10,000 bail to appear along with Tucker before the grand jury.

While these arrests were taking place, a rather strange advertisement was appearing in the newspapers of the city:

Rifles!!   Rifles!!

I would respectfully call the public attention to the fact that I manufacture and have for sale Rifles with self adjusting, expanding, elongated ball, which are far superior in point of accuracy and power to any military rifled arms now in use with Minnie ball. I warrant them to shoot seventeen hundred yards.

HORACE E. DIMICK

After reading this same advertisement in the daily newspapers for two weeks, the authorities decided that it was too dangerous to allow such notices in a city which could explode at any moment. So Mr. Dimick was visited one afternoon by a detachment of the Reserve Guard and his goods removed. Two furniture wagons were loaded with powder, percussion caps, cartridges, and shot and Dimick was told that he would be paid for them. No more ads appeared in the newspapers for RIFLES!! RIFLES!!

But the presence of rifles even in the hands of the federal troops continued to plague the Union officials and caused some tragic incidents. Early in the morning of June 16, a regiment of Union volunteers marched from the arsenal to the railroad station and boarded a train. They rode to the town of St. Charles on the Missouri River, reconnoitered the area during the day and left a guard to prevent any more bridge burning. The five remaining companies in the regiment returned to St. Louis, arriving at the depot at 9 o'clock the next morning after spending some 28 hours on duty. They had had very little to eat or drink and had been on their feet most of the time. The soldiers were tired and nervous, wanting only to get back to the barracks and get some sleep.

As they were marching through the center of the city toward the arsenal, a half-drunk civilian began insulting them and using abusive and threatening language. Some of the troops went over to him and told him to be quiet. But a captain came up and when the civilian protested that he meant no harm, the captain told the troops to let him go. The troops knew, however, that violent attacks had been made on German regiments passing through this section of the city and as they started marching once again several of the soldiers in the rear ranks began capping their rifles, in order to be ready for trouble. At this moment they were passing the corner of Seventh and Olive Streets, where the Recorder's Court was in session.

In St. Louis in 1861 the Recorder's Court heard criminal cases and at the moment the troops were passing by, a burglary case was in progress. As the soldiers passed down the street, several people in the courtroom stepped out on the balcony overlooking Seventh Street to watch them. At that moment, one of the soldiers accidentally stepped into a gutter and his rifle went off with a loud bang. The bullet hit the wall beside the balcony and threw up a small cloud of dust which looked to the soldiers exactly like a puff of smoke from a pistol being fired at them. Someone among the volunteers yelled, "Fire," and the troops suddenly swung their rifles around and pointed them directly at the balcony of the Recorder's Court. One of the men standing there shouted, "My God, they are going to fire here." Everyone on the balcony dove for the doorway as the soldiers fired point-blank at them. They all made it except one man, a witness in the burglary case, who fell with a bullet through his heart.

Complete pandemonium broke loose in the ranks of the soldiers. The more they fired, the more bullets hit the walls, and the more panicky they became. They fired wildly at the puffs of dust and within a few moments were firing at pedestrians in the street. A confectioner whose store was nearby was watching the soldiers when suddenly several of them fired directly at him and he fell dead. Another man, walking nearby when the firing started, was hit in the temple and died instantly.

As the firing continued, the prisoners in the Recorder's Court saw their chance and made a dash for freedom. The deputy marshal of the court took after one of them who was charged with murder. The volunteers saw the prisoner and the marshal race out of the building, and fired. They missed the prisoner completely, but shattered both legs of the deputy. A captain of the volunteers standing beside his company suddenly noticed that his troops were firing directly at him. He dove for safety but a bullet caught him in the shoulder.

Very soon the officers began to realize what was happening. Their shouted orders to cease firing slowly took effect and the troops marched out of the vicinity. Soon the dead-carts were back at their work and the incident was given the name of the Seventh Street Tragedy. It had not lasted more than a minute or two, but five dead were left in the street and several others were wounded.

The walls of the surrounding buildings were pocked where Minié balls had torn chunks of brick and stone away. Bullets had crashed through the windows of the Recorder's Court, a nearby drugstore was completely littered, and the local firehouse was covered with gashes. One man was hit by what appeared to be buckshot and several small pellets were removed from his leg. Since none of the soldiers were carrying a shotgun, it seemed that someone else must have fired on the volunteers. But it later developed that a Minié ball had ricocheted against a wall and had shattered into many pieces before hitting him. The Seventh Street Tragedy was entirely an accident, brought on by fatigue and nervousness on the part of the troops.

By early July, business in St. Louis had ground nearly to a halt, and unemployment had become a major problem in the city. The Mississippi River was blockaded at Cairo and there was no trade with the South. The Corn Exchange was silent and the wharves were quiet. The Union troops were unpaid and ununiformed. Even travel by train had been greatly impeded as a result of the bridge burnings. Most of the factories in St. Louis lay idle. A large portion of the population faced starvation. Patriotic ladies organized soup kitchens, rolled up their sleeves and went out to cook for the poor. The war had shattered the economy of St. Louis.

During this difficult period, the existence of the Missouri *State Journal* and its editor, Joseph Tucker, became more and more precarious. In June, as we have seen, Tucker had been arrested by civil process and was under $10,000 bail. But in early July, his newspaper began posting dispatches telling lurid stories of attacks on Union troops out in the state and great rebel victories. The street in front of the office became a gathering spot for Southern sympathizers and more and more Union men called for the suppression of the newspaper. Finally, it was decided that the paper must go.

At four o'clock one morning, Colonel McNeil and some 250 men in his regiment marched from Turners' Hall, the downtown fortress of the Union troops, to the office of the newspaper. Guards were put at the entrance of the building, and a small party entered the composing room. They stopped work on the paper and seized the copies that had been printed. The forms and papers were placed in a furniture wagon and taken to Turners' Hall.

Later during the morning, rumors began to spread in the city that the "Dutch" had sacked the *Journal* office and wrecked the paper. By 9 A.M. a large crowd of southern sympathizers had gathered near the office and was becoming more and more angry. There was a threat of mob action, but Mr. Tucker appeared at the window and pleaded with his friends to keep cool. The mob finally quieted and later in the day, the *Journal*'s compositors issued a small sheet called the *Bulletin,* giving the news which had come in by telegraph, but leaving out the secession editorials.

A statement was also issued by the Union authorities justifying the suppression of the newspaper. It said that the paper had continually given aid and comfort to the enemy by appealing to the people to take up arms against the United States and by its constant publication of news known to be false. It accused the newspaper of attempting to overthrow the United States —

> . . . by fraud, by deception, by the fabrication of false intelligence, by its open communication with those confessedly engaged in this rebellion, by its publication of such correspondence inducing the weak to believe in the safe and successful accomplishment of treasonable acts and designs, and by its skillfully contrived and inflammatory appeals to passion and prejudice, to secure the entire subversion of the federal authority in the State of Missouri.

All in all, this was one of the most explicit statements made in the entire war justifying the suppression of a newspaper. But Tucker was not arrested.

By the middle of July, St. Louis and the state of Missouri were being fought over and bled over. Thousands of men were under arms and rioting and killing were commonplace. Two large armies were maneuvering, preparing for the great battle that would determine the future of the state.

Yet at this same time there was another border state, Kentucky, in which peace reigned supreme. As war raged all around, this state stood like a sheltered, fragile, house of leaves, untouched by violence. But the passions that were sweeping the nation were being felt and with each passing day they threatened to turn Kentucky into a bloody battleground.

CHAPTER 9

THE LINCOLN GUNS

A LARGE MAN was pacing up and down in front of a house in
Louisville, Kentucky, early one morning in May, 1861. He
was enormous, some 6 feet 3 inches tall and weighing nearly
300 pounds. Inside the house was the wife of a man whom
President Lincoln had known for many years, Joshua Speed. As
Mrs. Speed watched this enormous man walking back and forth
she became worried for fear he might have evil intentions. Her
husband was known as a strong Union man in Kentucky and
passions were running high so soon after Fort Sumter.

Finally, the man came to the door and rang the bell. When
the servant answered the door and the visitor inquired for Mr.
Speed, the servant replied that Mr. Speed had already left
for his office. The visitor then asked how he might get to the
office and, as soon as he was given directions, started off with
a resolute step.

Mr. Speed was sitting at his desk a few minutes later when
this large man entered his office, looked around, and asked for
Joshua Speed.

"That is my name," was the response.

"Is there another room to this office?" asked the visitor.

"There is."

"Is there any one in that room?"

"There is not."

"I should like, Mr. Speed, to see you in that room for a short
time."

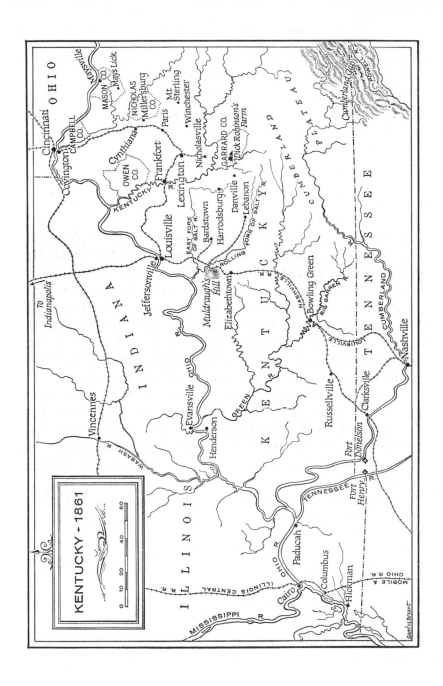

KENTUCKY · 1861

Sam'l Bryant

When the two men went into the other room, the stranger locked the door and forcefully started talking. He was Lieutenant William Nelson of the United States Navy, a citizen of Kentucky, and a man with a plan for saving the state from the secessionists.

The great danger that faced the Union forces in Kentucky was the fact that the state militia was completely under the control of the secessionists and all the guns and ammunition belonging to the state were in their hands. Although there were large numbers of Union men who had been organizing themselves into Home Guard companies, they had no weapons. It was feared that by a sudden coup the secessionists would take the state out of the Union.

To stop them Lieutenant Nelson had developed his plan. He had gone to Washington and met with President Lincoln to whom he proposed that muskets be shipped into Kentucky by the federal government and put directly into the hands of the Union Home Guard companies. If enough of them could be provided, there would be a standoff between Union and secessionist elements and the state would not slip into secession.

Lincoln had been considering such a plan himself and immediately approved it. He asked the huge lieutenant where he could find a man who would undertake the task of distributing the arms. "Cast your eyes," said Nelson, "on a little man of my size." Lincoln, who took great pride in his own height, did indeed cast his eyes upon the very large Nelson who was almost as tall and much heavier than he. He decided that the brusque, energetic Nelson was just the man he was looking for. He issued an order that same day for 5,000 muskets to be given to Nelson immediately and the plan was put into effect.

More than anything else Nelson needed to be put in contact with the prominent Union men in Kentucky who could arrange for distribution of the guns to the right men. Lincoln therefore suggested that Nelson meet with Joshua Speed to

arrange for the necessary meeting. And so Nelson had gone to
Louisville and was now outlining his plan to Speed. Speed
proceeded to arrange the meeting immediately. They agreed
to take the train to the state capital at Frankfort that afternoon. As soon as it had been arranged, Nelson, who wanted
the matter kept highly secret, turned to Speed and said in his
curt manner, "I do not wish you to speak to me on the cars this
afternoon, as we go to Frankfort; if you do I'll insult you."
Nelson's tendency toward rudeness was to get him in much
trouble during the months to come. But he was able to get
things done during this eventful May of 1861.

That very night the meeting was held in Frankfort with the
Union legislators from all over the state. Present were a group
of men destined to play a large role in the affairs of the nation.
The meeting took place in the law offices of the Honorable
James Harlan, father of John M. Harlan, later appointed to the
United States Supreme Court. Joshua Speed's brother, James,
was also there, a man destined for a cabinet post under
Lincoln. Senator John J. Crittenden, who had been working
on the last great compromise to avoid war, was there, as well
as several Kentucky Congressmen. Each man agreed to provide
the names of the Union men in his section of the state
to whom guns should be shipped. Special emphasis was placed
on the northern and central section of the state, where Union
elements were particularly strong. It was agreed that all would
observe secrecy until enough guns had been obtained to insure
that the state remain loyal. When the meeting finally broke up
at daybreak, someone remarked that this was perhaps the most
important meeting ever held in the state of Kentucky.

Distribution of the guns was begun immediately. In
Louisville, they were entrusted to the mayor who passed them
out to the Home Guard companies that had been forming in
the city. Scarcely a week after Nelson's conversation with
Lincoln in the White House, the Home Guard units in Louisville were drilling on the streets of the city with weapons
in their hands.

The remainder of the guns were shipped directly across the river from Cincinnati to Covington, Kentucky. At that time, Cincinnati had a large volunteer patrol which had taken upon itself the duty of preventing any arms from being shipped across the river in aid of the rebellion. Nelson and his wagons were stopped by the patrol and told they must turn back. But Nelson was not a man easily deterred. He demanded to know where they got the authority to stop an officer of the United States Government. The local volunteers were no match for him and during the night all the guns were ferried across to Kentucky. At 11 P.M. the train left for Paris and Lexington, Kentucky, with guns and ammunition. They arrived safely the next morning and, as one newspaper put it, their arrival "was the signal of great rejoicing, manifested in the form of wasting ammunition by many discharges of musketry." From Paris and Lexington, the guns were hauled in wagons into the country towns not served by railroads, such as Winchester and Mt. Sterling. Other guns were shipped from Cincinnati up the Ohio River to Maysville for the Union men in Mason and Nicholas Counties. Within a few days, the guns had been widely distributed throughout the eastern and northern regions of Kentucky and the Union forces were no longer helpless.

News of the sudden appearance of muskets spread like wildfire in Kentucky. The 5,000 muskets that had been ordered by Lincoln compared with some 11,000 muskets and 3,000 rifles in the hands of the state militia. However, rumor magnified the number of Lincoln guns being distributed to several times their actual number. The psychological effect of the weapons was therefore tremendous.

By the middle of May, the Kentucky legislature was forced to consider the matter of the Lincoln guns. The legislature itself was about evenly split in sentiment between North and South. The Southern sympathizers introduced a resolution stating that several members "have received information . . . that a large number of guns and munitions of war have been received from Northern States at Lexington and Paris . . . to be placed in the hands of organized bodies of men unknown to the militia laws of the state." The resolution provided that a committee of five men be empowered to investigate the matter and make a full report.

The Union members countered, however, by amending the resolution to add that the committee should also report whether an organization, known as the "Knights of the Golden Circle" was in existence in the state, "and if so, what were its purposes, who were its officers, what obligations it imposed on its members to oppose the United States government." The Knights of the Golden Circle being an organization which the secessionists did not want to have investigated, the resolution was allowed to die a natural death.

In the meantime, distribution of the guns continued to additional counties as arms were requested. Captain Speed Fry of Danville had a Home Guard company but no arms. He heard that Nelson was distributing arms and went to Cincinnati to see if he could obtain some for his company and for the other Union companies farther south and east, near the mountains of eastern Kentucky.

Because of the excitement in Cincinnati over the shipment of the muskets, Nelson had been forced to put all of his arms in a boat and move them up the river fifty miles to Maysville, Kentucky. He now gave an order to Speed Fry for seven hundred guns and told him to go to Maysville and pick them up. But from Maysville, there was no railroad on which the guns could be shipped south. They would have to be carried by wagon through territory that contained many Southern-minded Kentuckians. For ninety long miles, the wagons would be vulnerable to attack where any small group of secessionists could easily overcome the four men in the wagons and seize the weapons. Everything about the loading and shipping of the guns was public and word of their advance preceded them into every town.

Fry procured two wagons, loaded the seven hundred muskets on them and started on the journey. The first town they came to was Mays Lick where there was considerable excitement in the air. The streets were filled with Southern-minded farmers who had come in from the surrounding countryside to watch the guns pass. As the wagons entered the town a man opened the door of his house and waved to Captain Fry to come over. When Fry reached him, he whispered in a tone barely loud enough to hear, "Do not go into the town with those guns," and disappeared. Fry and the other men held a council of war but after talking it over, they decided to go on. So they drove bravely into the town, halted their wagons in front of the only hotel, and while Fry stood sentry duty over the wagons, the others went into the hotel and had breakfast.

One of the crowd walked up to Fry as he stood there and asked in an insolent tone if "they hadn't better take some of these guns?" Fry replied firmly, "There they are; take them." But the stranger turned away and there was no other disturbance.

They traveled the rest of the day and all was quiet until late in the afternoon when they approached the area of Millersburg. Kentucky in 1861 was spotted with alternating Union and secessionist areas. Millersburg was well known as one of the secessionist regions and some kind of trouble was anticipated. As the wagon train came into town, a large crowd of people stood watching the guns pass. But the only defiance came from an old lady who was sitting in her doorway. She raised her clenched fist and shook it at them as they passed, shouting, "If I was a man I would not let them guns pass without taking some of them."

Paris was their destination that night. Several miles out of town a messenger met them to say that a rebel company had been parading the streets of Paris that day and if they tried to pass through during the evening, there might be an attempt to seize their guns. So they camped by the roadside and early next morning went through the town. The streets were almost empty but they learned that the Union men in Paris had been preparing to defend the wagons if an attack were made on them. They continued on their journey and passed through Lexington without trouble. The next morning they reached Nicholasville, where a company of Home Guards joyfully received its guns. Fry and the wagons then continued on the turnpike to Dick Robinson's farm, where Home Guard units from Garrard County were given muskets. Dick Robinson was a staunch Union man whose farm was strategically located at a point from which troops could be assembled to control the main turnpike leading southeast toward the Cumberland Gap. Not many months later, this same farm was to be the most famous in the state and the name of its owner was to become a national symbol of Kentucky's resistance to secessionism.

The wagon train continued on and reached Danville late that night, after a three-day trip from Maysville. Most of the community was asleep when the men arrived but the guns were safely deposited with the members of the Home Guard company. This company was soon drilling in the streets with its muskets, much to the dismay of the secessionists in the town. As Captain Fry later put it, "It would be impossible for any one to describe, in language sufficiently strong, the consternation expressed in the countenances of these people, when they beheld my company of a hundred men file down the street, with bayonets glistening in the sunlight, pointing above their heads, and nodding to and fro as they kept 'step to the music of the Union.' "

The guns gave hope to the Union elements in Kentucky and brought despair to the secessionists. Of all the states where the Union sentiment had to be encouraged, none was more important than Kentucky. For it lay in the very center of the Union, not only between North and South, but also between East and West. Kentucky was destined to be the base for the campaigns that eventually broke the back of the South. With Lee guarding the narrow approaches to Richmond, his genius plus the closeness of the mountains and the sea would turn the war in the East into an early stalemate. To the West, in the empire beyond the Mississippi River, great battles would rage, but no Union victory in Missouri would ever destroy the South. Kentucky, stretching four hundred miles across the center of the nation, held the only key to victory.

Perhaps it was more than chance that caused Kentucky to be the original home of so many men who controlled the destiny of the nation in the years leading up to the Civil War. Kentuckians liked to call their state the "First Born of the Union," to honor their admission to the Union as the first state after the original thirteen in 1798. Within the next few years, Kentucky gave birth to the future presidents of the Union and the Confederacy, Lincoln and Davis. Two other major figures represented the state in the Senate, Breckinridge and Crittenden. In the end, one of them went South and the other remained with the North.

Like the eye of a hurricane, Kentucky during the spring of 1861 was quiet. It was an ominous quiet, surrounded by enormous pressures. But in Kentucky there was no fighting. For there was no Kansas on its border to inflame the passions of its citizens, as was the case in Missouri. And Union troops did not have to cross the state on their way to Washington, as was the case in Maryland. And so Kentucky rested secure, believing that no war could be fought if it remained neutral. It was thus allowed to remain for nearly five months after Fort Sumter, an island of tranquility in the midst of a raging sea. The cornerstone of Kentucky's policy was armed neutrality and no one in the state dared to question its wisdom.

This concept of armed neutrality was endorsed equally by all elements of the state government in the spring of 1861. Both the governor, Beriah Magoffin, and the state legislature had been elected in 1859 on issues entirely different from the overriding question of the Union, which was so crucial in 1861. As it turned out Governor Magoffin was Southern-minded, and refused to furnish troops to President Lincoln after Fort Sumter. In this action he was endorsed by the legislature. But the state legislature was fairly evenly split, with the house of representatives more secessionist and the senate more Union-oriented.

The people of Kentucky had their first opportunity to vote on the issues of 1861 in the election in early May for delegates to the Border State Convention. This convention had been organized to give the border slave states an opportunity to bring about a reconciliation between North and South. In Kentucky, two sets of candidates were put forward, one Union and the other Southern Rights. It soon became clear, however, that the Southern Rights slate would lose. As the voting drew near, the secessionists became more and more discouraged and five days before the election, the Southern Rights candidates were all withdrawn from the canvass. The Union candidates went on to score a rousing victory, receiving some 110,000 votes, more than two-thirds of the total vote cast for all the Presidential candidates the previous November. Kentucky was clearly in favor of remaining with the Union.

Although there was a strong secessionist minority in the state, and both the Union and the secessionist sentiment was opposed to the war, it was apparent that Kentucky would never secede from the Union in a free election. And the Lincoln guns insured that the Union men could not be coerced. And so the people of Kentucky waited for something to happen.

CHAPTER 10

PEACE IN KENTUCKY

T HE THEORY of armed neutrality had been tried in other border states in the early days of the war. It received its first test in Baltimore during the insurrection. But Marylanders had paid a heavy price for trying to keep Northern troops out of their state, and were never during the entire war to live down the perfidy of this act. As one newspaper put it, Maryland did "lie so low, there's none so poor to do her reverence."

And armed neutrality was all that Price had been seeking in Missouri. He wanted only to keep Lyon and Blair penned up in St. Louis and the rest of the state under the control of state militia. Lyon was specifically fighting armed neutrality when he made his famous remarks in the Planters' House meeting: "Rather than concede to the State of Missouri the right to demand that my government shall not enlist troops within her limits, or bring troops into the State whenever it pleases . . . I would see . . . every man, woman and child in this State dead and buried." And so the war came to Missouri.

But in Kentucky, for a time, armed neutrality worked. The state lay safely nestled in the center of the Union, looking with awe at the passions at work around her. As one newspaper reported, "Kentucky looks to the West and trembles as she beholds Missouri. She looks to the East and cowers like a frightened fawn when she sees the humiliating position occupied by Maryland." Kentuckians were agreed that the only answer lay in armed neutrality. To give power to armed neutrality, the state legislature passed an act establishing a "military board" and provided $1,600,000 for the purchase of arms and munitions to repel any aggressors, be they from the North or South. But the legislature was so evenly divided that arms were ordered to be distributed in equal amounts to the Union Home Guard companies and the rebel state militia companies.

In the similar vein, Governor Magoffin issued a proclamation on May 20 which formally declared and established armed neutrality as the official policy of the state. The proclamation put the state in a "position of self-defense" and forbade "the quartering of troops upon her soil by either of the hostile sections." He then went on to warn "all the other States . . . especially the 'United States' and the 'Confederate States,' that I solemnly forbid any movement upon the soil of Kentucky, or the occupation of any port, or post, or place whatever within the lawful boundary and jurisdiction of this State . . . until authorized by invitation or permission of the Legislature and Executive authorities of this State." And he further counseled his fellow-citizens "to make prompt and efficient preparation to assume the armor and attitude presented by the supreme law of self-defense."

And where Maryland and Missouri failed, Kentucky succeeded. Neither Northern nor Southern troops attempted to occupy the state. The four hundred-mile-long powder keg of Kentucky lay dormant as the months passed.

But recruiting for the Confederate armies was going on actively within the state. In the legislature there was a senator named Lovell H. Rousseau who was outraged that this should be allowed. He rose to the floor of the senate one day and cried: "Troops leave Kentucky in broad daylight . . . to fight against our own government, yet nothing is said or done to prevent them. . . . I am utterly opposed to it." Rousseau finally decided that something should be done about it. He formed a camp (called Camp Jo Holt after one of Kentucky's most famous Union men) where he trained Union recruits from Kentucky. Because President Lincoln was not ready to force the issue of Unionism in Kentucky, the camp had to be located outside the state. So Rousseau set it up across the river from Louisville, on a high, grassy plateau in Indiana overlooking the "Falls of the Ohio." The men who enlisted could see the Kentucky shore from their tents. They drilled, read, wrote and conversed here, preparing for war. By the middle of July, Rousseau had some 800 men in his camp. Along the southern border of Tennessee, similar camps were springing up where the Kentucky recruits for the Confederate army were drilling and preparing for war. But within the state itself, neither Union nor Confederate armies dared to establish military camps.

As a result, the state turned into a great debating society. One man who lived through this period said that "during the summer of 1861 nothing was talked of in Kentucky except union or disunion. The courts were virtually closed. . . . Meetings were arranged for the street corners in Louisville. A band of music was employed to bring the people together. The speaker usually stood on a box obtained from some storehouse near by. It is safe to say that . . . I made at least fifty 'storebox' speeches for the Union cause." Treason and loyalty jostled each other in strange proximity. One man wrote that "at the hotel breakfast-table, you look up from your latest Tribune, forty-eight hours from New York, to find your nearest neighbor perusing the Charleston Mercury. . . . Stop to chat with an unconditional Union friend upon the sidewalk; and while he is telling you that Magoffin deserves hanging . . . some inebriated cavalier reels by, shouting 'Hurrah for Jeff Davis.'" In Louisville, a group of pale, long-haired young men would pass by on their way to the Southern army and a moment later a company of long-limbed fellows from the mountain counties would pass on their way to join the Union army. As one man put it, "It is wonderful that with all these combustibles in contact, no explosion has yet occurred in the Kentucky powder magazine."

No place else in the country, except here right in the center, was this happening. Yet somehow, the state remained peaceful. By the middle of July, fully three months had passed since Fort Sumter. But the equilibrium was not upset. The penalties were too great, the gory examples of Maryland and Missouri too immediate, and the balance too fine between North and South in this state.

President Lincoln realized this only too well. He was represented as praying: "Oh, Lord, we earnestly hope that Thou wilt favor our cause, but we must have Kentucky." He not only refrained from attempting to send troops into the state, but his entire policy on emancipation was dictated by the desire to win the state for the Union. For as long as Kentucky hung in the balance, the Union itself hung in the balance.

On June 20th, a special election was held to elect Congressmen for the special session called by Lincoln for July 4. The canvass was pushed by both the Union and States Rights parties, but when election day came, the Union men won an overwhelming victory. Of the ten candidates elected, nine were Union, and only one, Henry Burnett from the far western tip of Kentucky, was a States Rights victor. The election showed once again that Kentucky would never secede from the Union. Time was beginning to run out on the secessionists in the state.

As Lincoln watched this panorama, it seemed to him that he could afford to play the waiting game. He wrote that he wished to suppress the insurrection "with the least possible disturbance" to the people of Kentucky. "So far I have not sent any armed force into Kentucky, nor have I any present purpose to do so," he added. As the Union men gained dominance of the state, step by step, it seemed best to wait.

And so four hundred miles of access to the South was denied to the North, and its eyes became riveted on the narrow coastline between the Chesapeake Bay and the Blue Ridge Mountains as the most logical access route southward. And this fixation led to the Battle of Bull Run, the first great battle of the war, and one that set the stage for a convulsion of the North never equaled before or since in the history of the country.

CHAPTER 11

WASHINGTON AT BAY

NEVER DID any American President face a more critical situation after his inauguration than President Lincoln. The mind of this man was to be tested during the next twelve months as few men's minds have been tested. Nothing in his experience, nothing in his training, nothing in his background prepared him for the ordeal through which he was to pass. A man who had scarcley been in charge of any organization larger than a two-man law office was suddenly catapulted into a position where his subordinates were numbered in the hundreds of thousands. A prairie lawyer who had been concerned mainly with the problems of the county courthouse for several decades found himself in charge of the destinies of a great nation. He was surrounded by men who had in the past outshone him in everything he had attempted. As a lawyer, he had never been able to break into the ranks of the great, with men like Edward Bates, Edwin Stanton and Reverdy Johnson. His short career as a member of Congress had only served to show there were other men more capable in that body. William E. Seward, the Blairs, Chase, and many others had managed to come to Washington and stay on to become national symbols. But Lincoln had returned to Illinois to be forgotten.

And then suddenly he was catapulted over these men to the one position they all wanted more than anything else in the world. For when the moment of decision faced the nation in 1860, Lincoln showed that he understood more clearly than any of these others the central issues at stake. Away from the turmoil of Washington, away from the daily necessity of meeting the Southerners, of dealing with them, of appreciating their position, of compromising in order to make the wheels of government work, Lincoln was able to think through the problem of slavery as it engulfed the nation in the late 1850's. From his detached position on the Illinois prairie, he slowly evolved a belief that there was only one thing that counted. Slavery must not be allowed to expand into the territories. This one principle underlay everything he did and said from that point onward. His position was simple, easily understood and completely lucid. While others were vacillating, switching from one party to another and changing their position in an attempt to marry expediency with principle, in an attempt to save the South without losing the North, in an attempt to win the Presidency without compromising the party, Lincoln was able to see and concentrate on the nub of the problem. Nothing should be done to disturb slavery where it was, and nothing should be done to abolish it or to destroy it. But it must not be allowed to expand into the territories.

He expressed his position clearly and simply in his debates with Senator Douglas during 1858 and strangely enough, the man who could be so easily forgotten in Congress and on the prairie up until this time, was never again to be forgotten. This man and his policy haunted the country, and as the North prepared to stand fast on the issue of slavery, it decided collectively to stand fast on the position as stated so clearly by Lincoln.

But Lincoln's ability to think through and express himself on the issue of slavery did not mean that he could step into an entirely new environment in Washington and run the federal government effectively. He leaned heavily on his advisors during these early days. The chief among these, in military matters, was General Winfield Scott. In the days immediately after the inauguration, Scott had watched and worried over the safety of Washington. In early April, 1861, the city had only

500 regular troops for its defense. Scott ordered a few companies of regulars to the city but there were not many to draw on. The entire Department of the East, stretching from Michigan to the Atlantic and from Maine to Florida, had only 3,800 troops and many of these were needed elsewhere. But he did his best. Three days before Sumter, as the situation became more tense, he called up the militia of the city and they soon outnumbered the regulars.

Rumors were circulating freely in Washington that the rebels of Virginia and Maryland were to rise in arms and take the city when the attack on Fort Sumter began. In the midst of the turmoil and worry, President Lincoln asked General Scott to make a daily report to him on military movements. "Would it impose too much labor on General Scott to make short comprehensive daily reports to me . . . If not, I will thank him to do so." Scott immediately began a series of reports that reflected his unperturbable confidence in the outcome of the struggle. For Scott was a true professional. He knew that any show of uncertainty or fear from him would spread like wildfire and might paralyze the government. He had been born before the United States was founded, and had participated in every war after the Revolution. During the War of 1812, he served as a lieutenant colonel and was twice wounded. Afterwards, he rose to become a senior officer of the United States Army. His career had reached its climax during the Mexican War in 1848, when he led a brilliant campaign which ended with the capture of Mexico City. His retirement at this moment would have left his name a happy memory for the American people. But he remained in command of the Army and was nominated to the Presidency in 1852 on the Whig ticket. William E. Seward had actually written his acceptance speech. After Scott lost out in the Presidential campaign, at the age of sixty-six, the rank of lieutenant general was created especially for him. He continued as head of the Army until 1861 and when the Civil War began he was seventy-four years old. By this time the proud figure had been slowed. Scott now weighed nearly three hundred pounds, a massive figure, much plagued by what he referred to as "the disgusting subject — my many physical infirmities." He was unable to mount a horse, or to walk more than a few paces at a time. After Fort Sumter he lived in his office, sleeping as well as working there. He was unable to review troops, much less direct them in battle. Many said he was not a fit image of military leadership to put before a nation of young men who were expected to rush to arms under his command. But Scott retained his position, partly through the tremendous prestige which he had earned and partly through his ability to meld into the social life of Washington. His conversaton was always entertaining and he was full of anecdotes, including some that went back to the Battle of Chippewa in 1814, nearly a half century before.

When the blow fell on Fort Sumter, Scott had a handful of regulars, plus some fifteen companies of volunteers, to depend on. He knew he had approximately the same quality troops as the enemy. Even when Virginia passed the Ordinance of Secession, Scott was unmoved. On the 15th of April, three days after Sumter, his daily report to Lincoln was very short. "I have but little of special interest to report today, except that . . . [I believe] our means of defense, with vigilance, are sufficient to hold till reinforcements arrive." The next day he ordered another eight companies of volunteers into service in the District and reported to Lincoln that "these, I think, place the Capital a little ahead of impending dangers." By this time, of course, 75,000 volunteers had been called up in the North, and he indicated that three or four Massachusetts regiments would arrive within a few days.

Scott's confidence was the most stable factor in the city of Washington during this period. For he knew that although his volunteers were not the best trained fighters in the world, they were probably a match for any that Virginia had on hand. And fighting from defensive positions around the city, they could give a good account of themselves.

Then came the insurrection in Baltimore. The panic that

struck Washington at this moment was almost overwhelming. It had become an island completely surrounded by rebels. Edwin Stanton, who was later to become Lincoln's Secretary of War, wrote that "no description could convey to you the panic that prevailed here for several days after the Baltimore riots. . . . Women and children were sent away in great numbers; provisions advanced to famine prices." All kinds of rumors were circulating. The mob which had attacked the Sixth Massachusetts was reported to be coming over to burn the public buildings and sack the town. Confederate vessels were reported on their way up from Norfolk to bombard the city. Confederate troops were supposed to be on the road from Richmond and Harpers Ferry, to seize the city. Frederick Seward, son of the Secretary of State, later wrote that forty thousand "Virginia volunteers armed with bowie knives" were supposed to be attacking across the Long Bridge over the Potomac River. "Business was at a standstill," he added. "The railway station was silent, the wharves deserted. Groups of people gathered at street corners exchanging, in low tones, their forebodings of disaster, or their hopes of relief." Scott distributed his troops around the city where they were most needed. Batteries of light artillery were posted to stand guard at the bridges. The Capitol was barricaded, and the Massachusetts Sixth was assigned to defend it. Two additional companies of volunteers were hastily formed by visitors at the hotels and they patrolled the streets and performed regular guard duties. The Richmond *Examiner* editorialized that "capture of Washington City is perfectly within the power of Virginia and Maryland . . . our people can take it — they will take it."

But Scott did not share in the panic. The day after the riots he reported to Lincoln that "we are in advance of all preparations for an attack upon us." He went on to say that he had sent orders to Butler and his Massachusetts troops to get to Washington as fast as possible. Butler was ordered to come by train if possible, but if not to march overland immediately.

The next day Scott thought he detected signs of massing of Virginia troops across the Potomac from Washington. He estimated that some 10,000 troops were preparing to attack but again added, "I feel confident that with our present force, we can defend the Capitol, the Arsenal and all the executive buildings." He had some 7,000 troops by this time, mostly volunteers and he felt that they could hold the enemy.

But Scott had no news from Butler in Annapolis and nobody could understand why it was taking so long for the Massachusetts troops to get to Washington. Scott reported to Lincoln that he was reluctant to release men from the vital defense of Washington, but he was considering sending a force sufficient to "release the troops hemmed in at Annapolis." Butler, who had encountered absolutely no resistance, had found other activities to engage in, and took six days to cross the short forty miles from Annapolis to Washington.

Then, on April, 26, a week after the riot in Baltimore, a train came roaring into Washington, blowing its whistles and loaded with Union troops. It was greeted by an enthusiastic crowd. Some 1,600 volunteers arrived in the city that day and the capital and nation breathed easier. At the same time Scott reported that he had heard "through very respectable channels" that Virginia had decided against invading the city of Washington and was thinking in terms of armed neutrality. The city's most acute crisis had passed and it was now safe. Troops were pouring in by the thousands.

The great fear and worry of the preceding days was followed by a wave of optimism. At the end of April Scott reported that "not a gun had been mounted, nor a breastwork commenced" across the Potomac River from Washington. He ordered that the call on Pennsylvania for twenty-six additional regiments which had been made during the emergency be withdrawn as they were not needed. He felt that 20,000 troops would be adequate to defend the capital against any enemy known to be within twenty-four hours of the city, especially in view of "the favorable change said to have taken place in the temper and purposes of Maryland."

But the fear and panic which had spread throughout the city were enough to start a wave of arrests, and several men were imprisoned without due process by the military. Toward the middle of May, a visitor from New Jersey got drunk and began harassing some members of a Newark regiment about taking up arms against the South. They became suspicious and had him arrested. The colonel of the Newark regiment ordered him kept under guard during the night and planned to let him go in the morning, but General Scott directed that he be turned over to the Marshal of the District of Columbia and lodged in jail to await further orders.

As soon as the United States Attorney heard about the incident he wrote a letter to Lincoln complaining that the military authorities were arresting, trying and imprisoning citizens in the District. Lincoln received the note and wrote on it, "Unless the necessity for these arbitrary arrests is *manifest,* and *urgent,* I prefer they should cease." The prisoner was released but the arrests continued. For it was a problem not easily solved.

By the time Congress convened in special session, on July 4, Lincoln had formally suspended the writ of habeas corpus along "any military line which is now . . . used between the city of New York and the city of Washington." And there were by this time a number of major arrests which Congress might question. Emmet McDonald of St. Louis and John Merryman of Cockeysville were the two major cases in which the legal aspects of the problem had been explored. In addition, Ross Winans, Marshal Kane and the Baltimore police commissioners had been arrested in Maryland.

So Lincoln raised the question in his Message to Congress. He said that he had suspended the privilege of the writ of habeas corpus in order "to arrest and detain without resort to the ordinary processes and forms of law . . .[anyone] considered dangerous to the public safety. This authority has been purposely exercised but sparingly." He said that he had seriously considered the matter before taking action. But the laws which he had sworn to execute faithfully were being resisted in nearly one third of the states. He asked whether they should be allowed to fail because "some single law made in such extreme tenderness of the citizen's liberty . . . should to a very limited extent be violated?" Or, to put the matter more simply, "Are all the laws but one to go unexecuted and the Government itself to go to pieces lest that one be violated?" He said the Constitution clearly provided that the privilege of the writ could be suspended in case of rebellion and the only remaining question was whether the President or the Congress had this power. He did not believe "the framers of the instrument intended that in every case the danger should run its course until Congress could be called together."

But he did not propose that Congress suspend the writ. He concluded simply by stating that "whether there shall be any legislation upon the subject . . . is submitted entirely to the better judgment of Congress." In order to arm himself for the struggle over the suspension of the writ, the President asked his Attorney General, Edward Bates of Missouri, to give him an opinion as to his authority to suspend the writ. Bates was an eminent lawyer who had been seriously considered as a possible candidate for the Presidential nomination in 1860 by some Republicans. He was an old man, at sixty-eight the oldest in the cabinet, who epitomized the conservative element of the party. Nominated to a cabinet post to please the border states, particularly Missouri, Bates held that Lincoln had the power and could make arrests without fear of judicial interference. He concluded that "the judiciary department has no political power and claims none, and therefore . . . no court or judge can take cognizance of the political acts of the President or undertake to revise and reverse his political decisions. . . . I think it will hardly be seriously affirmed that a judge at chambers can entertain an appeal in any form from a decision of the President of the United States, and especially in a case purely political."

This opinion, which entirely disregarded the concept of balance of powers on which the Constitution was based, was read and then largely ignored. In the great debate on habeas corpus that was brewing in the country, Bates's opinion commanded no respect from either camp. It remained some months later for a man of greater legal ability, an octogenarian Philadelphia lawyer named Horace Binney, to lay the legal groundwork to support the President in his course of action.

But in the session of July 4th, Lincoln turned the whole matter over to Congress to take action. Senator Wilson of Massachusetts proposed Joint Resolution No. 1 in the Senate which was designed to approve all the acts taken by the President since the firing on Fort Sumter. This resolution approved his calling up the militia, instituting a blockade of the Confederacy and increasing the size of the Regular Army. These provisions were not matters of serious dispute in the Senate, which numbered thirty-two Republicans against fifteen opposition. But included in Joint Resolution No. 1 was a provision approving his suspension of the privilege of the writ of habeas corpus, and the Senate boggled over approving it. Despite the large Republican majority, there were a number of Senators who simply could not bring themselves to agree with it. Senators from the border states, such as Powell and Breckinridge of Kentucky, Polk of Missouri, Kennedy and Pearce of Maryland, and Bayard of Delaware were entirely against the provision. Some of them were to go South after the session ended, and others had seen their constituents snatched up and sent to prison without trial or conviction. Their opposition was to be expected.

But not quite so expected was the reaction of men such as Senator Lyman Trumbull of Lincoln's own state, Illinois, who said he was prepared to give the Administration all the necessary power to suppress the rebellion, but "I am not disposed to say that the Administration has unlimited power and can do what it pleases, after Congress meets." To this Senator Morrill of Maine replied, "I am inclined to concur with the gentleman from Illinois." And Senator Latham of California said that "so far as the violation of the writ of habeas corpus in the State of Maryland was concerned, I refuse to give him my sanction for that act." And Senator Sherman of Ohio, brother of General William T. Sherman, said he did "not believe the President of the United States has the power to suspend the writ of habeas corpus. . . . I shall therefore be compelled to vote against the resolution."

Slowly sentiment built up against the clause which approved and legalized the suspension of the writ and it was removed from Joint Resolution No. 1. And so died the first attempt to obtain Congressional approval of the suspension. The Senate adjourned without passing any legislation on the subject and the House of Representatives never even got around to discussing the matter.

While the Senate was debating this question, two armies were preparing for battle just outside Washington. This great clash of arms was to stagger the North and make the habeas corpus issue one of the burning questions of the day. But Congress had failed to assert its authority in 1861 and as a result the legislative branch had no impact on the program. The executive branch was forced to do alone what it felt had to be done.

CHAPTER 12

BULL RUN AND McCLELLAN

B<small>Y THE MIDDLE</small> of July, Union arms were everywhere triumphant. It seemed that the war was nearly won. The entire North had responded to the call for troops after Fort Sumter and an enormous number had rushed to defend the capital. After the twin defeats of Charleston and Baltimore, everything began to go well for the Union. Baltimore had been retaken and Union troops were occupying the state of Maryland. Washington was safe and Union volunteers had crossed the Potomac and occupied some high ground across the river from the city. Harpers Ferry was seized once again by Union forces.

Far to the west, Frank Blair and Nathaniel Lyon had taken Camp Jackson and captured the entire body of state militia camped there. Then Lyon had started out into the state, chasing General Price, Governor Jackson and the legislature out of the state capital. By mid-July he was somewhere in western Missouri, in hot pursuit of the rapidly retreating Price. The western anchor of the Union line was secure.

Even in Kentucky there was ground for optimism. Delivery of the Lincoln guns had inspired the Union elements and the Congressional elections in June had resulted in an overwhelming victory for the Union. Kentucky seemed to be moving inexorably toward the North.

But it was in western Virginia that the most remarkable events were taking place. A young West Point-educated general, George B. McClellan, had been named commander of the

Ohio militia and just across the river from that state lay the mountain regions of western Virginia. These regions contained an entirely different population from the Virginia of the tidewater area. Here there were few slaves and most of the farmers hated the rich planters in the eastern part of the state. They had voted against secession and were ready to take up arms for the Union. McClellan did not intend to let this rare opportunity slip from his grasp.

All of his life he had been successful. A high-ranking graduate of West Point, he had served under Winfield Scott in Mexico and was breveted for gallantry. In 1855 he was sent to Europe as an official Army observer in the Crimean War. This gave him an unusual opportunity to learn something of European methods of fighting. In 1857, when he had risen to the rank of captain, he resigned his commission and entered the railroad business. By the time the Civil War began he was President of the Ohio and Mississippi Railroad Company, at the very good salary of $10,000 a year.

When McClellan took over command of the Ohio volunteers in April, he realized the key nature of his post. With the exception of some mountainous terrain in western Pennsylvania, Ohio was the only free state that bordered directly on a seceded state. For two hundred miles, only the Ohio River separated the people of western Virginia from their friends and neighbors in Ohio. This part of Virginia was ripe for invasion and General McClellan was quick to seize the initiative. He moved across the Ohio River with several regiments and quickly cleared the region of Confederate troops. Then he advanced into the mountains and attacked two Confederate detachments drawn up in the passes. One withdrew and the other surrendered, and McClellan overnight became famous. The groundwork had been laid for creation of the new state of West Virginia, which was admitted to the Union later in the war. To celebrate this victory he congratulated his troops for having "annihilated two armies . . . entrenched in mountain fastnesses." His success was the culminating victory for Union arms during the early days of summer. Everywhere along the thousand-mile line that separated North from South, the Union was winning. The power of the North seemed invincible.

And so the stage was set for an advance into Virginia. The war was to be won in a single battle, just as Napoleon had toppled whole empires with his great victories. For the Napoleonic figure haunted the North during this period. The concept of a single, decisive battle was his legacy. The Union, it was felt, had only to marshal its forces, meet the enemy in battle, and the war would be over.

All of the pressures called for an attack into Virginia. It was impossible to restrain the demand and President Lincoln had no desire to do so. Failure to attack would mean that the Southern policy of armed neutrality had succeeded. Even a delay of six months could destroy the Union. There was no alternative to an attack and it had to be soon. The great mass of three-month volunteers who had been called to duty in April would be mustering out in July. And so under a general named Irvin McDowell, the Union armies were ordered into Virginia and they lurched forward. As it happened, they got only a few miles into the state and ran into the Confederate army at Manassas Junction. Because they fought alongside a creek named Bull Run, the battle took this unusual name. It was fought on Sunday, July 21, and it was on this day that the Civil War really began.

The Northern defeat would have been difficult to avoid. For three long years, it would prove nearly impossible for any Northern general to take his armies into Virginia without being defeated and equally impossible for any Southern general to take his armies into Maryland or Pennsylvania without being defeated. With the Minié rifle and improved artillery, the defense was already ahead of the offense, a trend which would reach its climax in World War I. Massed infantry attacks were to fail amost every time they were attempted in the Civil War and they would frequently destroy the attacking army. Unfortunately, the image of Napoleonic warfare which possessed the American generals and people, with its emphasis on attack and on the goal of a single decisive battle, did not coincide with the realities of the day. It is perhaps well that President Lincoln and others around him did not see this, as they might have shrunk from the carnage that lay ahead.

As a result, when the untrained troops of July, 1861, were sent into Virginia, they had little chance of victory. For they did not face a Baltimore mob, or an unarmed Camp Jackson or even a disaffected western Virginia. They faced determined men, defending their homeland with devastating defensive weapons, and they were routed. As they came straggling back into the city of Washington on the evening of July 21, the North realized that the summer lark, with its friendly camaraderie around the campfire, was over. War, in all its stark reality, had come.

The next morning as the Senate met just a few miles from the battlefield, gloom and anxiety filled the chamber. The Army had been defeated, the three-months' men were about to go back to their homes, and the capital was in danger. Horace Greeley, the foremost Republican editor in the country, wrote to Lincoln asking, "Can the rebels be beaten after . . . our late awful disaster? . . . If the Union is irrevocably gone, an armistice . . . ought at once to be proposed." A secessionist newspaper in the North wrote that Bull Run "will be the crowning victory of the contest. The Federal forces remaining in Washington cannot retrieve a disaster so terrible. . . . The fall of Washington City is not at all improbable."

In the midst of this wave of despair, the victories of McClellan in western Virginia seemed almost miraculous. He alone had been able to win. The day after Bull Run, Lincoln asked him to come to Washington.

Into the Napoleonic miasma which had transfixed the North, McClellan fitted perfectly. Overnight he became "the young Napoleon." Small in stature, with an air of supreme confidence, he was a dashing, brilliant figure, only thirty-four years old. At the moment when the nation needed someone to believe in, he appeared on the scene and became an idol. The man who had been a captain in the Army just a few years before, suddenly found himself responsible for the military destinies of the entire nation. He wrote privately: "I find myself in a new and strange position here: President, cabinet, Gen. Scott and all deferring to me. By some strange operation of magic I seem to have become the power of the land." And later, "I went to the Senate . . . and was quite overwhelmed by the congratulations I received and the respect with which I was treated. . . . It seems to strike everybody that I look young. They give me my way in everything, full swing and unbounded confidence. All tell me that I am responsible for the fate of the nation."

But McClellan soon found that they did not really give him his way in everything. Old General Scott was still running the Army, and McClellan's position was that of a subordinate commander of the city of Washington. The two men were soon clashing over plans for the future and over the basic question of who was to run the Army, Scott or McClellan. During his first days in Washington, Scott had ordered McClellan to bring discipline to the troops in the city, many of whom were drunken and demoralized after the battle of Bull Run. As one of his first official duties, McClellan made a trip around the city, personally visiting the outposts and encampments. He found that the troops in the northern and western parts of the city had made no preparation for defense. The camps had not been dug in and none of the approaches were guarded. As he put it, "All was chaos, and the streets, hotels and bar-rooms were filled with drunken officers and men absent from their regiments without leave — a perfect pandemonium."

McClellan was greatly shocked at this and believed that a small enemy cavalry force could take the city of Washington by surprise. He expressed his belief in conversation with Senators and cabinet members, hinting that Scott had failed to attend to the defenses of the city. He brought in Allan Pinkerton to spy for him in Virginia, and Pinkerton, perhaps responsive to his chief's wishes, submitted exaggerated reports of troop concentrations across the river from Washington. These reports supported McClellan's repeated warnings that Washington was in imminent danger of capture. The strain between McClellan and Scott grew with each passing day as the authorities in Washington bypassed Scott, and McClellan tasted the sweet elixir of being singled out as the new American Napoleon. McClellan wrote to his wife: "I receive letter after letter — have conversation after conversation calling on me to save the nation — alluding to the Presidency, Dictatorship, etc. . . . I would cheerfully take the Dictatorship and agree to lay down my life when the country is saved. . . . Scott is the most dangerous antagonist I have."

Then on August 8, just two weeks after his arrival in Washington, McClellan sat down at his desk and composed a letter to Scott that was to shake the nation. He began by painting the danger to Washington in the darkest terms. He said that in his opinion, the "enemy intend attacking our positions on the other side of the river, as well as to cross the Potomac north of us. . . . I am induced to believe that the enemy has at least 100,000 men in front of us." This was some three times the number of troops available in Washington. If it were true, it meant that instead of having a rough balance between Union and Confederate forces, which Scott felt to be the case, the Union army was completely outnumbered. And so McClellan went on: "Were I in Beauregard's place . . . I would attack the positions on the other side of the Potomac, and at the same time cross the river above this city in force. I feel confident that our present army in this vicinity is entirely insufficient for the emergency and is deficient in all the arms of the service." In view of the "imminent danger" to the city, he urged that "not an hour be lost" in moving all available troops to Washington. As a kind of afterthought, he proposed that his own department be expanded to include Virginia, Maryland and Pennsylvania. To make sure the letter would not be ignored, he sent a copy directly to President Lincoln. McClellan had "thrown a bombshell," as he later referred to this letter.

General Scott was old but not too old to realize that McClellan was on the move. He forwarded a letter to Secretary of War Simon Cameron which, he said, would be his "only reply" to McClellan. He said that McClellan had "stood on his guard" in meetings with him and had not indicated any of his views. But McClellan had spread "in high quarters" his views on the danger to Washington. And, he added, "I am confident in the opposite opinion." Relying on the Union troops, the forts and the Potomac River as a protection, and considering "the stream of new regiments that is pouring in upon us . . . I have not the slightest apprehension for the safety of the government." But Scott realized that his hour had passed and that younger men must take over. And so he added that his age and infirmities had caused him to "become an encumbrance to the Army." He asked that he be placed on the retired officers' list so that he could quietly "lay myself up — probably forever." He closed the letter with "God Save the Union."

These two letters were dumped in Lincoln's lap. Although recognizing that the young hero would have to be given precedence over General Scott, Lincoln was never one for precipitous action. Scott's name held magic, particularly as he was a Southerner and the border states were crucial. So Lincoln intervened to smooth the situation over. He called in General McClellan and asked him to withdraw the offensive letter. McClellan did so cheerfully, writing to Lincoln that he would not think of doing anything that would "give offense to General Scott." He said that he had accepted his command in the "humble desire to serve my country. . . . Every moment's reflection and every fact transpiring convinces me of the urgent necessity of the measures there indicated." He added that since the government and his superior officer had been apprised of what he conceived to be necessary, he would withdraw the letter.

Armed with this letter of withdrawal from McClellan, such as it was, the President asked Scott to withdraw his resignation. But Scott insisted that in view of the many offenses and slights that McClellan had given him he could not withdraw his resignation. He felt that the prospect of "filing daily complaints against an ambitious junior" would not befit the dignity of his position or of his years. He added that McClellan had "very high qualifications for military command. I trust they may achieve crowning victories in behalf of the Union."

Although Scott was eventually induced to remain in his position, McClellan's major point had been made. He was given an expanded command and from this time on, McClellan was running the Army. He devoted himself tirelessly, with the backing of the nation, to the training and equipping of the Army. The dispute with Scott fell into the background as the old general accepted his fate.

But the fear for the safety of Washington continued to grow. As the number of troops in the city increased to the point where it was no longer possible to say that they were outnumbered, the danger reverted from Washington to Maryland. It was rumored that the Southern armies would cross the Potomac above the city and sweep across Maryland, with the aid of the mob in Baltimore, and cut Washington off once again from the North. The danger seemed to grow and grow, even after McClellan had taken command.

Panic is a strange thing. Once it has started, it is very difficult to stop. Of all the requirements of a general, none is more important than that he exude confidence and inspire his troops to the belief that they are the best in the world. McClellan had risen to the top by displaying doubt and uncertainty. In doing so, he set the stage for the phantom invasion of the North that occurred during the fall of 1861. Although no invasion took place, the effects of this attack were nonetheless real politically and psychologically in the North. A closing together of the ranks occurred, and all opposition was snuffed out. Hundreds were sent to prison as the North waited in fear of the blow to fall.

CHAPTER 13

RIOTS IN THE NORTH

WHILE McClellan was spreading uncertainty in Washington, another force was at work in the rest of the country. The volunteers who had been called to Washington immediately after the fall of Fort Sumter had finished their three-months' tour and were moving back to their homes in late July and early August. Not only had a bond developed between them, but they tended to have a collective chip on their shoulders. They were, after all, part of a defeated Army. Now they were returning home to find that the cheers with which they had been sent off in April were dimmed. Newspaper editors who favored letting the South go in peace frequently compared the Northern soldiers unfavorably with the Southern. Some editors even had the temerity to ridicule the patriotism and ability of the local regiments. This was too much for the Union soldiers, many of whom had left their families on a moment's notice and rushed off to defend their capital while these editors remained behind and sniped at them. Led partly by the returned soldiers, a wave of lawlessness swept the North in August, 1861, directed particularly against the anti-war newspapers.

The loss at Bull Run had had a tremendous impact on the North. Many of the doubters had their doubts confirmed. It suddenly became possible to question the wisdom of fighting a war. One Union editor wrote a private letter to William E. Seward in early August after making a tour of the North:

"There is no longer observable that feeling of unanimity in support of the Administration . . . or that confidence in the war and its ultimate issue, which pervaded the popular heart a few weeks ago. . . . There is an anti-war party slowly but surely forming all over the North."

The initial focus of this anti-war feeling appeared in the newspapers of the day. Outside the larger cities, these newspapers consisted mainly of small printers who tried to make a little extra money putting out a weekly gossip sheet folded double to make a total of four pages. These weekly sheets were rarely very successful and the printers who put them out were usually held in low repute. In the bigger cities, where more initiative was evidenced, editors were considered to be a positive menace to peace and order. They went to all lengths to stir up fights, adopt crusades, criticize and condemn. Many of the better citizens would walk across the street in order to avoid passing them. Their motto was simple; they would do anything that might help circulation. Horace Greeley, who was one of the most successful of the city editors, was inconsistent about everything, slashing at this and that, never adopting any single political or social philosophy, except perhaps the philosophy that anything that sells newspapers is good.

From Horace Greeley down to the editor of the meanest little weekly printer's sheet, however, these men seemed to have a penchant for politics. They were not loathe to express their opinion and if they happened to be opposed to the war, it was usually a vociferous, outspoken opposition, which belittled, condemned and degraded everything remotely related to the war.

Such a man was the editor of a paper called the *Democratic Standard*, which was published in the fair city of Concord, capital of New Hampshire. Why fate should have chosen this paper as the object of the first rioting in the North is difficult to say. However, the editor was a man of biting sarcasm and he used his pen not only against the men in far-off Washington, but against the local soldiers of the First New Hampshire Regiment who had just returned to Concord after the completion of their three-months' tour.

On August 8, the same day that McClellan was penning his letter to General Scott complaining about the defenses of Washington, the *Democratic Standard* issued its regular weekly paper with some stories that made the soldiers' blood boil. The paper ridiculed "a certain Northern New-England regiment" that had mutinied before leaving for Washington, because the men had been denied passes to see their friends on a Sunday. The same edition also said that "our Southern papers are filled with heart-sickening accounts of the murders and robberies which individuals in Old Abe's Mob are perpetrating on the Southern people. Innocent women and children are shot on their own door steps. . . . No wonder the Northern people run, when the honest men of the South march toward them."

When the soldiers read these words they angrily began to gather in front of the printing office of the *Democratic Standard*. As the crowd grew, several people went up to the third-floor room where the paper was printed to try to get in. But they found the doors locked. Within a few minutes, however, the four publishers of the paper, printers all, appeared at their windows armed with revolvers and guns. One of the printers was reported to have reached out with his revolver, and told the mob that he and his fellow printers were prepared to defend themselves to the last extremity. At this, the mob let out a bellow, shouting "Fire, you traitor, you rebel and secessionist."

The city marshal and several prominent citizens arrived at the scene to prevent the soldiers from attacking the building. But they had no success. The soldiers climbed up the stairway to the printing office and started breaking down the door. Firing broke out and several people in the mob received minor bullet wounds. As the rioters got into the building, the printers beat a hasty retreat, escaping through an attic. The mob then began demolishing the office, throwing type, desks, papers and

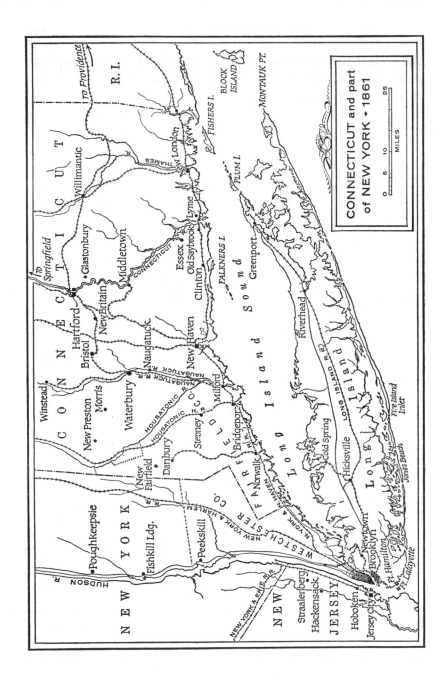

CONNECTICUT and part
of NEW YORK • 1861

0   5   10   25
MILES

R. I.

to Providence

BLOCK
ISLAND

MONTAUK PT.

FISHERS I.

PLUM I.

New London

THAMES R.

Willimantic

FALKNERS I.

Greenport

CONNECTICUT

Lyme
Old Saybrook
Essex
Clinton

Glastonbury

Middletown

Riverhead

Springfield

Hartford

NewBritain

Bristol

Naugatuck

New Haven

L o n g   I s l a n d   S o u n d

LONG ISLAND R. R.

to Springfield

Winstead

Morris

New Preston

Waterbury

NAUGATUCK R. R.

HOUSATONIC R.

Milford

Stepney

Bridgeport

Cold Spring

Hicksville

Fire Island
Inlet

Jones Beach

C O N N E C T I C U T

L i t t o r a l

Danbury

New
Fairfield

A Norwalk

Newtown

L o n g   I s l a n d

Poughkeepsie

Fishkill Ldg.

Peekskill

HUDSON R.

N E W   Y O R K

NEW YORK & HARLEM R. R.

WESTCHESTER CO.

N. YORK
HAVEN R.

N'YORK

Brooklyn

Ft. Hamilton

Ft. Lafayette

Straalenberg

Hackensack

Hoboken

Jersey City

N E W
J E R S E Y

NEW YORK & ERIE R.R.

everything else they could find, down on the sidewalk from the office. The refuse was set afire and the entire pile burned as the soldiers and citizens went about shouting joyfully.

When this job was done, the soldiers set out to find the printers. But some citizens came to their rescue and hurried the printers to the police station at a fast run, with the crowd following and shouting, "Lynch them, lynch them." The printers were placed in the city jail and later that night were transferred to the State Prison for safekeeping. In front of the printing office a flag was hung: "The Doom of Traitors."

Not far away in Bangor, Maine, a similar scene occurred a few days later. The Bangor *Democrat* was run by a man named Marcellus Emory, who took his politics seriously and was opposed to the war. His newspaper articles had irritated the people of Bangor for some time without causing any incidents, but when the news of the Concord mob reached town, the men of Bangor felt they were at least as good as the men of Concord.

On Monday morning, August 12, everything seemed to be quite normal to editor Emory as he proceeded to print his weekly paper. He finished the job, handed out the papers to his newsboys and left his office to have lunch at his boarding house a half mile away. While he was eating he heard the firebells ringing and ran out to see what the trouble was. He arrived in front of his office to find that all of his property had been thrown from his upstairs shop into the street below. The square in front of his office was filled with nearly two thousand people and in the center of the square was a large bonfire consuming the remains of what Emory claimed had been "one of the largest and finest printing offices in the State." He made his way through the crowd to the entrance of his private office and found that crowbars were being used to get it open. He was allowed to open the door, and the mob followed him in, seizing everything it could lay its hands on. The work of destruction was soon complete and when Emory returned to the sidewalk, he heard cries of "Hang him. Tar and feather him."

But his friends gathered around and escorted him through the mob to safety. When it was over and Emory had seen four years of toil swept away, he lamented, "thus hath the freedom of the press been stricken down here in Maine."

Four days later a Peace meeting was planned in Old Saybrook, Connecticut, a town near Long Island Sound. The schedule called for raising a Peace flag and listening to a rousing anti-war speech. When word got around that the meeting was planned, Union men from all over that section of the state set out for Old Saybrook to break it up. Some two hundred of them came from New Haven, Lyme, Essex, Clinton and other towns, met in Old Saybrook and marched down the street holding aloft a large Union flag. They soon arrived where some seventy-five Peace men were holding their meeting. The Union men rushed in and started tearing down the Peace flag and raising the Union flag. A fight broke out between the two groups but the Union men outnumbered the Peace men and it wasn't long before the Union flag was flying from the flagpole. The Union men took over the grounds and proceeded to hold their own meeting. One man got up on a wagon and urged "steady support with money and life of our Government and its flag." Fortunately, no one was seriously injured.

By the middle of August, the Peace movement was in full bloom and Peace meetings were being held in many parts of the country. In Danbury, Connecticut, the ladies of the town held a meeting and raised their own Peace flag, a white banner with the motto "Peace and our Country" inscribed on it. They passed a resolution stating that whereas "Civil War is now raging in our midst; laying waste to our land, demoralizing our people, prostrating our business," it was necessary that it should "be brought to an immediate close. . . . We cannot believe that a war like the present can ever reconstruct the Union." The meeting did not cause any rioting but showed the temper of some of the people of Danbury.

Feelings continued to build up as newspapers printed their

anti-war editorials. Then suddenly on August 19, there erupted a torrent of mob action. On that day, three newspaper offices were gutted. The first was in Haverhill, Massachusetts, where the Essex County *Democrat* had gained quite a reputation as a pro-Southern newspaper. After the experience in Concord and Bangor, it appeared to be only a matter of time before the citizens of Haverhill would get around to doing something about the editor of this paper.

On the night of August 19, Mr. Ambrose Kimball, its editor, was walking down the Main Street of the town with some friends when he was suddenly surrounded by an angry crowd. Kimball's friends got him into a carriage with some difficulty and he started off at top speed for his home. As he drove off, a cry of fire was raised and the large crowd chased the carriage down the street. Kimball got home but the mob was right behind him and gathered in front of his house. A cry went up for Kimball to come out and when he refused, they went in after him, dragging him out into the street.

Kimball was carried to the center of the town where he was asked if he regretted what he had published. He made no reply. Then he was asked if he would acknowledge that he had been wrong, and promised not to "further outrage the sentiment of the community." Kimball declined and was instructed to remove his clothes.

While he stood in the center of town with nothing on but his drawers, the mob covered Kimball with a coat of tar and feathers, mounted him on a rail and rode him around town for some time. After suffering this indignity, the editor was asked once again whether he regretted his conduct. Properly chastised, he replied that he did. He was then required to kneel down, raise his hand and repeat: "I am sorry that I have published what I have, and I promise that I will never again write or publish articles against the North and in favor of secession, so help me God." He was then escorted to his home.

The same day that Mr. Kimball was being tarred and feathered in Massachusetts, another mob was venting its anger three hundred miles away in Easton, Pennyslvania. A Democratic county meeting in Easton had led to some fist-fights and by nightfall a group of Union men were on the rampage in the town. This mob, some two thousand strong before it had finished its work, started off by visiting the home of the local Congressman, Philip Johnson, whose remarks at the meeting had indicated something less than 100 per cent Union sentiment. They raised an effigy in front of his house and set fire to it, while Johnson sat on his front step and watched. As the effigy burned, part of the mob charged up onto the porch after Johnson with the thought that perhaps they would do the same thing with him. But Johnson ran into his house and a few moments later appeared at an upper window with a small Union flag in his hand, and assured them of his loyalty. This appeased the mob somewhat and it began to drift away from his house. Then suddenly the cry went up, "To the Sentinel."

The *Sentinel* was another of the newspapers which was opposed to the war and had no hesitancy in so stating. After the defeat at Bull Run, it had become particularly strident in proclaiming its conviction that the Union could not be restored by arms. With the mob in Easton in its present state of mind, the *Sentinel* was doomed. They charged into the office and completely gutted it. Type, cases, desks, stands, stoves and everything that could be moved were thrown out into the street. Within a few minutes, the office was a complete wreck and the street in front looked like a dump. Then the mob went to the office of two other local newspapers to wreck them. But these papers had been less offensive and only a little damage was done. It was agreed that the editors would be allowed to publish statements affirming their Union sentiments.

The same night another group of men in West Chester, Pennsylvania, just outside Philadelphia, decided to do something about the conduct of the *Jeffersonian*, a local anti-war newspaper. Six men quietly entered the office in the darkness and cleaned out all the type in an attempt to prevent the paper from publishing. They were not successful, however, as the paper was back on the streets in a few days.

Out in Ohio, another newspaper was severely damaged a few nights later when a group of Union men, including some volunteers, broke into the office of the Stark County *Democrat* and threw the type, cases and stands out into the street. The whole pile was set on fire and made a huge blaze.

In Connecticut, an undercurrent had been building up for some time in Fairfield County in the southwest portion of the state. The area was mainly composed of prosperous farmers who were much opposed to the war. The center of the area was Bridgeport, where there was published a very highly respected newspaper called the *Farmer*, which had been in existence some fifty years. It had a circulation of over five thousand, very large for a country paper. The Bridgeport *Farmer* was utterly opposed to the war and had a strong influence on the thinking of the whole region. The Peace advocates in the area became very active after Bull Run, holding meetings and raising peace flags throughout the county. The Bridgeport *Farmer*, now edited by a young man named Nathan Morse, actively promoted the Peace movement in its columns and kept the people in this part of the state well informed as to Peace activities. As a result, one New York newspaper said that there was probably "no territory of equal extent north of Mason and Dixon's line, where so many secessionists can be found as in the County of Fairfield."

Connecticut's Third Regiment came from this region and when its volunteers returned from Washington in mid-August, trouble began almost immediately. The *Farmer* had called the troops "hirelings, miscreants and incarnate fiends" when they had been called up and the newspaper was now giving prominent space to Peace meetings taking place all over the state. The paper reported that five hundred men attended a Peace meeting in New Preston and said that the people of the county "are aroused; they have made up their minds that this unfortunate war must be terminated; that our difficulties can and must be settled without further bloodshed — or we are ruined as a people." At another meeting in New Fairfield, Connecticut, a white flag with the words "Peace and Union" was raised on August 24, while three hundred Peace men watched. Some forty Union men from Danbury, a few miles away, made the trip over to New Fairfield to prevent the raising and there was a fight with shovels, pickaxes, and stones in which several people were seriously injured. But the Peace men outnumbered the Union men and forced them to return to Danbury. That night the Peace flag was still flying in New Fairfield.

On the same day a Peace meeting was held in nearby Stepney. This meeting was announced in the Bridgeport *Farmer* and 125 Union men made the trip to Stepney to break it up. When they got there, they found that the Peace flag had already been raised and Ellis Schnabel, a well-known Peace speaker, was about to start speaking. The Union men from Bridgeport drove up, jumped out of their carriages and headed for the pole with the Peace flag on it. There was a fight but the Union men finally got the Peace flag down and raised the Stars and Stripes in its place. P. T. Barnum, one of the Union men, got up on the platform and called for the speaker who had been advertised for the Peace meeting, saying that if he were for the Union he would be defended, but if he spoke treason he should expect the just deserts of traitors. The originally scheduled speaker, Ellis Schnabel, when he heard this, shouted, "That's a lie," and somebody gave him a kick. Barnum and the other Union men then sang "The Star-Spangled Banner" and passed a resolution which condemned all "peace meetings" as "really intended as secession demonstrations," proclaiming that "there are but two parties — Loyal men and Traitors — those who sustain the Union . . . and those who oppose . . . through falsely called peace meetings."

The Union meeting was then adjourned and the men returned to Bridgeport where they held a triumphant procession, with the fallen "secession banner," as they called the Peace flag, trailing in the dust behind them amidst the cheering of their fellow citizens. This was heady wine, particularly for the volunteers, and they decided it was time to destroy the office of the Bridgeport *Farmer*. The cry "To the *Farmer* office" went up. Several hundred men moved down the street to the building where the *Farmer* was printed, followed by a mob several thousand strong. The printing office filled three floors in a brick building and the men went to work on it. The doors were forced open and for some twenty minutes the rioters tore apart the printing establishment. They threw everything into the street that could be found. Type, job presses, ink, paper, books and other equipment were tossed out the windows. Every time a large item came crashing down, the mob outside let up a lusty cheer. Two presses too heavy to lift were smashed with sledge hammers. Then the men climbed out on the roof and tore down the signs. By the time they had finished the *Farmer* office was a wreck.

Their work done, the crowd dispersed, after giving three cheers for the Union and singing "The Star-Spangled Banner." Nathan Morse, the young editor of the paper, had escaped across the rooftop and hidden during the rioting. The next morning the streets were thronged by excited groups of men, and Mr. Morse was vigorously groaned at when he appeared on the streets. Sensing that he was not the most popular man in town, he put his things in his carpetbag, walked to the railroad station with the groaning crowd at his heels, got on the train and left town. New arrangements for publishing the paper under loyal auspices were made. Following the Bridgeport riot, most of the Peace flags that had been raised in the county were torn down by Union men.

By the end of August, many of the planned Peace meetings were being cancelled. In Newtown, Long Island, a Peace meeting which had been advertised was cancelled at the last moment. But Union men showed up at the scheduled time and held their own meeting. They invited any Peace speakers to have their say, but no one offered to speak. Some Union resolutions were passed to the effect that "there are but two sides to this question — the 'Government' or 'Rebellion'" and demanding the purging "alike of Southern rebels and Northern traitors." Some two thousand people formed a procession at the head of which was carried an illuminated coffin, with the inscription on the sides: "Newtown Secession, died Aug. 29, 1861." The procession called on the leading Peace advocate in town who obediently made a good Union speech and hung out the Stars and Stripes. Then the crowd dispersed.

In New York City, several newspapers with Peace sympathies were threatened with violence. The office of the New York *Daily News* was guarded by police for some time to prevent its destruction. Other newspapers, including the *Journal of Commerce* and *Daybook* were worried about mob action but none developed.

By this time the Union newspapers in the North reflected the general feeling that this type of mob action could not be tolerated. The New York *Herald* cried out that "there can be no justification . . . of mob law," and the New York *Times* called directly for action by the federal government: "If these newspapers are to be suppressed, let it be done by virtue of public law, and not by a reckless violence. . . . If their continued existence puts the Government in peril, let it be arrested; but let it be done by the law and its agents and not by a mob."

Throughout the North, therefore, the mob violence of August, 1861, was directly raising the issue of whether the federal government could continue to stand aloof from the question of loyalty. Unless the federal government stepped in and took some action, mob law could be the only result. But any action by the federal government would require a radical readjustment in the balance of power between the states and the federal government. And so it was to this question that the Lincoln Administration was forced to address itself.

CHAPTER 14

THE POLICY OF REPRESSION

THE CIVIL WAR began at a time when men showed little respect for federal power. As one writer put it, "the extension of the federal power during the three-quarters of a century preceding the Civil War was met with resistance from every quarter of the land." The list of attempts by states to nullify federal power prior to the Civil War was a long one and included actions by Northern as well as Southern states. Examples included the Whiskey Rebellion in Pennsylvania, resistance to the Window Tax, nullification of the Alien and Sedition Laws by Virginia and Kentucky, the threat of secession in 1814 by New England at the Hartford Convention, the Ordinance of Nullification in South Carolina in 1833, and the resistance in the North to the fugitive slave laws of Congress during the 1850's. And in 1861, of course, came the greatest threat in the form of secession of the entire South.

Responding to the threat of disunion in 1861, the Lincoln Government did not at first attempt any radical readjustment of its power relationships with the states of the North. When the call for troops went out after Fort Sumter, it was a call from the federal government requesting the governors of the various states to furnish troops. It could be accepted or rejected as the individual governors saw fit. In fact, two states that remained with the Union, Missouri and Kentucky, did summarily reject it. Even in the states that sent troops, provision of supplies, purchase of guns and ammunition, and procurement of transportation as they rushed to the defense of Washington, were largely in the hands of the states. Each state, and in fact, each company, had its own uniform. The Sixth Massachusetts, as it had marched through the city of Baltimore, had been clothed in a variety of uniforms ranging from the black pants and white pompoms of Company A through the dark blue and red French-style uniform of Company I. Out in Missouri, the men at Camp Jackson fought without either uniforms or pay. The states were still sovereign. The federal government in 1861 was a weak and incomplete thing compared with the government we now know — almost without power except as provided to it voluntarily by the states.

Within this framework, the Lincoln Administration found itself being propelled into radical actions as fear for the safety of Washington spread throughout the government and mob law threatened to become worse in the North. Exactly how the federal government would go about injecting its power into the equation against the Peace movement, however, was unclear. And then, at just the right moment, the Administration was offered a perfect opportunity to take action.

The first step in any program against the anti-war newspapers had to start with the muzzling of the New York press. The New York City newspapers dominated much of the nation. Although some of the larger newspapers such as the *Tribune*, *Herald* and *Times* supported the war, a few of the major journals did not. The most important of the opposition papers was the *Journal of Commerce*, which claimed to have the largest daily circulation of any newspaper in the city. It had been in existence nearly thirty-four years and was widely read and admired as a commercial newspaper. Another opposition paper was the Democratic political organ, the *Daily News*. The *News* was published by Benjamin Wood, a Congressman from New York and brother of New York's Mayor Fernando Wood, who had proposed in January 1861 that New York secede from the Union and form a free city.

These two newspapers, the *Journal of Commerce* and the *News*, were the heart of the opposition press of the nation. It was common practice for newspapers all over the country to fill their pages by reprinting articles taken from other papers. The opposition press represented a coterie of similar opinion and Peace newspapers in New York, with their enterprise and resources, tended to dominate the Peace press of the nation. Any attack on the opposition press would have to start in New York.

And as luck would have it, it was in New York that the Administration was presented with its golden opportunity. Twenty federal grand jurors had been sitting in New York City since the beginning of May making investigations and bringing indictments. Most of these involved offenses dealing with customs, mails and other similar matters, but just before their term ended in August the *Journal of Commerce* published a list of over one hundred newspapers in the free states which opposed "the present unholy war." This so enraged the Union men on the grand jury that they drew up a document asking the federal judge what action the grand jury could take with regard to such newspapers. The grand jurors added that if using such phrases as "unholy war" is not a crime, then "there is a great defect in our laws." The jury asked if such conduct was subject to indictment and punishment.

The judge, in his turn, asked the jury if they wanted instructions from him on the subject or whether they would merely like to bring it to the attention of the next grand jury when it convened two months later. The foreman of the jury answered that they had been in session for a long time and would like to be discharged of their duties, but would like to have it brought to the attention of the next grand jury. So the judge thanked the grand jury and discharged them. Nothing further was ever done about the request.

But this small action set in motion a series of events which shook the North. Without citing any laws, without actually receiving any opinion from the judge, and without taking any evidence, the grand jury succeeded in giving an aura of legality to the general hatred of the Peace press. The action was legally a "presentment," the same word which covers a formal indictment, and thus it was made to appear that laws existed and evidence had been taken. Here was an opportunity for the Administration to step in and muzzle these newspapers, thereby setting an example for the rest of the anti-war newspapers in the free states.

Arbitrary suppression, however, was not undertaken immediately. Instead, it was decided in Washington to deny these newspapers the use of mail facilities. Montgomery Blair, the Postmaster General, issued an order to the postmaster at New York City directing that the newspapers presented by the grand jury be excluded from the mails. In addition to the *Journal of Commerce* and the New York *News*, there were three smaller papers named in the presentment.

Almost the entire distribution of newspapers in 1861 was done through the mail. Denial of these facilities meant that the newspaper probably would not survive. Furthermore, this blow came at a time of grave financial crisis for all newspapers. As uncertainty had spread throughout the country in 1861 and trade with the South was disrupted, advertising revenue, the life-blood of the newspapers, had fallen off greatly. By August many newspapers were struggling for survival from economic causes alone. When in the midst of this crisis the government ruled that the newspapers could not be carried through the mails, it very clearly meant their end.

An agonizing crisis confronted the august *Journal of Commerce* as it faced this decision. The driving force behind the newspaper was Gerard Hallock, who had become editor and proprietor of the newspaper in 1828, some thirty-three years earlier, and had nursed it to its present eminent position. It was his Peace editorials that had brought the wrath of the government down on his head. Negotiations were commenced with the postal authorities to find out what would satisfy them. They insisted that Hallock sell his part ownership of the paper and withdraw. He agreed and within two weeks the *Journal of Commerce* was restored to the mails by the Post Office Department. In a farewell editorial, Mr. Hallock wrote that "the times are out of joint" and added that he could not "contend with the government." And so he retired and his paper lived.

The next opposition newspaper excluded from the mails was the New York *News*, which published a daily and weekly edition. This paper was quite different from the *Journal of Commerce*. It was much smaller, had few loyal readers, and was essentially a Democratic political organ heavily supported by the city advertising which Mayor Fernando Wood was able to give it. Ben Wood, its owner, knew that the newspaper would have little value once deprived of his political connections. And so nothing would be salvaged by his withdrawal except its demise.

Wood decided to fight the order with every possible weapon. For he was heavily committed in opposition to the war. When the extra session of Congress had met in July, the *News* objected to its "endorsing the most stupendous series of frauds, political villainies and usurpations of power, that have been perpetrated in any civilized country since the days of Henry the Eighth." The paper also had stated that Congress had "given its sanction to murders, massacres, illegal imprisonments [and] robberies of the Treasury." As for Lincoln, he was an "unscrupulous Chief Magistrate" whose special message to Congress was "an ocean of falsehood and deceit" interlaced with "ghastly jokes and hypocritical slang."

Such talk did not set well with the people of New York and the circulation of the *Daily News* suffered. But the notoriety that attended the order excluding it from the mails increased its popularity in the border states, where a larger anti-war sentiment existed. Wood made a vigorous attempt to send the newspapers west and south by private express and recruited newsboys to deliver them to customers. Whether this strategy would have worked was not revealed because it was decided in Washington to use force against the paper. The United States marshals in cities throughout the country were ordered to seize and confiscate all copies of the *News* that were delivered by express. Public opinion was so aroused at the *News* that it became difficult for men to buy and read the paper in public. Newsstands were told not to handle copies and one newsboy in Connecticut was arrested and sent to prison for selling it.

Finally, in the middle of September, Ben Wood and the *News* gave up. In his last editorial he complained that, with the mails cut off, express transportation denied him, and his newspapers "confiscated by Government officials, acting without warrant or process of law," he had no choice except to quit. James Gordon Bennett's *Herald* was "gratified to announce" the death of the paper. The New York *Times* added that Ben Wood should be thankful he could "walk the streets with as much impunity as if he were a true man."

The third newspaper excluded from the mails was the *Daybook*, which claimed to have thirty thousand subscribers scattered across the country from Maine to Oregon. The newspaper was published by Van Evrie, Horton and Co. in New York and the company proposed to the postal authorities that the name and editorial policies of the paper be changed. Instead of opposing the war, the newspaper would be devoted only to a discussion of the slavery question and would take as its motto the words attributed to Stephen Douglas, "I hold that this Government was made on the white basis, by white men, for the benefit of white men and their posterity forever." Van Evrie then requested that the paper be allowed to circulate through the mails. Since the war in 1861 was not being fought on the question of slavery but to preserve the Union, the request was approved. And so a new newspaper appeared on the streets called the *Weekly Caucasian*, having full mail privileges.

The fourth newspaper included in the presentment was the Brooklyn *Eagle*. Brooklyn in 1861 was a separate city, the second largest in the United States after New York. The *Eagle* was a leading newspaper in that city and the order denying it the use of the mails quickly brought about the desired result. The publishers agreed to cease publishing anti-war views and the *Eagle* was restored to the mails.

The toughest of the editors in New York, however, was a man named James McMasters, the editor of the fifth and last newspaper included in the presentment, *Freeman's Journal*. This was a small paper, published weekly by McMasters and two friends in their printing shop. It was a religious paper, as were a great many papers published in that day, and McMasters fought with religious fervor against the war. When the order denying it the use of the mails came through, McMasters changed the name of the paper to *Freeman's Appeal*, reduced it in size by one half (an economic necessity) and continued without any change in the tone of the publication. He vowed to continue his paper in this form "till the press can be free." His flaming opposition to the war continued another three weeks. In the middle of September he proclaimed that he felt the newspaper had "by God's favor, a long career" ahead of it. But a copy of the *Freeman's Appeal* was sent to Secretary Seward in Washington and the question was asked, "What is your opinion in regard to . . . [his] arrest?" Seward's reply was brief but clear. "You will arrest and send him to Fort Lafayette."

Arresting McMasters was quite an experience. He had a high temper and was a very forcible man. When four deputies arrived at his office and placed him under arrest, he demanded to see their warrant. They told him they had orders directly from Secretary Seward to take him to Fort Lafayette. McMasters said that if Seward were there, he would shoot him. McMasters then demanded that he be handcuffed and allowed to walk down Broadway in the center of a hollow square, composed of four deputy marshals, to display his handcuffs to the best advantage. He was told that it was a long walk to Fort Lafayette and he finally agreed to go in a carriage. But whenever he saw an acquaintance during the ride he would thrust his manacled wrists outside the carriage to show what had happened, and shout "This is Seward's work."

McMasters remained in prison for over a month. While he was there his wife requested that she be allowed to publish the paper without any editorial content. This was agreed to, and the use of the mails was restored to the paper.

Other newspapers which had opposed the war saw the handwriting on the wall and made the necessary changes. A French-language newspaper in the city, the *Courier des Etats-Unis*, had been outspokenly opposed to the war. But when the action was taken against the five papers presented by the grand jury, the editor of the *Courier* resigned his position and turned it over to men who could support the war. In his farewell editorial, he said that the "desertion" of the other newspapers "leaves the *Courier des Etats-Unis* completely isolated in the position it had assumed in common with them." It became useless, he added, "to keep up a warfare at once without aim and without echo."

One German-language newspaper in the city, the *National Zeitung*, was also strongly opposed to the war. In a typical article, it attacked the Administration without restraint: "Terror against all citizens who do not bear allegiance to the usurper [Lincoln], becomes more rampant every day. . . . To render complete the system of Asiatic despotism, nothing is wanting now but secret executions." A county grand jury was sitting in Westchester County, just north of New York City, in September. Leaning on the experience of the New York grand jury, it stated that the *National Zeitung* was printing information which "prevented enlistments for the war, which would otherwise have taken place." The grand jury requested that a copy of its presentment be transmitted to the United States District Attorney in New York with a view to commencing proceedings against the paper. The district attorney recommended to Seward that some of the editors be arrested and at one time Seward asked for their names. He was given three names, but never took any action against them, as he did not want to alienate the tremendous support for the war that was coming from the Germans generally throughout the nation. And so the newspaper continued to publish without interference.

Generally speaking, however, the newspapers in New York which opposed the war had been silenced by the end of September, 1861. The *Journal of Commerce* reported that "there is now no Opposition press," a statement that contained a great deal of truth.

Having cut off the head of the opposition monster, the Administration proceeded to attack whatever tentacles remained alive. Out in Greenport, Long Island, a well-known young Democrat named Henry Reeves edited a newspaper called the *Republican Watchman*. He was very much in favor . of the institution of slavery and opposed to the war. He therefore filled his newspaper with eulogies of Jefferson Davis and abuse of President Lincoln. In August, there had been rumors that his print shop would be mobbed and he had felt it necessary to request protection from the sheriff. No violence had occurred at that time, but one issue of the paper was forwarded to Seward in Washington. An immediate order for his arrest was sent out. Mr. Reeves was picked up on his way to a Democratic Convention in Syracuse and sent to Fort Lafayette. His Congressman interceded strenuously for him, pointing out to Secretary Seward that he was basically loyal and that his mother and sister were entirely dependent on him. After a month in the Fort, he was released.

Another newspaper causing trouble was nestled against the

Canadian border in northern New York State. In the town of Malone, there were two brothers, both staunch Democrats, who had a tremendous influence on opinion in that area. They were Joseph Flanders, a lawyer with a flair for public speaking, and his brother Francis, who ran the Franklin *Gazette*. During the summer months, as the war began to heat up, they organized Peace meetings throughout Franklin County, gave speeches, wrote articles for their newspaper and were completely outspoken in their opposition to the war. Even before Bull Run, their paper had spread anti-war talk throughout the county: "There is but one course to pursue — pronounce against the war, denounce the usurpation and military despotism at Washington, demand peace."

After Bull Run the Flanders brothers became even more active and under their influence only one company of volunteers was raised in the entire county. Seward was continually besieged with requests that something be done about them. The Congressional representative from the district, the United States attorney in Potsdam and others joined in the clamor. Seward first suggested to the Postmaster General that the newspaper be denied the right to use the mails; when he learned that this had already been done he ordered the arrests of the Flanders brothers. They were sent to Fort Lafayette and remained in prison some five months while their paper languished.

Farther south in New York State, the Tompkins County *Democrat* was being published in Ithaca and the United States marshal sent copies of it to Seward, asking "What shall be done with the editor?" Seward gave his usual prompt reply, "Arrest and send [him] . . . to Ft. Lafayette." Before the order had been carried out, however, it was countermanded and the editor was never sent to jail. Many of the arrests Seward directed were in his home state of New York and a surprisingly large number of them were not far from his hometown of Auburn. He evidently felt much more at ease sending familiar faces to prison than unfamiliar.

The mania for arrests soon spread outside New York State. Pennsylvania suffered greatly because it was Simon Cameron's home state and he, like Seward, found it easier to send men he knew to prison than men he did not know. At the time the New York press was being brought under control, Cameron was singling out his first Pennsylvania victim, Pierce Butler. Butler was a wealthy man-about-town in Philadelphia who was related to the South Carolina Butlers, and owned property and slaves in that state. After the firing on Fort Sumter, he made a trip to South Carolina to clean up his business there. Returning to Philadelphia in mid-August, he was arrested by order of Simon Cameron. Butler, of course, knew Cameron and felt that this was a personal matter between them but made no effort to resist. As he was leaving his house, his house-keeper asked, "Mr. Butler, when will you return?" His reply was, "When the war is over, Madam." But he was unduly pessimistic. He was released from Fort Lafayette in about a month and showed up in the office of the New York *Herald* where a reporter noted that he looked quite "fresh, young and buoyant." After his release, Butler brought suit in the state court against Simon Cameron for false imprisonment. This was considered a very serious matter in Washington because illegal arrests were being made all over the country and if Butler's suit were successful it might bring them to a halt. President Lincoln officially stated that the arrest was made by the Secretary of War "under the President's directions and deemed necessary for the prompt suppression of the existing insurrection." The United States District Attorney in Philadelphia was directed to give special attention to the defense of Cameron. But before the test occurred, Pierce Butler dropped the case.

Butler's arrest was only a prelude to the main event. On August 22, a major compaign was undertaken by Marshal Millward in Philadelphia. He and his deputies first stopped at the railroad station to meet the train from New York. As part of the drive against the New York *Daily News*, they went aboard the train and seized all copies of this paper, including one thousand copies on the way to Louisville and five hundred destined for Baltimore and Washington.

From there the marshal went to the office of the *Christian Observer*, a Presbyterian newspaper that had been published in Philadelphia for twenty-two years. This newspaper had been preaching peace for months: "The first question is for peace, with or without Union, on any terms not disgraceful to Christian States." Stories had also been printed in the paper telling of the "gross, brutal fiendish demoniac outrages perpetrated by the chicken-stealers" sent to ravage the South. Marshal Millward and his deputies arrived outside the building at twelve noon and told Amasa Converse, the editor, "We want to look at your Printing Office." "Very well," said Converse, "I will conduct you." When they got to the office, the marshal said, "Mr. Converse, I have an order from the government for your arrest." Then he read the order directing him to take possession of the office and its contents and close the paper down. Mr. Converse said he would not resist but would like to know what charge was preferred against him. The marshal simply reiterated that he was acting on orders from Washington, and proceeded to lock the office and take the keys. Converse was allowed to go free later in the day. He met with his lawyers, who advised him to write a letter to the President stating his case and asking for the return of his property. If he got no answer he should commence a suit against the editors of the *American Presbyterian*, a competing newspaper within the Presbyterian church which was also published in Philadelphia, and which Converse believed to be responsible for the seizure of his newspaper. He penned the letter to the President and eventually got his paper back after giving the usual guarantees as to his loyalty.

Upon seizing Converse's paper, however, Marshal Millward's day was not finished. That night he went out to West Chester and seized the printing shop of the *Jeffersonian*, one of the newspapers which had been attacked earlier in the month by some Union men. He took possession of the office and locked up the press.

The day's work in Philadelphia indicated that the government meant business about suppressing treason. As the New York *Tribune* editorialized, these actions "helped public confidence in believing that the Government means something." Even the country's leading editors refused to rise in defense of their stricken comrades.

Next came Washington's turn. In the Southern city of Washington, there had been a few arrests of civilians, but no attempt had been made to strike at the social leaders. The Democrats had been in power for years, and the city had been substantially under the control of the South for decades. A Southern elite had developed, including some of the finest families. When Abraham Lincoln arrived on the scene in early 1861, he was considered by them to be an uncouth backwoodsman, without any of the graces that typified the best circles. Many of the practical businessmen, lawyers, traders, and others that flooded into the city from the North with him were beyond the pale of Washington society.

Among the social leaders in Washington in 1861 was a Southern woman with a captivating personality, Mrs. Rose Greenhow. She was the widow of a former librarian at the State Department who had died some fifteen years earlier. After his death she had remained in Washington and had risen to the top layers of society. In the middle of August, 1861, Allan Pinkerton, the Chicago detective, was called in by an Assistant Secretary of War and asked to keep an eye on Mrs. Greenhow. She had been speaking openly against the Union, declaring that she saw the Stars and Stripes only as a "symbol of murder, plunder, oppression and shame." And there was suspicion that she was sending information to the Confederacy on troop movements in and around Washington. Some Union men even accused her of having caused the defeat at Bull Run.

Pinkerton took some operatives with him and staked out Mrs. Greenhow's house on the corner of 13th and I Streets, just a few blocks from the White House. He kept a close watch on everyone who entered and left the house for about a week. Then one night, Pinkerton was watching outside the house with some of his men when a tremendous thunderstorm hit the city of Washington. In the darkness, he had taken his shoes off and was standing on the shoulders of one of his men, so that he could see inside the house. On this particular night, he saw that Mrs. Greenhow had a caller, a young captain of the Washington garrison, who was obviously infatuated with her. He saw them exchange an affectionate greeting and then sit and study a map. Then they disappeared elsewhere within the house for an hour before the captain came out of the house in a great hurry. Pinkerton followed him through some of the more fashionable sections of Washington. But the captain finally got away when the barefoot, soaking Pinkerton was picked up by a patrol as a suspicious character.

Pinkerton spent the night in jail, and as coincidence would have it, the captain who had charge of him was the same captain he had seen at Mrs. Greenhow's. He managed to slip a message out of the jail to the War Department and was released the next day. He had the captain arrested and Mrs. Greenhow was quietly placed under arrest and confined to her home. She soon became one of the most notorious prisoners and was eventually sent south.*

At 4 A.M. the next morning, Mayor Berrett of Washington was arrested and sent to Fort Lafayette. Berrett was an ardent Southern sympathizer who had recently been made an ex-officio member of the Washington Board of Police Commissioners. As such he was expected to take the oath of allegiance. Berrett refused to do so, on the grounds that he had already taken an oath as mayor and no further oath was required. Attorney General Bates was asked his opinion in the case and

---

* Mrs. Greenhow was sent to England on a mission for the Confederacy and died in 1863 when the ship on which she was returning foundered off Hatteras.

he ruled that Berrett should take the oath. When the mayor still refused, he was expelled from the Police Board and that night arrested and sent to Fort Lafayette. His stay in prison lasted less than three weeks, but to get out he was forced to resign his office as mayor. The southern city of Washington was becoming less Southern with each passing day.

During the summer of 1861, Congress was also undertaking its own witch hunt. A special committee was set up to look into the employment of Confederate sympathizers by the government. This committee, known as the Potter Committee, began to meet in early July and continued during the entire session of Congress. During these hearings, charges against five hundred government employees were heard. The Committee did not pretend to be a judicial body, but merely listened while the clerks in the departments accused other clerks of treason. As the Committee said, "the parties charged were not examined by the Committee, nor were they notified of the charges preferred against them." It was felt that there would be endless wrangling if rebuttals were allowed. The Committee acknowledged that loyal men might become the victims of unjust suspicion, but added magnanimously that "the exigencies of the times demand great sacrifices."

All summer long, witness after witness paraded in front of the Committee and gave evidence. It was pointed out that one clerk was "decidedly opposed to the use of force on the part of the government," and another had said that "if the South attacked this city, he would not take up arms against the South." Washington in early 1861 was a nest of Southern sympathizers and many of them were fired or forced to resign their jobs as the result of the Committee's hearings. But radical Republicans on the Committee were never satisfied with the actions taken by the Administration in getting rid of the people whose loyalty had been called into question. At the end of the year they still felt that a large number of secessionists were drawing government pay.

Even Secretary of the Treasury Salmon P. Chase, a radical

Republican himself, could not satisfy the Committee. It sent him a list of sixty-four people in his Department "against whom the evidence is deemed conclusive" and a list of ten names "against whom the evidence furnishes a well-grounded suspicion of their disloyalty." Of this total of seventy-four, Chase later reported that twenty had either resigned or been removed. Most of the remainder, Chase said, had letters endorsing their loyalty by Republican Congressmen. He added that he did not consider the evidence taken by the Committee as "absolutely reliable." The strong-willed Mr. Chase did not like to have Congress meddling in his affairs.

But the main course of events was controlled by the Administration and as summer came to an end in 1861 arrests grew more frequent. The American political society was slowly changing as the impact of the federal government was being felt all over the North. The main result of the change was to see more and more power move into the hands of the federal executive. Neither Congress nor the judiciary were meeting the crisis effectively so all the praise and all the blame for what happened were to fall directly on a few of the men who were running the Lincoln Administration.

CHAPTER 15

SEWARD AND LINCOLN
CONTROL THE NORTH

T HE HAND of Abraham Lincoln can be seen but dimly in the policy of repression. Always, it was the cabinet members, the generals, the United States marshals and district attorneys who ordered and carried out the arrests. Yet in August and September, 1861, the arbitrary arrests were headlined in newspapers all over the country and stories of multiple arrests in New York, Philadelphia and Washington were printed and reprinted everywhere. The New York *Herald* on August 26 devoted nearly its entire front page to stories of arbitrary arrests and discussion of political prisoners and prisons. A major pamphlet debate even occurred over the Administration's policy of repression.

Yet, despite Lincoln's inevitable awareness of what was going on, he was scarcely touched by it personally. The many volumes of the *Official Record of the War of the Rebellion* rarely mention his name in connection with the program. The diaries of the cabinet members largely ignore the entire problem. Lincoln's own personal papers include very few letters on the subject.

For Lincoln played a unique role as President and Chief Executive of the Union. He had, after all, come to Washington from the prairie, with no intimate understanding of the workings of the executive branch, or of Washington politics. He did not have personal friendships with men all around the government, such as Seward, Chase, Cameron and many others had. He was in a new, strange environment, facing the gravest crisis in the nation's history. He therefore surrounded himself with strong men capable of running their own departments effectively by themselves. For himself he reserved the role of arbitrator. He was not by nature an aggressive, domineering man and although he always retained the final authority on important matters, he was reluctant to interfere in the day-to-day administration of the affairs of his cabinet officers. As a matter of policy, he felt that the arrests were a necessary evil. But he rarely suggested that any single individual be arrested or released. He left this almost entirely to others.

It was Seward who seized upon this opportunity, eagerly and effectively. Seward had the thirst for power that Lincoln lacked, and he was not reluctant to interfere in the most minute affairs of the smallest community in America. It had fallen to Seward to order the arrest of Southern diplomats as they returned to New York from Europe after the war started. Men like Charles Faulkner, Virginia-born minister to France under Buchanan, were detained on Seward's orders on their way home to join the Confederacy. Seward rapidly expanded his authority until he was ordering nearly all the arrests being made in the free states. Cameron directed a few arrests as Secretary of War, but he lacked the aggressive character necessary to carry out a large-scale policy of repression. Attorney General Bates, who might have become a key man, chose to remain aloof on this question.

The whole program, then, swirled around the head of William E. Seward, Secretary of State. Indeed, many people considered Seward the real leader of the Republican party and the nation during this period. For Seward had all the prestige and experience that Lincoln lacked. He had served as Governor of New York and United States Senator during the years before the Civil War and had helped organize the Republican party. But the American custom of denying the presidential nomination to the leading legislative spokesman of the party had worked against Seward and in 1860 the Republicans had picked the relatively unknown Abraham Lincoln over him.

In 1861, however, Seward was Secretary of State and many of his actions reflected his own conviction that he was destined to save the Union. In no field was this more apparent than in the policy of repression. As panic and mob rule swept the North in August and September, 1861, it was the strong will of Secretary Seward that rose to overcome them. In doing this, he carried his power to incredible lengths, seemingly unrestrained by any factor save naked political expediency. In effect, he was the President's cabinet officer for internal security and everyone accepted him in this role. There was a widely circulated story that Seward had boasted of his power to Lord Lyons, the British Ambassador. "My lord," he was reported to have said, "I can touch a bell on my right hand and order the imprisonment of a citizen of Ohio; I can touch a bell again and order the imprisonment of a citizen of New York; and no power on earth, except that of the President, can release them. Can the Queen of England do so much?" Whether the story is true or not, there is no doubt that Seward could honestly have said it. He could send anyone to prison, keep them there as long as he liked and let them out whenever the whim struck him. There was no law, no precedent and no judicial proceeding, nothing except the knock on the door in the middle of the night and the clanging of the gates at Fort Lafayette. For six months Seward had more arbitrary power over the freedom of individual American citizens all over the country than any other man has ever had, before or since.

By the middle of September, 1861, arrests were occurring in many cities of the North. New York, however, seemed to be getting more than its share. Recommending candidates for arrest in New York was a man who knew Seward well and worked very effectively with him, Superintendent John A. Kennedy of the New York Police. Kennedy was a staunch Union man who took a personal interest in seeing that Southern sympathizers were kept under control.

In New York there was a large element opposed to the war. Manufacturers, merchants, and traders who had gotten rich in trade with the South, and to whom the Southern planters were heavily in debt, were often bitterly opposed to the war. One description of the political sentiments of Wall Street was typical:

At a sugar-broker's office in Wall Street, a few secessionists are in the habit of meeting and talking, daily, over the war news, in which they take sides very strongly with treason. At another office in the same street the loquacious senior partner daily discourses on the horrors of civil war and denounces the Beechers, Sumners, Lovejoys, etc. . . . A Broad-street commission-house has recently become obnoxious to the business community on account of its Southern tendencies. Among the flour and grain brokers two well-known friends of the traitors, who could be named, have lost the business of Union men on account of their disloyal course.

In the face of such sentiment, arrests in New York continued during most of 1861. Wall Street bankers, priests, merchants, policemen, and anyone else who expressed disloyal sentiments were subject to arrest. Speechmakers in Central Park, men talking under their breath to soldiers, anyone carrying Confederate currency, all were suspected and many arrested. New York's mayor, Fernando Wood, came within a hair of being arrested. Wood had been under suspicion for some time, and after he made one particularly obnoxious speech Seward was showered with letters recommending his arrest. Marshal Murray wrote that he had been requested by some of the most respectable people in New York to arrest Fernando Wood and added, "I await your instructions." But Wood, a rather shady politician with many of the attributes of an eel, managed to squirm out of this predicament. He wired Seward that his speech was reported incorrectly in the newspapers and claimed that he was staunchly for the Union. Wood remained a free man.

But many other arrests were made. They became so common and information on proposed arrests spread so rapidly that the New York Police Department finally ordered that no information on them was to be given out. Occasionally, the truth about men who had been imprisoned was hidden even from the police themselves and of all the arrests that occurred during the war, none was more bizarre than the case of a well-known New Yorker named Marcus Cicero Stanley. For Marcus Stanley was a Union man, tried and true, who had never uttered a disunion sentiment. His arrest was the result of a carefully contrived plot carried out by some New York underworld characters to get personal revenge on him.

The story began during the period following Fort Sumter, when New York was a beehive of recruiting activity. In those days a young man did not just go to an army recruiting station and offer his services. The most common method of enlisting soldiers was for a prominent man who was well-known in the community to offer to raise a regiment. If his offer were accepted, he was given the rank of colonel and would open his own recruiting office. His previous military experience was a matter of little concern. The important thing was that he was well known enough to bring the young men of the city flocking to his banner. Since the men who would qualify best for such work were usually in public life, it soon developed that a large proportion of the colonels in the army were former politicians.

The officers, however, had to come from somewhere when the 15,000-man Army of early 1861 grew almost overnight to a force of several hundred thousand. This particular method of giving commissions produced great results in some instances. Frank Blair, out in St. Louis, was an outstanding example of a politician turned colonel. He raised troops very effectively and later became an excellent officer. But at the other end of the spectrum, there were some horrible examples. One of the worst was Andrew Sheehan, a professional gambler and pugilist in New York City, who was well known in the

sporting world. He offered to raise a regiment and state officials, pressed for troops, did not look too carefully at him.
His request was granted and he went to work.

As Sheehan knew, there were great opportunities open to
a man who raised a regiment. There was no more glamorous
undertaking during the Civil War. It immediately placed a
man high in his own community and indicated that he was a
leader under whom young men wanted to serve. But there was
more than prestige involved. In May and June of 1861 there
was no central organization of this rapidly expanding Army, no
central commissary and no central procurement office. A man
who had successfully raised a regiment would be given substantial amounts of money by the state for the purchase of food,
ammunition, uniforms, and perhaps even weapons. Just how this
money was spent depended largely on his own integrity, and if he
was not in particularly long supply of this commodity he could
make quite a bit of money for himself.

All of these considerations caused Andrew Sheehan to offer to raise a regiment, but he did not figure on Marcus Stanley.
Stanley was another sporting figure in New York who hated
Sheehan and considered him a criminal. When Sheehan started
to raise his Empire City Regiment, Stanley promised to break
it up if it took all the money he had. And so he started offering bonuses to lure members of the Empire City Regiment into
other units. It wasn't long before there was no Empire City
Regiment and Sheehan was being ridiculed as a man who hadn't
been able to raise his regiment.

This enraged Sheehan and a few months later, as the wave
of treason arrests swept New York City, he saw an opportunity
to get even with Stanley. Sheehan swore out a statement
against Stanley which gave only enough of the story to make
Stanley look like the worst possible secessionist. Stanley had
"tampered" with his men and prevented the regiment from
being organized. He added that he believed Stanley sym-
pathized with the Confederacy and asked that he be arrested.

This statement found its way to Seward who, with his usual gusto, replied: "Arrest Marcus C. Stanley . . . and send him to Ft. Lafayette." The United States marshal in New York picked up Stanley in a saloon on Park Row and sent him off to prison. Stanley was well known in the city as a Union man and everybody assumed that his arrest was a deep plot by Seward to put his own spy in Ft. Lafayette. Superintendent Kennedy of the New York Police wrote Seward that if Stanley had been put in Fort Lafayette for this purpose "he is just the man for the business. I know of none who could exceed him in tact and general capacity. What he did in breaking up the Empire Regiment he deserves the thanks of the community for." In Fort Lafayette, Stanley was treated as a Union spy by the other prisoners and they refused to speak to him. Upon investigation, it was discovered that the state military board had been glad to see the Empire City Regiment broken up, and Stanley was released. When he got out he said he was satisfied with the action taken by the government. But the arbitrary Seward was to make many such mistakes. They were the inevitable result of his method of operation.

Boats frequently arrived in New York harbor from Europe with suspicious characters aboard. Although the naval blockade of the South was in effect, it was still possible for Southerners to dock in New York and slip through the lines southward unless a close watch was kept on arrivals. Passenger lists were scrutinized carefully to see that this did not happen. One passenger who caused a great deal of interest was a wealthy businessman named Thomas Serrill. Although a Pennsylvanian by birth, Serrill had spent many years in New Orleans and was now returning from a trip to England where he had arranged for bank credit to open a new business in Philadelphia. However, on the trip home from England, two drinking acquaintances had become rather troublesome to the other passengers. Serrill had an argument with them about their conduct and they decided to get even with him. When the boat docked, they denounced him to the police as a traitor and when his baggage was searched he was found to be carrying £40,000 currency. He was arrested under judicial warrant and held in jail overnight awaiting a hearing.

The next day an order was received from the State Department to send him to Fort Lafayette. It was believed that the £40,000 was a loan negotiated to buy goods for the South. Serill remained in Fort Lafayette for about three weeks while his friends interceded with the authorities in Washington. When he was released he went to Washington to pick up his £40,000 and had an interview with President Lincoln. During the interview the greatest courtesy was extended to him. He told the President the state of affairs in England, intriguing Lincoln with his stories so much that Seward was called in to hear him. Then they sent Serrill home to Philadelphia, still a Union man.

One of the most difficult decisions to make in Washington concerned a former Senator from California, William Gwin, and his friend, Calhoun Benham. Senator Gwin believed in letting the South go in peace. He had written earlier in the year that "the cotton States are out forever. The border States will follow. . . . The chances are there will be two republics, North and South, with amicable relations. Time will probably turn it into three." Gwin decided to come East from California and while he was making the trip, some bizarre incidents occurred. Gwin and Benham were accused of hurriedly throwing overboard some charts and papers and were put under gentleman's arrest. Meanwhile, the overland mail had informed Kennedy that they would soon arrive in New York and he wired Seward asking what he should do when they docked. Seward replied that the question "has not yet been decided upon." After Gwin and Benham arrived in New York the question was once again posed by Kennedy to Seward: "Have you any order to give me?" Seward replied, with an indecision that was completely out of character, to keep them on their

ABRAHAM LINCOLN. Faced with the possible destruction of the Union in 1861, Lincoln allowed Seward and others to make arrests at will. The result was a radical readjustment in the balance of power between federal and state governments which made possible the winning of the war.

General Benjamin Butler, above. The first arbitrary arrests of the Civil War were made under the command of this Massachusetts politician.

Secretary of State William H. Seward, top right. Dominant in the policy of repression, Seward had more arbitrary power over the personal destinies of individual citizens all over the North than any other man has ever had, before or since.

Chief Justice Roger Taney, bottom right, whose objection to the arbitrary arrests of the Lincoln Administration caused one of the supreme moments of drama in American judicial history.

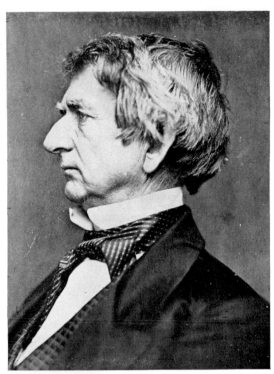

FT. LAFAYETTE. This grim fortress in New York harbor was filled with political prisoners in 1861 and became a symbol of the power of the federal government.

SENATOR GWIN, a former United States Senator from California, was arrested during the time of panic in 1861 but was released after Lincoln intervened in the case.

BENJAMIN WOOD, United States Congressman from New York and publisher of the *Daily News*. His paper was forced to cease publication when United States marshals seized the copies and arrested the newsboys.

GERARD HALLOCK (above) had been editor and part owner of the New York *Journal of Commerce* for thirty-three years during which time he had made it the leading commercial paper in the North. His anti-war editorials brought the wrath of the Administration down on him, and he was forced to sell the paper to prevent its being suppressed.

MAYOR BERRETT of Washington, D.C., was arrested and sent to prison as a Southern sympathizer.

THE LINCOLN CABINET. Of the eight men in the cabinet, five were involved in the policy of repression during the time of panic in 1861. The program was carried out under the permissive guidance of President Lincoln, seated in the center. Secretary Seward standing next to him, dominated the program as he dominates this picture. Secretary of War Cameron, seated next to Seward, ordered many arrests, particu-

larly in his home state of Pennsylvania. Next to him is Attorney General Bates, who sent a legal opinion to Congress in which he held that no federal judge should "entertain an appeal in any form from a decision of the President of the United States" making an arbitrary arrest. At far left is Postmaster General Blair, who put many newspapers out of business when he denied them the use of the mails.

GENERAL JOHN ADAMS DIX. A man of lenient temperament, Dix opposed the policy of arrests until orders came directly from Washington to arrest and imprison the leading Peace advocates in Baltimore.

GENERAL NATHANIEL BANKS was bluntly ordered to break up the Maryland Legislature and arrest all the members who opposed the war. He carried out his orders to the letter.

S. Teackle Wallis, dean of the Baltimore bar and member of the Maryland state legislature, composed the "Wallis Resolutions" which excoriated the Lincoln Administration for making arbitrary arrests. He spent fourteen months in prison.

Ross Winans, a millionaire manufacturer, was elected with nine other men to the Maryland legislature in a special election in 1861. All of them, including Winans, were in Union prisons within five months, except for a single legislator who escaped into exile.

SECRETARY OF WAR EDWIN M. STANTON. One of his first acts in office was to provide for a general amnesty and release of political prisoners early in 1862.

parole until he had had a chance to review the case. And the third time the cock crew, as Kennedy insistently wired once again: "Do you mean they shall be released?" To this urgent request, Seward replied that they should be arrested. But then, later in the day, he had a change of heart and sent another wire saying that if the order had not been executed, it should be suspended. In the end, however, Gwin and Benham were sent to Fort Lafayette for a week. Rarely had Seward shown such an appalling inability to make up his mind.

The real reason for Seward's indecision was the strong pressure being brought to bear on behalf of Gwin and Benham. Not only was Gwin a man with many friends in high places, but Benham was the brother-in-law of George Prentice, the publisher of the Louisville *Courier*, the most important newspaper in the most important state in the Union, Kentucky. After the arrest, Prentice arranged for his brother-in-law to come to Washington for an interview with the President. When Lincoln met them, he exercised his well-known leniency and said that Gwin and Benham "might go their several ways, they to ask no questions nor any questions to be asked of them, and the pending affair between them and the Government growing out of their arrest and parole to be thus entirely disposed of and ended." This was one of the very few cases in which President Lincoln intervened personally to make a decision. Gwin and Benham went free.

In upstate New York, there was a man named George L. Bowne living in Cooperstown. Bowne had led an eventful life. A native of New York, he had developed consumption in his twenties and had been forced to move to Florida for his health. He settled in Key West and became quite wealthy operating a shipping company. He was elected to the Florida legislature and as a member of that body voted against the resolution calling for a state convention to consider seceding from the Union.

For many years Bowne had returned to New York State during the summer to visit his family and friends. He was very highly thought of in Cooperstown and was considered to be almost one of its citizens. During the summer of 1861, however, while making his usual visit, a resident of the nearby town of Richfield Springs sat down and wrote a letter to Seward. He said that Bowne had signed the secession ordinance in the legislature of Florida and concluded: "He is rich, and is a spy. He travels that he may gain facts for Jefferson Davis."

This letter had the desired effect on the mercurial Seward. To the United States marshal, he telegraphed: "Arrest G. L. Bowne, of Key West, who is said to be at Cooperstown . . . and send him forthwith to Ft. Lafayette." Two United States marshals, a local sheriff and a deputy went to Bowne's house about 6 P.M. on the night of September 8 and knocked on his door. When Bowne answered, he was placed under arrest and asked to turn over all his papers. Bowne was startled, but he got his papers and packed some clothes while the posse waited for him. Meantime the word spread in Cooperstown that Bowne was being arrested and an angry crowd of some fifty to sixty persons assembled outside the house. They had some sharp exchanges with the officers and one man even offered to whip the marshal. Bowne finally stepped in and asked his friends not to make any trouble, as he was happy to go. The marshal told the crowd he was taking Bowne to Rochester because he knew he would never get his prisoner out of Cooperstown if they realized he was going to Fort Lafayette. The party was finally permitted to leave and Bowne was soon in Fort Lafayette.

When the news of Bowne's arrest was published, there was a tremendous storm over the incident. Letters flowed to Seward from all over New York State protesting against the arrest. Bowne's New York attorneys contacted Seward and asked for an interview with him to determine how they might get their client out of prison. They especially asked for speedy action, inasmuch as Bowne had been a sick man for twenty

years and "his confinement in Ft. Lafayette for any very considerable length of time might be fatal to him." Seward
ordered Bowne's discharge two weeks after his arrest and he
was allowed to return to Cooperstown.

One legal attempt was made to free the political prisoners.
The Baltimore police commissioners and Marshal Kane were
in Fort Lafayette, in Kings County, New York, where the local
judge, Samuel Garrison, favored the normal processes of law.
Rumors of an attempt to use force in serving a writ of habeas
corpus reached Colonel Burke, in command at Fort Lafayette
and Fort Hamilton, a companion fort on Long Island. So
Burke wired General Scott, asking what he should do if he
were attacked. Scott's reply was very firm: "Hold your prisoners to the extent of all your means of defense." Scott then
sent word to the commanding officer in New York City that
Fort Lafayette was threatened with an attack by the local
sheriff and his posse. "Send him a reenforcement . . . without delay," Scott sternly ordered.

Meanwhile, back in Kings County, Judge Garrison asked
the general of the local militia whether it would be possible
to capture the Fort. The militia general looked over the federal
ramparts and reported that the whole strength of the brigade
which he commanded was only 1,500 men, and he did not
think he could take the Fort with this number. He said that all
the siege guns in New York State would not have the slightest
effect on the fortification. The sheriff of Kings County therefore decided to dispense with the troops and went by himself
to serve the writ.

When he arrived at the gates of the Fort, he was followed
by a large, curious crowd. The guard denied him entrance to
the Fort when he tried to serve the writ and he returned to
Judge Garrison with the information that the writ could not
be served. This ended the attempt by Kings County to free
the prisoners in Fort Lafayette. However, a man who had
urged Judge Garrison to issue the writ was a well-known New

York City businessman. Marshal Murray sent some deputies to arrest him a few days later and he was soon inside the Fort with the Baltimore prisoners.

On September 13, a young man was arrested who was so obviously inoffensive and helpless that he served as a kind of symbol for the opposition throughout the war. His name was George Hubbell and he was a newsboy. The United States marshal in Connecticut had been ordered to stop the sale of the New York *Daily News*, but he ran into trouble with Hubbell, who was selling the newspaper at the railroad station. Marshal Carr wrote to Cameron that Hubbell was "doing great mischief by his treasonable talk." He had violated Carr's order forbidding the sale of the *Daily News* and was said to have bragged about it. Carr added to Cameron that "all I want is an order from yourself or Mr. Seward to arrest and take him to some of the forts in New York." He said that such an order would "do more good than any order that has yet been issued" in Connecticut.

Cameron thought the request a reasonable one, and wired the marshal: "Arrest the man . . . and send him to Ft. Lafayette." And so George Hubbell, the crippled newsboy who had managed to anger a United States marshal, was sent to prison and soon became a national symbol. His brother, a Republican ward worker in New York, wrote to President Lincoln that George Hubbell "has been a cripple from his youth with a spinal deformity, and is the sole help of his poor mother who is in the deepest sorrow." He said that the remarks for which he had been arrested were uttered "in the heat of passion to people who advised him to stop selling the News, because he regarded it as none of their business." Seward ordered Hubbell's release within a week.

The inconsistencies in the entire program were highlighted by the Hubbell arrest. The New York *Tribune* editorialized that the use of "lettres de cachet" was acceptable for arresting editors who opposed the war, "but when you descend to newsboys, can the game be worth the ammunition?" Several papers pointed out how silly it was that the newsboy should be in prison while the editor of the paper which he was arrested for selling, Ben Wood, should be, as one of them put it, "sunning himself on . . . the pleasanter side of Broadway." Very few national figures from the free states were arrested. Men like Congressman Clement L. Vallandigham, a fiery anti-war agitator, and Senator Jesse Bright of Indiana, who was later expelled from the Senate, remained at liberty during this period. New York's own Benjamin and Fernando Wood, Congressman and mayor, were never sent to Fort Lafayette.

Another of the minor figures who got into trouble was Ellis Schnabel. Schnabel was a lesser Pennsylvania politician who had been the featured speaker at a meeting in Old Saybrook that was broken up by Union men. A few days later, he spoke at a meeting in Morris, Connecticut, where he gave a two-hour speech in which he proved that in seventy years the Negroes in the South would increase to eighty million. He also unfolded his Peace plan under which the North was to call for a national convention to settle all matters in dispute. After his speech, some Peace resolutions were passed which declared the war to be unholy and recommended peace. At the end of the meeting Schnabel was arrested by the local sheriff who turned the prisoner over to the United States marshal and Schnabel was promptly shipped off to Fort Lafayette.

Schnabel knew Cameron well and claimed that the Secretary had had him arrested "for private reasons." But he was quickly offered his freedom if he would sign an oath with an added phrase stating that he would "not by speaking or correspondence interfere with the measures of the Government for suppressing the existing insurrection." He refused to sign this special condition, saying that it would force him to support the Republican party. He said he would surrender his constitutional rights "only with my life." Schnabel kept sending Seward long letters setting forth his constitutional position and Seward finally released him after some six weeks in Fort Lafayette.

Across the Hudson River in New Jersey there were more problems. A company of men, some forty strong, had armed themselves in military fashion in the small village of Straalenberg, near Hackensack, and reports were reaching the United States District Attorney that they were secessionists. A posse of twelve good Union men was formed, under the leadership of the deputy marshal, to visit the village and disperse them. When they arrived in Straalenberg they were told that the company was at that moment off parading in another village. However, at the local "armory," they found a lieutenant and a private together with forty-three muskets. The muskets were seized and the militiamen were given the oath and discharged. The deputy loaded the muskets on a wagon and took them back to Jersey City. This threat to the Union was completely eliminated.

Further down state, another nest of Peace men had developed around Burlington, New Jersey. As was usually the case, the problem centered around the leadership of one man, James W. Wall. Wall was the son of a former United States Senator, Garrett Wall, who had been one of Andrew Jackson's principal advisers thirty years before. For decades, the Wall family had been the leading family in Burlington. The younger Wall was a man of passionate convictions, eloquent pen and persuasive speech. As the war got under way, Wall became a leader of the Peace movement and his influence turned the whole area to his views. He became a leading editorial writer for the New York *Daily News,* and his speeches echoed throughout the state. He was unalterably opposed to the war. As he put it in his speeches, "The war has a fourfold object. First, power; second, plunder; third, negro equality; and fourth, Southern subjugation. . . . The rights of the States and constitutional liberty will find their graves."

Wall's influence was having a bad effect on his part of New

Jersey and Simon Cameron, whose home in Philadelphia was just a few miles from Burlington, ordered his arrest. Cameron's order was very short and simple: "You will please forthwith arrest James W. Wall, of Burlington, N.J., and convey him to Fort Lafayette." It is difficult to believe that this order and the events that followed could have occurred in the United States. Yet we see them unfolding before us. The officer with a posse of six men went to Wall's house and arrested him as he was standing on his front porch. When Wall asked for a few minutes to go back into the house and say goodbye to his family, the marshal said there was no time for this, as they had to catch a train leaving Burlington in ten minutes. Wall flew into a rage, wrenched himself loose and rushed back into his house. He got as far as the hallway when he was overpowered and, as he later described it, "torn from my home, from a sick wife and frantic children" and "dragged to the railroad station." He was taken to Fort Lafayette, leaving the cities of Burlington and Trenton considerably excited over his arrest.

Once in the Fort, Wall devoted himself to writing letters to everyone he knew. He particularly addressed himself to Simon Cameron. "What is my offense?" he asked. "I come from Revolutionary blood on both sides and would scorn to do an act that would compromise or cast dishonor on such a birthright. I long for peace and a cessation of this terrible strife. If such be a crime then I am a criminal." He referred to his physical infirmities, saying that imprisonment for a few weeks could aggravate an internal disorder from which he was suffering and be "fatal in its results."

Governor Charles S. Olden of New Jersey interceded for him and within two weeks Wall was out of prison. When he returned to Burlington, he was welcomed by a thousand people at the railroad station. There was a great celebration which ended in a torchlight parade to escort him to his home. Even after his release, Wall refused to let his arrest be forgotten. He continued to write long, argumentative letters to Cameron, demanding that he be informed of the charges against him. But Cameron made no reply. When the New Jersey legislature convened, Wall addressed a very effective memorial to it which expressed his view that the federal authority had usurped states' rights. After describing his arrest and imprisonment in detail, he said that it was up to the state legislature to decide what action it should take "in reference to this wanton outrage upon the constitutionally guaranteed rights of one of your citizens." He concluded dramatically:

> I speak earnestly because I feel so. I have been made to know the insolence of arbitrary power. The most degraded criminal in any of your prisons could not have been treated as I have been, without an outcry of indignation from every honest citizen in the State. I have been arrested without the form of legal warrant — condemned without the shadow of a trial, punished by a degraded imprisonment of weeks, without at this hour even knowing the nature and cause of the accusation against me. . . . If such an act can be done in a republic, without redress, and with the approval of its citizens, then I know no difference between it and the vilest despotism upon earth, save only, that the latter is the more honest government of the two.

Thus spoke James Wall, with passion, feeling and great success. For the New Jersey Legislature did indeed do something about it. It elected him to the United States Senate and sent him to Washington to help make the laws governing the nation. Needless to say, he became one of the most outspoken critics of the policy of arbitrary arrests, joining other Democrats in the Senate to oppose every arbitrary arrest by the Administration. His experience was frequently cited by the opposition as an example of the alleged tyranny of the Lincoln Administration.

Far, far away, in the little village of Freedom, Maine another man was stirring up his community. His name was Bob Elliot, a man who had been a Peace candidate for the state senate in Maine. He lost the election, but only grew more and more defiant. When the question of war taxes and the military draft became burning issues, Elliot raised a company of soldiers in little Freedom and boldly announced that they were being trained to resist both measures. Secretary Cameron ordered the United States marshal to go to Freedom and arrest Elliot. Although the marshal was told that he would be lynched if he went to Freedom, he made the trip successfully, arrested Elliot and took him to Fort Lafayette where his prisoner spent nearly two months. Finally Governor Washburn of Maine wrote that although he considered Elliot's arrest to have been fully justified, he could see no further reason for keeping him in prison. And so Elliot was allowed to return to his home.

Eighty miles away in the seacoast town of Yarmouth, Maine, another problem had arisen. Cyrus Sargent was a boat builder as well as a Breckinridge Democrat who did not hesitate to express his opinions on the war. He denounced the government roundly for not bringing it to an immediate end. As a result, he was accused of having entered into a contract to furnish supplies to the rebels and of building a boat to carry the supplies south. As soon as this accusation was brought to Cameron's attention, he ordered an immediate arrest.

The United States marshal in Portland received the instructions and proceeded to Yarmouth with some deputies. He hurriedly arrested Sargent, put him in a carriage and headed for the nearest railroad at Saco, hoping to get him on the train ahead of any intervention by the local judiciary. However, before he got to Saco, the local authorities caught up with him and took Sargent away on a writ of habeas corpus. The prisoner was taken back to Yarmouth and turned free, but the federal authorities bided their time. Two weeks later, after things had quieted down a bit, Seward directed the marshal to arrest Sargent once again. This time the marshal was successful and Sargent was safely deposited in Fort Lafayette.

After he had spent some six weeks in prison, the United States District Attorney made an investigation of the case. His report was fascinating. He said that the entire case against Sargent appeared in letters from two men, both of whom relied for their statements on information furnished by still another man in Pittsburgh, Pennsylvania. The district attorney wrote letters to all three men asking for information. The first two did not reply, but the man from Pittsburgh wrote back willingly enough. He said he had no knowledge of the affair, but that he was certain the charges against Sargent were false. The district attorney concluded that "such are the results of my efforts to make certain and definite the accusations upon which the Government ordered the summary arrest of the prisoner, and such may be considered at this stage the whole strength of the Government case." The day Seward received this report he ordered Sargent's release.

Far to the west, another small Peace community had sprung up in North Branch, Michigan, a village some sixty miles north of Detroit. The ringleader of this group was Dr. Guy S. Hopkins. There were reports that a small band of men in North Branch openly justified the rebellion and hurrahed for Jeff Davis. In fact, one report was circulating all over the state that the men in North Branch had actually hoisted an old pair of white underwear on a flag pole. In the suspicious days of 1861, this was a Peace flag and could only lead to trouble.

One night, Hopkins' office was ransacked by some Union men. His anger thus aroused, Hopkins became greatly irritated by stories printed in the Detroit newspapers about widespread Democratic treason and, as he referred to it, "the universal reign of suspicion." He decided to churn up a little suspicion himself by writing a letter to the Detroit newspapers, full of dark, secessionist innuendos and hints, by way of a practical joke on the Detroit press. And so Hopkins sat down and wrote his letter. But it turned out that he was playing a practical joke on himself. His handwriting was discovered and he and two of his Peace friends were arrested and sent off to Fort Lafayette where they remained for several months.

One of the paragraphs he included in the letter went: "President P - - - - - in his passage has drawn many brave and influential men to the league. P - - - - - - y, of the L.C.D - - - - - - - t, sent a line to Dr. F - - - - (by H., the Mormon elder)." This letter was forwarded to Seward after Hopkins' arrest and Seward took it seriously enough to send to the former President of the United States, Franklin Pierce, living in Concord, New Hampshire. Pierce was a Democrat who had shown less than complete support for the war, and Seward had no particular regard for his feelings. He wrote to Pierce that Hopkins' letter would seem to indicate that "you were a member of a secret league the object of which is to overthrow the Government. Any explanation upon the subject which you may offer would be acceptable." Seward, in his usual abrupt way, was calling Pierce a traitor. One can just imagine Seward considering the possibility of sending a telegram to the local district attorney which might read: "Arrest President Pierce and send him to Ft. Lafayette." But no such highhanded action was taken. When Pierce received Seward's letter, however, he was quite shocked by the accusation (and probably by the manner in which Seward chose to handle it) and replied that "nothing but the gravity of the insinuation, the high official source from which it emanates and the distracted condition of our recently united, prosperous and happy country could possibly lift this matter above ridicule and contempt." He added that "my loyalty will never be successfully impugned so long as I enjoy the constitutional rights which pertain to every citizen of the Republic." Seward took no further action in the matter.

A man named Thomas B. Lincoln of Texas checked into a hotel in Cincinnati while the wave of suspicion was at its height in the North. Word had been sent ahead to keep a close watch on him, as he had invented a gun which was patented in Richmond earlier in the year. In Cincinnati he was arrested under warrant and a document was found on him which reverberated throughout the North. It was a letter from United States Senator Jesse D. Bright of Indiana to Jefferson Davis. The date was 1 March 1861 and it said:

My Dear Sir:
Allow me to introduce to your acquaintance my friend, Thomas B. Lincoln of Texas. He visits your capital mainly to dispose of what he regards a great improvement in firearms. I commend him to your favorable consideration.

This letter revealed that a United States Senator in March had recommended to the President of the Confederacy that he arrange to buy a new, improved gun, at a time when the Confederacy was preparing for war against the Union. Particularly interested in this bit of evidence were the Union men in Kentucky. They had been cursed by the entire North for the widespread disloyalty in their state and they were glad to see that Indiana had a Senator of questionable loyalty. Kentucky newspapers and others throughout the country took up the cry that Senator Bright should be arrested, but Seward couldn't bring himself to do it. A few months later the Senate expelled Bright, but even then he was not arrested. As for Thomas B. Lincoln, he was released after a short hearing.

Out in Iowa another man was caught in the meshes of Union suppression. He was William Hill, tripped up by fate in a rather improbable sequence of events. Hill had close connections with the South and when the war broke out his family was visiting in Virginia. Hill decided to bring his family home and in order to pave the way and prevent trouble with the Virginia authorities, he wrote a letter to the local newspaper in the town where his family was visiting. In it he said that the war had been brought on by "the demons in the shape of Black Republicans and Abolition rulers." Conservative citizens of Iowa, he said, "justify the course the South is taking and condemn this Black Republican Administration for wag-ing this unholy and unjust war." The letter was returned to the dead letter office in Des Moines, where it was opened and read by postal authorities. Hill was indicted and brought to trial for treason. Marshal Hoxie in Iowa wrote to Seward that Hill would never be found guilty because there was a large secession element in the jury. "Under the circumstances," he added, "I believe it would be better for the Government to enter a *nolle* and have him committed to military custody by order of the State Department." Seward agreed so Marshal Hoxie arrested Hill and escorted him on the long journey from Des Moines to Fort Lafayette. As he was leaving Des Moines, Hoxie just evaded a writ of habeas corpus designed to take his prisoner from him.

When Marshal Hoxie got back to Iowa, he found that a $1,000 damage suit had been instituted against him under the provisions of the Iowa habeas corpus act, for disregarding the writ. He wired this information to Washington and the reply came back: "What are the names of the attorneys who have commenced proceedings against you for refusing to obey a writ of habeas corpus." Hoxie gave the name of the lawyer handling the case and Seward ordered his arrest.

Meanwhile, both of the Iowa Senators and the entire Congressional delegation requested that Hill be released from prison. They did not succeed immediately, but Hill was eventually released after some four months. To get out, however, Hill was forced to stipulate that he would drop his case against the United States marshal for disregarding the writ of habeas corpus. In those days, it simply didn't pay to fight the system of arbitrary arrests.

In the entire program, there was no semblance of order. Some of the arrests were ordered by Seward and some by Cameron. Recommendations on candidates for prison came from private citizens, marshals, district attorneys, and city police. Actual arrests were made by all kinds of officers, local, state and national.

Furthermore, the arbitrary arrests did not stop the Peace

talk. Some of the arrested men, such as James Wall of New Jersey who later became a Senator, actually derived benefit from their imprisonment and never stopped talking against the war. Many of the newspapers that were suppressed soon started publishing again under another name and continued to cause trouble to the Administration during the entire war.

Nevertheless, the policy of repression did have a tremendous impact on the nation. It fundamentally altered the balance of power between the federal and state governments, laying the groundwork for such actions as the national draft and the federal income tax. At the outbreak of the war, the federal government was not a real source of power. But when the arm of the Lincoln Administration reached into Cooperstown, New York, and took away George Bowne, when it slipped into Freedom, Maine, and spirited away Robert Elliot, when it proved powerful enough to send three citizens of North Branch, Michigan, to Fort Lafayette, and imprison, without any recourse to law, a man in Des Moines, Iowa, it was apparent that the federal executive, after all, had real power. The wave of lawlessness that had swept the country in August abated as Union men all over the country began to realize that there was some other remedy available besides mob action.

Fort Lafayette became a national symbol for federal action. When an editor of a newspaper wished to attack a Peace man he would suggest him as a candidate for Fort Lafayette. When a Union man heard a Peace speech, he knew it was not necessary to interfere. He would simply pass by with the remark that the speaker had better watch out or he would end up in Fort Lafayette. This relaxed the country, this certain knowledge that someone in Washington was watching out for traitors. The frustration, the indignation, the sense of outrage that had been engendered after Bull Run whenever someone suggested peace, began to abate. A sense of lawfulness returned to the country as a result of the lawless acts of William E. Seward. As each day's newspaper told of more men being arrested, confidence built up among the people that this new power, the federal government, would do what had to be done.

And so the balance of power inexorably changed and William E. Seward, under the permissive guidance of Abraham Lincoln, altered the fundamental workings of the American political system. He changed them the only way it can be done, by changing men's attitudes toward their political institutions. After the leaves had fallen in 1861, the general consensus in the free states was that the Lincoln Administration was on top of the traitor problem. The image of an alert, all-knowing government had been created. "Father Abraham" had been born to the American people.

CHAPTER 16

THE DEATH OF
THE MARYLAND LEGISLATURE

JULY 21, 1861, was a warm, pleasant Sunday in Baltimore. The city was enjoying its usual Sunday with many families out walking in the streets. Reports had been coming in from Washington for several days that the Union army was moving into Virginia and that the Confederates were preparing to meet them. A feeling of uneasiness settled over Baltimore as some 50,000 soldiers maneuvered for position. Many of the Sunday strollers stayed near the newspaper offices to read the latest bulletins.

The first news that filtered through indicated that the Union armies were winning. Then reports indicating the exact opposite started coming in. The Confederate troops had met the Union attack at a place called Bull Run and had stopped it. The Northern army was retreating. Then, unbelievably, a total, disastrous Union rout was reported, with Northern troops fleeing before the invincible Confederates. The Union army was straggling back into Washington, the front had collapsed, Washington was in danger, the war had been lost.

All night and into the next day reports were received. As the Southern men of Baltimore read the news, they could scarcely believe it. Then slowly the confirmation was received. The Union army had suffered a tremendous defeat. And the secessionists in Baltimore went wild with joy and started parading through the streets cheering for Jeff Davis and the South. Secessionist flags appeared everywhere and pictures of the Confederate leaders appeared as if by magic in the streets. Rumors spread through the city that Congress had adjourned to Philadelphia and that Beauregard had reached Washington. Something akin to the atmosphere of April 19 was reasserting itself in the city when a sudden heavy rain drenched Baltimore and forced the celebrators indoors. There was no riot and the Union men, with their army behind them, slowly regained control.

Just as the news of the Union disaster was reaching the people in Baltimore, the city was given a change of commanders. General Nathaniel P. Banks was ordered to western Maryland to guard the Potomac River and General John Adams Dix was sent to replace him in Baltimore. Dix had an illustrious career behind him, including a period as United States Senator from New York. In January, 1861, after some of the Southern members of Buchanan's Administration had withdrawn from the cabinet, Dix was offered the job of Secretary of the Treasury. While he held this job, the Southern captain of one of the Treasury Department's revenue cutters refused to bring his ship north from New Orleans. Dix sent an order to the head of the Customs House that the captain should be arrested, and added, "If anyone attempts to haul down the American flag, shoot him on the spot." Actually, this order accomplished nothing in New Orleans, where the flag was hauled down and the cutter became part of the Confederate Navy. But coming as it did from the wishy-washy Buchanan Administration, it caught the fancy of the North and established Dix as an uncompromising Union man.

After Lincoln's inauguration, Dix was made a major-general of the New York militia and old General Scott at one time considered giving him command of the forces around Washington. But Dix was quite old and without military training. Stories were circulating that he could not ride a horse which, although untrue, were fatal to his chances of getting an important command. So he was assigned during the last days before Bull Run to the quiet post at Baltimore where it was thought his political abilities could be put to use. When he arrived in the city two days after the Battle of Bull Run, however, Baltimore was a seething volcano, and it turned out that Dix had been given one of the most important assignments in the Army.

As soon as General Dix had had an opportunity to look over the situation, he informed Washington that he would need 10,000 troops to keep the city quiet. Then he began visiting all the regiments personally, to persuade the men to remain for a few days beyond their three-month tour, so that he would have time to get reinforcements. In this he was only partly successful, but he strengthened the defenses of the Union camps in the city and had Federal Hill crowned with fifty heavy guns. The huge cannon stared down into the center of Baltimore and effectively dominated everything. One day, he exhibited to some secession-minded ladies an immense columbiad, which he had installed in Fort McHenry, and informed them that it was pointed to Monument Square, and if there were an uprising he would immediately begin firing directly at the Square.

There was no uprising, but the secessionist feeling in Baltimore had once again come out into the open and the city would have to pay the penalty. The Northern press started another campaign against the Maryland city. It was reported that the rebels there were only waiting for a Confederate advance across the Potomac River to rise against the Union troops. When some Southern prisoners of war were taken through the city one day, on their way north, it was reported that they were given an informal escort by secessionists singing rebel songs and giving cheers for Jeff Davis. This and every other incident that occurred was given prominent mention in the Northern press.

Officials in Washington were quite worried about the city and General Dix soon found himself in a running battle with the authorities over the advisability of making arrests. Dix was basically a kind, gentle man (one paper referred to him as an old fogey) who hated to make arrests. He wrote to the War Department that in his opinion men should not be arrested "unless we have evidence sufficient to convict them before a court." He even referred to the possibility of bringing on a political Bull Run in the city if arrests were made. But he was given orders to arrest anyone if there was good reason to be suspicious, "even when there is a want of positive proof of their guilt."

During August, Congressman Henry May of Baltimore had a party for Senator John C. Breckinridge, who had not yet joined the Confederacy, and Congressman Clement Vallandigham of Ohio, a man of brilliant oratory who was completely opposed to the war. During the visit, Breckinridge tried to give a speech from the balcony of Eutaw House, but the crowd in the street was split between Southern sympathizers and Union men and there was so much shouting, cheering and booing that he could not be heard. A few days later, General Dix issued an order that any person who made a public demonstration "by word or deed" in favor of the Confederate Government was to be arrested.

During early September, however, no important arrests were occurring in Baltimore, even though men were being sent to Fort Lafayette from all over the North. Dix was accused of having a "kid glove" policy with regard to Maryland and one Union paper in New York noted that while the government was arresting "an obscure editor of a contemptible weekly secession paper at Greenport, Long Island . . . three or four daily secession organs in Baltimore, of the most rapid type, are permitted." And so the day of reckoning for Maryland came nearer and nearer. But the final push that made the move inevitable came from still another source, the wave of fear that followed General McClellan's accusations that Scott was not adequately defending Washington.

Of all the events that occurred in the Civil War, none is more remarkable than the absolute certainty with which everyone in the North, from the highest officials down to the most lowly newspaper reader, confidently expected an invasion of Maryland, an uprising in Baltimore, and an attack upon Washington in September, 1861. This was the cloud behind which every action was taken in Maryland, and it prompted many things to be done that would never have been done otherwise. Among the documents being passed around in official Washington was a remarkable piece of paper, written in the first person (undoubtedly thought to be Jefferson Davis) which laid out a careful plan to do exactly what everybody thought the Confederates were planning to do. This document sent prickles of fear up the spine of everyone who read it. It stated that the signal for the invasion of Maryland was to be an ordinance of secession by the Maryland legislature and added:

> After the act of secession I will claim Maryland and make good her state action at all hazards and cross two columns over the Potomac one above and one below Washington, not attacking Washington unless McClellan divides his forces — it would be a political error to attack Washington till Maryland has reassumed control over the soil of that city and would weaken the cause — we contend for States Rights. The Eastern shore of Maryland is thoroughly secession and the lower two counties of Delaware are pledged to Civil War.
>
> The upper column will march on Chambersburgh, the lower on Annapolis — Baltimore must burn the bridges — We have over 300,000 men in Virginia all told — 232,000 are fully armed and efficient, the rest are without arms and are in Camps of instruction at Lynchburgh and elsewhere. I fully appreciate the risk of the advance but we need the stores now in Baltimore and must take the risk.

Almost exactly the same story was printed over and over again in the Northern newspapers during this time of panic.

The New York *Times* headlined: "The Real Rebel Design. Closing up the Potomac. Maryland to be Invaded. Washington to be cut off from the North." The story pointed out that "the Capital is not out of danger. . . . The Rebel force in Virginia outnumbers ours, and it is daily increasing." The New York *Tribune* gave another version of almost exactly the same story, with the rebel movement on Frederick, where the Legislature would "legislate the State out of the Federal Union into the Confederate Union, and thus formally complete the rebellion."

And so panic spread throughout the Administration to President Lincoln and a review was made of the situation to see whether the Maryland legislature should be suppressed. This legislature had met in Frederick immediately after the Battle of Bull Run and even then, with the Confederate army triumphant, no secession move had been proposed. But this had been before the virus of fear was spread as McClellan made his move to replace Scott, and so no federal action had been taken. It was during this session that the legislature managed to deliver an annoying thorn into the side of the Lincoln Administration.

The new tactics of opposition in the Maryland legislature were worked out by S. Teackle Wallis, the Baltimore lawyer who had been elected in the special election during the insurrection. Replacing the leadership of the extreme secessionists who had gone south by the end of July, Wallis moved deftly to attack the Lincoln Administration at its weakest point — its arbitrary arrest and imprisonment of Maryland citizens. As Chairman of the Committee on Federal Relations, he proposed a resolution which told the story of the imprisonment of the police commissioners and Marshal Kane "under frivolous and arbitrary pretexts, without oath, warrant, presentment of a Grand Jury, or lawful cause disclosed or trial had." It said they were prisoners of state, held at the arbitrary pleasure of the President of the United States. It closed with a stirring appeal:

We appeal . . . to the whole people of the country, of all parties, sections and opinions, to take warning . . . and come to the rescue of the free institutions of the Republic, so that whatever may be the issue of the melancholy conflict which is now covering the land with sacrifice and sorrow, and threatens to overwhelm it with debt and ruin, there may at least survive to us, when it is over, the republican form of government which our fathers bequeathed to us, and the inestimable rights which they framed it to perpetuate.

This document, known as the Wallis Resolutions, was passed by the House of Delegates 42 to 7 and by the Senate 12 to 6. Some 25,000 copies were ordered to be printed and it was directed that copies should be sent to all Senators and Representatives in Congress and to the governors of the various states, with the request that they be submitted to the respective legislatures. The Maryland Legislature then adjourned until the fateful day of September 17, 1861.

By September Maryland was in the iron grip of federal troops and Mayor Brown of Baltimore later wrote that in view of the position of the state at that time, the idea of secession was "so absurd that it is difficult to believe" that anyone seriously entertained it. But in Washington, the decision was finally made to prevent the Maryland legislature from meeting. At this point the figure of President Lincoln steps out of the background and comes to the fore. He personally directed the move and participated in making the arrangements with the generals who were to carry out the orders. Lincoln sent Seward over to Baltimore to explain the decision to General Dix and make sure there would be no slip-up. Seward took with him the plan of invasion of Maryland which was attributed to Jefferson Davis to emphasize the importance of the arrests.

A few days later, in early September, President Lincoln slipped out of his office and took a carriage ride with Seward and McClellan. Also in the carriage was Frederick W. Seward,

Assistant Secretary of State and son of the Secretary. He tells this story of the incident. They drove out past Georgetown toward Rockville, Maryland, and the President observed, "General Banks is expecting us, I reckon."

"Yes, sir," replied General McClellan. "I have telegraphed him. He will meet us at his headquarters, at Rockville, and will provide a quiet place for conference."

"I suppose," queried General McClellan, in turn, "that General Dix has his instructions also."

"Yes," said Mr. Lincoln. "Governor Seward went over to Baltimore a day or two ago, and spent some hours with him at Fort McHenry. So he is fully informed."

"Then he will take care of the members in that part of the state?"

The Secretary of State smiled: "General Dix's views on the subject of hauling down the American flag are pretty well known. He can be depended upon."

The carriage continued on for some hours and finally drew up at the door of a tavern in Rockville, which was General Banks' headquarters. Banks greeted the visitors and led them into a small grove nearby, where they could converse freely, without being overheard. The whole plan was laid before Banks at this time, and he was told that it rested with him to prevent the legislature from meeting. He was not to interfere with the movements of loyal members of the legislature, but he was to watch carefully the movements of any disunion members and if they started toward Frederick they were to be "quietly turned back toward their homes." It was felt that there should be little difficulty, as Mr. Lincoln remarked, in "separating the sheep from the goats."

It was late in the evening when the party returned to Washington. If Frederick Seward remembered this conversation correctly, the decision to turn back disunion members to their homes was changed radically during the next few days. For on September 11, Secretary Cameron started the cataclysmic events in Maryland with a short dispatch to Banks which is certainly one of the most remarkable in American history:

Washington, September 11, 1861

Major General N. P. Banks,
  Commanding near Darnestown, Md.

GENERAL:

The passage of any act of secession by the legislature of Maryland must be prevented. If necessary, all or any part of the members must be arrested. Exercise your own judgment as to the time and manner, but do the work effectively.

Very respectfully,
your obedient servant,
SIMON CAMERON
SECRETARY OF WAR

On the same day Cameron sent a message to General Dix at Baltimore:

You are directed to arrest forthwith the following-named persons, viz: T. Parkin Scott, S. Teackle Wallis, Henry M. Warfield, F. Key Howard, Thomas W. Hall, Jr., and Henry May, and to keep them in close custody, suffering no one to communicate with them. . . . You will also seize their papers and cause them to be closely examined.

This message was hand-carried to Baltimore by Allan Pinkerton, who was given overall responsibility for the handling of arrested persons and inspecting their papers. Of the six men named, the first three had been elected to the legislature during the insurrection, the next two, Howard and Hall, were editors of pro-Southern newspapers in Baltimore, and the last, Henry May, had been elected to the United States Congress in the June election. The day of reckoning had arrived for Maryland.

Pinkerton arrived in Baltimore so late in the evening

of September 11 that the operation had to be deferred until the next night. The plans were carefully laid during the following day for a simultaneous descent on all the proscribed persons and at 9:30 P.M. General Dix sent a message to the Provost Marshal of the city to "arrest without an hour's delay" all the legislators in the Baltimore area. He also added the name of Mayor Brown to the list, due to the Mayor's insistence on paying the Baltimore police force which had been suspended in July.

It was a warm, clear evening in Baltimore the night of September 12, 1861. About midnight a detachment of thirteen policemen with a carriage set out for the residence of Baltimore's Conditional Union Congressman Henry May. When the police arrived at his house, Mr. May was in bed but he was awakened by the inevitable knock on the door after the police had surrounded his house. Upon being informed that he was under arrest, he dressed quickly, said goodbye to his wife, and left with a small package of clothing. As he walked out of the house he inquired as to the authority for his arrest and was told it was by order of the United States Government. He got into the carriage and was driven off to Fort McHenry.

Ross Winans, the munitions manufacturer and legislator from Baltimore was in bed by midnight that night. When the detachment of police arrived at his door and told him he was under arrest, he dressed and prepared to leave. But one of his sons became quite excited about the fact that his father was being taken away in the middle of the night and began arguing with the officers. The servants also prepared to enter the fray. Old Mr. Winans, however, told them all to be quiet, bid his family farewell, and rode off to the fort. This was his second imprisonment in the fort in four months.

Lawrence Sangston, another member of the legislature, was visited shortly after midnight by Captain Bishop of the federal police force. When the captain rang the bell, Sangston appeared at an upper window and inquired who was ringing his door bell. He said he would not come downstairs until told the nature of the business. He was then informed that he was being arrested upon the authority of the United States Government. At this, he dressed and came downstairs. When the police captain suggested that he take additional clothing with him, Sangston gathered a small package together and was driven off to the fort.

Mayor Brown had two homes, one in Baltimore and the other out at Relay House. At midnight his Baltimore home was visited by the police, who arrested his brother by mistake. The brother, however, soon convinced the police that he was not their man and he said that the mayor was at his country home south of the city. A police detachment immediately proceeded into the country to arrest him. When the police arrived at Brown's country home, they placed a guard in the front and rear of the house and an officer rapped on the door. Brown had gone to bed, but was still awake when they arrived. He rose and opened a bedroom window.

"What do you want?" he asked.

"We want Mayor Brown," was the reply.

"Who wants him?" Brown asked.

"The government of the United States," the police said.

"Do you have a warrant?" Brown asked.

"No, we don't," the police replied.

Brown then came downstairs and the police told him to get ready to come with them. He said goodbye to his wife and children and walked out to the carriage that was waiting for him. The police drove him back to the city and when he arrived at Fort McHenry he was greatly surprised to find himself a fellow-prisoner with so many of his friends.

Not all the arrests were carried off successfully. John C. Brune, President of the Baltimore Board of Trade and a member of the legislature elected during the insurrection, was warned of his impending arrest and managed to escape. He fled to Canada, and from there he went to England. He died in 1863 aboard a steamer on a voyage from England to Cuba.

Several other men whose arrests were planned for the night of September 12 were out of town. One member was at his country home when the police called at his house in the city, but he returned to the city the next morning and was immediately arrested. Another of the Baltimore legislators was out of the city and was arrested on his return the following morning. Most of the others were arrested without incident, including the venerable S. Teackle Wallis and T. Parkin Scott. They vanished "into anonymous night as though smitten by terror," as Carl Sandburg put it nearly a century later.

The editors who had been proscribed were also picked up during the night. A squad of police went to the home of Frank Key Howard, editor of the Baltimore *Exchange* and grandson of Francis Scott Key, author of "The Star-Spangled Banner" which had been written on another eventful night in Baltimore nearly fifty years earlier. Howard had persistently urged recognition of the Confederacy and had made strong objections to the federal occupation of Maryland. For his views, so publicly expressed, he was awakened at 1 A.M. on September 13 and arrested. As he left his house he said this was "a big thing, but not on ice" and then was taken away to be imprisoned in the same Fort McHenry which had inspired his grandfather to write his famous ode to "the land of the free." F. Key Howard later wrote that "the flag which he then proudly hailed, I saw waving . . . over the victims of as vulgar and brutal a despotism as modern times have witnessed."

Thomas W. Hall was the editor of *The South*, a newspaper born during the insurrection which openly advocated the secession of Maryland from the Union. His name was on the list that came from Washington and he was imprisoned during the night. The offices of *The South* were broken into by the police and Allan Pinkerton searched the editorial and press rooms for incriminating evidence. Nothing worthy of mention was found.

The next morning, General Dix sent troops north of the city into Baltimore County to arrest legislators living there. Three members were arrested at their country homes during the morning. During the following days, all secessionist legislators passing through the city on their way to Frederick were arrested. Two delegates from Cecil County arrived in Baltimore and were arrested in their rooms at the Fountain Hotel. A boat arriving from the Eastern Shore was met at the pier and three more delegates were taken from it and sent to the fort. The news of the arrests had reached them before they left the Eastern Shore but they felt it their duty to make an effort to reach Frederick on behalf of their constituents. For this pronounced sense of duty, they were to spend several months in prison.

Two days later, General Dix was ordered "to make any arrest that you may consider necessary even if you have not direct authority from the Government." The august Baltimore *Sun*, then as now the leading newspaper in the city, which had advocated calling a sovereign convention and had attacked the federal occupation of Maryland relentlessly, fell silent editorially. By never again expressing an opinion during the entire war it escaped suppression. The Baltimore *Clipper*, a sprightly Union newspaper, greeted the mass arrests with a very light pen:

> The most stupendous and important arrest of the time occurred between 11 o'clock on Thursday night and 11 o'clock Friday morning. The following parties to our recollection have been arrested on the charge of uttering and circulating treason, and are now snugly enjoying themselves in Fort McHenry:
>
> His Royal Highness, Mayor George Wm. Brown;
> S. Teackle Wallis, a member of the bar, but now supposed to be peeping through bars of a cell in Fort McHenry. . . .
> Lawrence Sangston, formerly a dry goods clerk, recently an unauthorized member of the Legislature, and now sojourning at Fort McHenry;

William G. Harrison, said to be a member of the Legislature
now in session at the Fort . . .

Naturally, the *Clipper* was not molested. The Baltimore *American*, a leading commercial newspaper in the city, which had supported Bell and Everett in the 1860 election, was now entirely
for the Union and was not disturbed.

The more Southern-minded newspapers suffered a different
fate. *The South* not only lost its editor to Fort McHenry but it
was suppressed. After six days of silence it resumed on a half
sheet and with a new editor. It managed to survive a few
months more with a muted editorial voice, but early in 1862 it
was suppressed for good. The *Exchange* lost both of its editors
to the inner recesses of Fort McHenry. The paper was suppressed for five days and then reappeared as the Maryland
Times with the same type, style and advertisements as the old
Exchange, except that it was silent editorially. The new editors,
who had been the business manager and pressroom foreman of
the *Exchange,* publicly announced that the Maryland *Times*
"has no connection whatever" with the *Exchange,* "nor are
those who were its editors and proprietors, and who are now
under arrest, in any way responsible for our action." With this
new policy, the paper was not disturbed again in 1861.

General Dix had done his job well. As Secretary Seward had
said, "He can be depended upon." In all, he had arrested
twenty-one men, including a member of Congress, a mayor, and
assorted state senators, delegates, editors and publishers. Several others had been forced into hiding or had fled the state.
But there still remained the job of actually destroying the legislature. Many lawmakers from the western and southern part of
the state could get to Frederick without passing through Baltimore, and others were feared to have escaped the dragnet. General Banks sent the Third Wisconsin Regiment to Frederick
under the command of Colonel Ruger and the day before the
session was scheduled to meet, Banks forwarded detailed in-

structions to insure the destruction of the Maryland Legislature:

IMPORTANT AND CONFIDENTIAL

HEADQUARTERS
Camp near Darnestown,
Sept. 16, 1861

Lieutenant Colonel Ruger.
Comdg. Third Wisconsin Regt.,
on special service at Frederick
SIR:

. . . It becomes necessary that any meeting of the Legislature at any place or time shall be prevented.

You will hold yourself and your command in readiness to arrest the members of both houses. A list of such as you are to detain will be inclosed to you herewith, among whom are to be specially included the presiding officers of the two houses, secretaries, clerks and all subordinate officials. Let the arrest be certain and allow no chance of failure. The arrests should be made while they are in session, I think.

You will upon receipt of this quietly examine the premises. I am informed that escape will be impossible if the entrance to the building be held by you; of that you will judge upon examination. If no session is to be held you will arrest such members as can be found in Frederick. The process of arrest should be to enter both houses at the same time announcing that they were arrested by orders from the Government. . . .

Any resistance will be forcibly suppressed whatever the consequences. . . .

N. P. BANKS
MAJOR-GENERAL

The legislative sessions were to be held in Kemp Hall, a building owned by the German Reformed Church. It had two fairly large rooms, one on the second floor in which the senate met and the other on the third floor for the house of delegates. There was only one door and one hallway leading up to the two chambers so it would be easy for a small squad of men to arrest all the legislators.

The moment of truth for the Maryland Legislature arrived at 1 P.M. on Tuesday, September 17. There were only three senators in town at that moment, the remainder having been arrested or frightened away. These three were staunch Union men who met in the Reading Room across the hall from the senate chamber and decided not to attend the session. At precisely 1 P.M., Mr. Kilgour, the clerk of the senate, rose in the chamber and called the roll, name by name. Twenty-one names were intoned and only the echo of his own voice answered. Upon completion of the roll call, he solemnly announced: "There being no quorum present, the Senate stands adjourned until noon on Wednesday."

The house of delegates also convened at 1 o'clock. The Union members in Frederick did not want to attend it, but when they saw several opposition members moving toward the hall, they followed. Thomas H. Moore, the reading clerk, called the house to order at 1 P.M. and proceeded to call the roll. Just eleven members were present in the hall and of the seventy-four names he called out, only four answered. Mr. Long, a Union delegate, moved that the house adjourn until noon the next day and this was agreed to.

Meanwhile, in Colonel Ruger's headquarters, the small attendance at the session was causing some worry. He did not want to make the arrests while the senate and house were in session and let all the other legislators escape. So he decided to seal the entire town off. As the members were leaving Kemp Hall they noticed small squads of Wisconsin troops marching through the streets toward the outskirts of Frederick. In about half an hour the troops had thrown a cordon of armed pickets around the entire town, with instructions to allow no one to pass without a written permit from Colonel Ruger.

As soon as the cordon was in place, a squad of federal policemen from Baltimore, accompanied by a military escort, began to search for the members and clerks of the legislature. The first man found was Milton Y. Kidd, the aged Clerk of the House, suffering in the last stages of consumption. He was arrested and taken to the guard house at the railroad depot. William Kilgour, who had called the roll in the senate, was also arrested, along with his assistant. The search for the delegates took somewhat longer. Many of them had made arrangements to stay at private homes or in rented rooms in Frederick and their location was not known to Colonel Ruger. He was forced to spend quite a bit of time tracking them down, but slowly and inexorably he found them.

The first legislators apprehended were Josiah Gordon of Allegany County and Richard Maccubin of Anne Arundel County. Both were arrested and sent to the guard house. Then came three Frederick County delegates, all farmers, two of whom had voted for the Wallis Resolutions. The third man, who lived near Frederick, had not voted for the Resolutions and had deliberately stayed away from the session on September 17. But he was considered a member of the opposition so he was sought out at his farm and arrested. When some of the citizens of Frederick objected to these high-handed proceedings, they were arrested and sent to the guard house.

The sudden embargo on egress from the town occasioned considerable excitement in Frederick. Pickets were stationed on every road and across every field surrounding the town and no one was permitted to leave without a special pass. One gentleman who lived only ten steps beyond the picket guard was compelled to return to town for his pass. At Colonel Ruger's headquarters, he joined the clamoring throng of citizens who had been stopped and turned back by the guards. Passes were given freely to those who could prove they were not Wallis adherents in the legislature and local citizens were called in to identify applicants.

During the evening, 25,000 copies of the Wallis Resolutions were found. They had been printed by E. Riley, the public printer and editor of the Annapolis *Republican*. All copies of the Resolutions were seized and Mr. Riley was arrested. The 25,000 copies were dumped in a big pile and burned that night, making a "grand conflagration," as one report noted.

The next morning General Banks sent a message to Washington:

> Darnestown, Md.
> September 18, 1861
>
> To Governor Seward:
> But four present at opening yesterday. Eighteen s—— only in town. Twelve secured up to 5 p.m. Probably all last night.
> N. P. Banks

That morning, the train from Baltimore arrived at 12 o'clock, with four more members of the house of delegates. Three of these had voted against Mr. Wallis's resolutions, but the fourth had voted for them and he was arrested. During the morning another delegate arrived from Washington County but he was a Union man and "approved the action of his Union colleagues." Indeed, many citizens of Frederick who had read of the fighting that had swirled around the legislature in Missouri were relieved to have the sessions removed from their town. Frederick was only fifteen miles from Virginia and the legislature, it was feared, would serve as a magnet to bring the Confederate armies down on the town.

Just before noon the last opposition legislator in Frederick, who had managed to elude his captors all night long, was arrested and sent to the guard house. The afternoon train to Baltimore, which normally left Frederick at 1 p.m., was delayed this September 18, waiting for its unusual cargo of prisoners. At the last minute, it was decided that only the legislators need be held in custody, and the others were offered their freedom if they would take the oath of allegiance. Mr. Riley, the Annapolis printer, and the chief clerks of the house and senate were released. Of the three assistant clerks, two were released, but the third refused to take the oath and was sent to Fort McHenry with the legislators. All the citizens of Frederick who had been arrested the preceding day were released on taking the oath.

At 3 P.M., the remaining ten prisoners were taken down to the railroad station and put aboard one of the cars. A soldier was seated next to each one and the remaining seats of the car were filled with additional soldiers. The train finally got under way for Baltimore and the legislative prisoners started out on what was to become an extended tour of Northern prisons. The guards around the town of Frederick were withdrawn and the city fell back once again into the control of the civil authorities.

President Lincoln was reported in the newspapers as having justified the incident by saying that no arrests had been made on mere suspicion, but "in all cases the Government is in possession of tangible and unmistakable evidence which will, when made public, be satisfactory to every loyal citizen." No such evidence, however, was ever made public. F. Key Howard called the statement a "baseless and atrocious lie."

After the Frederick arrests, General Banks sent a dispatch to Washington summing up his part in the destruction of the Maryland legislature:

> I have the honor to report . . . that all the members of the Maryland Legislature assembled at Frederick City on the 17th instant known or suspected to be disloyal in their relations to the Government have been arrested. . . . [Only] nine secession members were found in the city. . . .
> I regret the attempt at Frederick was not more successful.

General Banks need not have apologized. By the time he and General Dix had finished their work, practically the entire leadership of the opposition was in prison. The Peace Party had been stripped of its leaders in the city of Baltimore, and its representation in the state legislature and the United States Congress. All the newspapers supporting the party had been suppressed and their editors imprisoned. The Peace Party in Maryland had been completely broken.

CHAPTER 17

THE END OF FREE ELECTIONS

THE REGULAR ELECTION for members of the Maryland legislature was scheduled for November, 1861, and the canvass went ahead during the six weeks following the death of the old legislature. It was an eventful six weeks as the full power of the federal government was felt throughout the state. Scarcely a day passed in which the newspapers did not publish the name of at least one man who had disappeared into Fort McHenry. The speaker of the house of delegates, Mr. E. G. Kilbourn, had made no attempt to attend the session in Frederick, but he had been the very first delegate listed as voting for the Wallis Resolutions. Federal troops therefore arrested him at his home at Jessup's Cut and he was sent to the fort. Several of the leading merchants in Baltimore were arrested during the following days. Henry E. Johnson, President of the Baltimore banking firm of Johnson Bros. and Co., was arrested and sent to Fort McHenry. A Baltimore lawyer, a cabinet manufacturer and the bailiff in the office of the Tax Auditor were arrested within a few days. Dr. A. C. Robinson was ordered arrested but escaped and fled to Richmond. Throughout the state other arrests were being made. Dr. McGill of Hagerstown was arrested in early October and sent to Fort McHenry. He was a stubborn man who refused to take the oath and as a result was destined to spend many weary months in federal prisons. During this time he was imprisoned with Richard Alvcy, a leading lawyer in Hagerstown who had been arrested the previous June and was being held without anyone's knowing what he had been arrested for.

The arresting mania spread rapidly in Maryland. On the Eastern Shore, the army commander issued an order that "all persons who have lately uttered expressions of hostility to the Government or have spoken disrespectfully of the President of the United States are to be arrested." Under these instructions, several leading citizens in that area were imprisoned. A little later, General McClellan wrote a note to an army commander in Maryland that he "fully approves your course in arresting a man . . . who used offensive language toward your regiment."

Occasionally, an investigation was made with surprising results. General Dix arrested two men charged with open acts of hostility to the government "on testimony vouched by the United States marshal," and yet he found later that they were "two of the most consistent and active Union men in the neighborhood." He wrote to Secretary Seward that he had "become somewhat suspicious of charges against individuals unless they are well supported by statements from reliable sources." He added that he did not think men should be arrested for speaking disrespectfully of the President, as he believed there would be no man in the United States "more annoyed by it than the President himself."

One man arrested during this period was named Timothy Webster. As the incident was reported in the local papers, a detachment of Baltimore police took possession of a small hotel in that city and proceeded to search the place for articles of contraband. A number of letters and papers were seized, and Timothy Webster was arrested on suspicion of holding communication with persons in the Confederate states. His "wife" was arrested with him but released. He was put in a local jail, held a few hours, and then sent to Fort McHenry in the middle of the night. As one Baltimore newspaper described the event, "while the vehicle was in motion, he gave a sudden bound from his seat, and before the officer could seize him he was beyond his grasp. It is not known which direction he took, but he will scarcely be able to escape the city." Actually, Timothy Webster was one of Allan Pinkerton's operatives, and he had been sent to Baltimore to infiltrate the secessionist circles in that city. There was no Mrs. Webster, and Timothy was evidently combining business with pleasure at the Baltimore hotel. When he was arrested he managed to get in touch with Pinkerton, who arranged his escape. When he leaped out of the wagon, the guards "obediently took aim at a passing cloud and fired," as Pinkerton later recounted the event. Webster returned to his old haunts in Baltimore, by now assumed to be a true secessionist, since he had actually been arrested. Webster had spied in the South as well as in the North, but after this incident, Pinkerton said, he had to be more careful "when inside the Northern lines than while touring anywhere below the Potomac." *

As the November election drew near, the authorities in Maryland were busy working out plans to insure a resounding Union victory. Not only were most of the state legislative seats up for election, but also the governorship and some lesser state-wide offices. Hicks could not succeed himself and the Union men nominated Augustus Bradford, a Baltimore lawyer. The Peace Party nominated General Benjamin C. Howard, former commander of the Maryland militia, who had served as a captain with the Baltimore troops when the city was attacked by the British in 1812. He subsequently had been elected as a member of Congress and for the past twenty years had been Supreme Court reporter in which capacity his name adorned some twenty volumes of Supreme Court Reports. General Howard was one of the few leaders of the Peace Party who had not been arrested in September.

General Dix was greatly concerned with the canvass and ordered some shallow draft boats on which his troops could go up the numerous rivers of the Eastern Shore and break up Peace

---

* Webster's death came a few months later in the South, however, when he was caught and hanged as a spy in Richmond when McClellan's advance units were just a few miles from the city.

meetings. He ordered General Lockwood at Cambridge, Maryland, to respect the "just rights even of those disloyal" to the government, but said everyone should understand that "no act of open hostility to the Government will be tolerated for a moment." Orders were issued to General Banks in the western part of the state to send detachments of troops to the voting places "to protect the Union voters." Banks was told to "arrest and hold in confinement till after the election all disunionists who are known to have returned from Virginia recently." He was authorized to suspend the writ of habeas corpus for such election-day activities.

On November 1, General Dix issued his final orders covering the election. In them he said that it would be necessary to arrest all who appeared at the polls "to convert the elective franchise into an engine for the subversion of the Government." He especially warned the judges of election not to allow the ballot box to be "polluted by treasonable votes." Out in western Maryland, one States Rights candidate and twenty other Southern-minded citizens were arrested and locked up overnight to prevent too much electioneering. Finally, on November 6, the day of the election, posters were put up at all polling places in Baltimore inviting citizens to point out to the judges of election and to the police anyone who took part, on the 19th of April, in opposing the march of United States troops through Baltimore. Thus, everything was in readiness.

There was no free election in Baltimore that day. As the polling began, many public-spirited Union men were happy to stand at the polling places and point out disloyal persons as they tried to vote. Mr. John T. Robinson of 22 North Howard Street had a busy day accusing his neighbors. He stood at one of the polling places and as they filed by to vote, he accused one man of helping to incite the riot of April 19; he accused another of bearing arms on April 20; he accused a third of insulting soldiers. All three were arrested and taken to the police station where they were locked in cells.

Samuel Duer was at another polling place and when his neighbor, Charles A. Schwatka, tried to vote he said that Schwatka was a secessionist. Schwatka was arrested and put in jail. Another man was arrested for disorderly conduct and cheering for Jeff Davis when he tried to vote. Still another was arrested "as a riotous Secessionist and sympathizer with the South."

The secret ballot was not part of the electoral process in Maryland in 1861. Each party printed its own ballots with its own distinctive color. Many who attempted to vote the Peace ticket in Baltimore were arrested for carrying a ballot of the wrong color. The charge against these men was simply "polluting the ballot box." A number of men were arrested for this novel offense, and one of the judges of election was arrested for "failing to bar accused secessionists from voting."

All through the morning the arrested persons streamed into the police stations and charges were lodged against them. About 11 A.M. a rumor began spreading in the city that the Peace Party candidates had withdrawn from the election and this, plus the wholesale arrests, discouraged many Peace Democrats from trying to vote. By the end of the day, about 170 Peace Democrats had been arrested and were being held in the station houses. As soon as the polls closed, the justices appeared and disposed of the cases. By early evening nearly all who had been arrested were released without bail, and the charges against them dropped.

One of the few men not released immediately was Clinton James, who had been indicted by a federal grand jury for treason and was free on $5,000 bail. When he had attempted to vote, he was sent to Fort McHenry where he was held eight days and then released. Two other men spent the night in jail, Dr. F. A. McManus and his son, Samuel. When Dr. McManus tried to vote, he was challenged by a neighbor who said that Dr. McManus had boasted of helping to seize the Pikesville armory during the insurrection. At this, Dr. McManus turned slowly around, went up to his accuser and said in a loud voice, "Your doom is sealed." McManus was arrested and an hour later his son was seized for making a similar threat. The next morning they were brought before the justice who heard their case and held each to bail in sum of $1,000 to keep the peace. Then they were allowed to go home.

Similar scenes took place throughout the state. The various generals in command had their troops stationed at the polling places and many arrests were made. Most were released, however, during the evening. In the town of Prince Frederick in southern Maryland, August R. Sollers, former member of Congress, was arrested for using violent and treasonable language near the polls and for drawing a large knife with which he cut to the right and left. Several others were arrested in the same area for similar offenses.

When the votes were counted, it was found that every legislative seat in Baltimore had been won by the Unionists, and Augustus W. Bradford, the Union candidate for governor, had won the city with a vote of 17,480 to 3,430. He led in every county in the state except four, where the presence of federal troops had not been fully exploited. In the house of delegates, sixty-eight Union candidates were elected and only six Peace Democrats.

The election was a great triumph for the Union ticket and as the year 1861 drew to a close, the federal government was in an unchallengeable position in Maryland. The situation has been described by a man who suffered during this period. He wrote:

Spies and informers abounded. A rigid supervision was established. Disloyalty, so called, of any kind was a punishable offense. Rebel colors, the red and white, were prohibited. They were not allowed to appear in shopwindows or on children's garments, or anywhere that might offend the Union sentiment. If a newspaper promulgated disloyal sentiments, the paper was suppressed and the editor imprisoned. . . .

Very soon no one was allowed to vote unless he was a loyal man, and soldiers at the polls assisted in settling the question of loyalty.

It was in Maryland that the orgy of suppression reached its apex. For here were pitted two irreconcilable forces, the historically mercurial temperament of a Southern city, and the absolute necessity for survival of the federal government. Temporarily the insurrectionary audacity of Baltimore had been triumphant, and during this phase the blockade of Washington was complete. But in time, the overwhelming resources available to the North overcame this lone city and the ultimate subjugation of Baltimore was as complete as the blockade had been. As a result, Maryland was to stand throughout the war as a symbol of oppression, and its martyrs were to provide unlimited ammunition to those who criticized President Lincoln for his "tyranny" and his Administration for its abuse of freedom.

CHAPTER 18

RELEASE OF MARYLAND PRISONERS

WHAT DOES a democratic society do when it is accustomed to operating through due process of law and suddenly these laws are cast aside? Arrests can be made easily enough, but what is to be done with the men who are in prison? During the Civil War, these questions haunted the Lincoln Administration and many attempts were made to answer them. Developing a system for getting people out of the prisons proved much more difficult than arresting them in the first place.

As soon as a man was arrested and held without recourse to law, the pressures began to build up for his release. Letters poured in to the authorities from his friends, many of whom were good Union men, pointing out that he had many fine qualities, that he was a relatively harmless person, that his family was starving, that his business would be ruined, or that his health was bad and he might die in prison. Personal solicitations were made to President Lincoln, Secretary Seward, Secretary Cameron, General Dix, or any other person in a position to influence the decision. Many of these solicitations were made by governors, Senators, Congressmen and prominent businessmen. In the American political society, which operates through a system of pressure balances, these solicitations were of great importance. Indeed, it required considerable will power to keep any of the political prisoners in jail more than a few days.

A few Marylanders were released very quickly as a result of this process. Ross Winans, the Baltimore manufacturer, was sixty-five years old, and extremely wealthy, and the pressures for his liberation were tremendous. One of the leading figures in Maryland, Reverdy Johnson, interceded strenuously in his behalf. Within eleven days of his arrest, Secretary Seward gave in and ordered his release on parole.

Congressman Henry May was in very poor health when he was taken into custody. Two of his brothers had died of consumption and Henry May had been suffering a lung infection for six months at the time of his arrest. Early in October, his brother wrote to President Lincoln that May was being confined in a crowded casemate with thirty-two other prisoners. He said that unless May were given exercise and fresh air, he would die. The risk of having a United States Congressman die in a political prison was one that Seward did not relish. A month after May's arrest, as if to reinforce his case, the third brother died of consumption and Secretary Seward ordered May's release to attend his brother's funeral. May gave his parole to "return to the fort if required by the Secretary of State." He was never asked to return, however, and he continued to represent the state in the halls of Congress as one of the most outspoken opponents of the policy of summary arrests in the House of Representatives.

Most of the Maryland prisoners were not so fortunate. They remained in confinement long enough to complete the grand tour of the federal prisons. This tour began with a few days in Fort McHenry in Baltimore harbor, followed by a few more days in Fortress Monroe, a federal fort on an island off the tip of the Virginia peninsula. From here the typical prisoner was taken by sea to Fort Lafayette in New York harbor. After six to eight weeks at Fort Lafayette, the prisoner was sent to Fort Warren in Boston harbor. Usually, he remained at Fort Warren until his release.

This grand tour was made by most of the Marylanders who had been arrested, for their release was not seriously considered until after the November election. But when the state voted staunchly Union, the question of releasing the less dangerous prisoners was revived. Many were men of moderate talents and not to be feared. One such man was George W. Landing, delegate to the Maryland General Assembly from the Eastern Shore. Congressman Crisfield, a Union man, represented the same area in Congress, and he wrote a letter to Secretary Seward pointing out that Landing was "uneducated, very ignorant and entirely incapable of conceiving or executing any scheme at all dangerous." As a result of this ringing endorsement, Landing was released in December after spending eleven weeks in prison.

Leonard G. Quinlan, a member of the house of delegates from Baltimore County, was ill most of the time he was in prison and his friends clamored for his release. General Dix considered Quinlan a "moderate man in talents, influence and political feeling," and after the November election, Seward ordered his release. Maryland State Senator John Heckart was an old man who had voted against recognition of the Confederacy in June. But his vote for the Wallis Resolutions had consigned him to prison and he was held for eleven weeks, until his release early in December.

The general amnesty in February, 1862, brought the release of most of the Maryland prisoners who still remained in custody. These men had been in prison some five months by this time. However, there were about a dozen bitter-enders who refused to give any kind of parole, on the grounds that it would imply guilt on their part. One of these was S. Teackle Wallis, the author of the resolutions which had created such havoc. When the general amnesty was proclaimed, he was offered his freedom but refused to sign any document and remained in prison during most of 1862 as a result.

The case of Mayor George W. Brown of Baltimore was perhaps the most distressing of all. A man of genial temperament, he had shown great courage in marching alongside the Massachusetts troops on April 19, trying to stop the bloodshed. He probably had more Union men as friends than any other prisoner. Within two weeks after his arrest, Secretary Seward was in a dilemma and he wrote to General Dix:

> No sooner is the conspiracy against the Government defeated than under the natural law of the human mind sympathy begins to rise in behalf of the agents of the crime held under duress. Among the prisoners recently arrested Mayor Brown is represented as having been harmless, unoffending and even loyal. Relying implicitly on your discernment and discretion I have to ask your opinion concerning the mayor and the reasonableness or unreasonableness of releasing him.

General Dix replied that the mayor was a "man of great amiability of character," and said he had behaved very well during the 19th of April riots. It was finally agreed between them that Brown should be offered his freedom if he would take the oath of allegiance, resign his office as mayor and reside in some Northern city.

Brown flatly refused. He felt that to resign his office would amount to a virtual confession that he had been disloyal. So there was another scramble to work out an acceptable formula for his release. After many discussions between Baltimore and Washington, the condition that he resign as mayor of Baltimore was dropped, but he was asked to give his parole not to return to the state of Maryland.

Brown refused once again, feeling that it would also be a confession of guilt. When he was moved to Fort Warren in Boston there immediately arose a clamor in that city for his release. Rumor had magnified his actions on April 19 to the point that he was supposed to have ordered the troops to fire on the mob. Petitions were signed by the men of the Sixth Massachusetts in an attempt to get him released. Captain Follansbee, who had led the marching troops on April 19, certified that during the attack "Mayor Brown was at my side and signified a willingness to take any position or to render any service in his power. I can bear witness to his patriotic and heroic conduct on that occasion." Everyone sent to review his case was impressed with

Mayor Brown and sought to arrange some sort of compromise. Indeed, there seemed to be great confidence in the mayor's judgment. While he was in prison, Mayor Brown became acquainted with a Baltimore boatman who had been imprisoned for contacting the rebels. The mayor recommended his release in a letter to President Lincoln on the grounds that he had "neither the power nor the disposition to do injury to the Government." Largely as a result of this letter, the man was released but Brown himself remained in prison.

In January, 1862, the mayor was given a thirty-day parole to attend to business matters. His Union jailers were hoping that he would not return and were willing to forget about his arrest, but at the end of the thirty days he promptly appeared outside the gate and was put back in his cell. When the general amnesty was proclaimed in February, 1862, he was offered his release if he would resign the office of mayor. Brown once again refused and the months in prison stretched into more than a year.

As Brown was approaching his second winter in prison, President Lincoln ordered the unconditional release of all Maryland prisoners and he was freed. His return trip to Baltimore was a restrained triumph. When he arrived at the railroad station in the city he was met by a happy, cheering crowd of 2,000 people. He made no speeches, however, and there was no disturbance. He merely got into his carriage, acknowledged the cheers with a wave of his hand, and proceeded to his home. After the war, he became Chief Judge of the Supreme Bench of Baltimore and lived many years as a political elder statesman in the city.

Others who remained in prison for more than a year included four men elected to the Maryland legislature during the insurrection. They spent fourteen months in prison. The two Baltimore editors, Frank Key Howard and Thomas Hall, also remained in prison until November, 1862, refusing to give their parole. After his release, Howard wrote a book entitled *Fourteen Months in American Bastiles*, which was suppressed by the authorities, but its author was not molested again.

The two men who spent the longest time in prison were William Gatchell, one of the Police Commissioners, and Marshal Kane, who had been arrested in June and July of 1861. They remained in prison for seventeen months, longer than any other political prisoners in the Civil War, before their release on November 30, 1862. Although Kane had been indicted by a federal grand jury for treason, he was never brought to trial. But he became quite a hero in the city and after the war was elected mayor of Baltimore.

Baltimore suffered more than any other city in the Union from arrests and arbitrary imprisonment in 1861. By contrast, the other great border state city, St. Louis, fared remarkably well. For St. Louis was far away from Washington and the pen of William E. Seward. During the first year of the war, this was one of the most significant geographical facts in the struggle for Missouri.

CHAPTER 19

A HERO COMES TO MISSOURI

ALTHOUGH THE Battle of Bull Run was fought some eight hundred miles away from Missouri, it disheartened the Union men in St. Louis and triggered a secessionist uprising in the northern part of the state. But the key to Missouri lay in the movements of General Lyon, the Union commander, and the retreating secessionist army under General Price in the southwestern part of the state. News of the approaching battle between Lyon and Price was eagerly awaited throughout the West.

While the two armies were maneuvering for position, the Missouri State Convention met in St. Louis as the supreme political body of the state, with the power to rewrite the state constitution, replace the legislature, or do whatever else it felt necessary. The Convention was in the hands of Union men and they voted by heavy majorities to vacate the offices of governor, lieutenant governor, and all the seats in the state legislature. Then they appointed a provisional governor of the state. By a vote of 68 to 0, Hamilton R. Gamble, a conservative Union man and St. Louis lawyer, was elected to this post. The military bill which the state legislature had passed immediately after Camp Jackson was repealed. Governor Gamble issued a proclamation on August 3 in which he noted that Missouri was being invaded by troops from Arkansas and Tennessee. He said these troops were in Missouri against the wishes of the people and asked them to depart. He asked all sheriffs and other local magistrates to arrest men who used violence against those with different political convictions. Then the convention adjourned, subject to the call of the new governor. When it was over, the entire secessionist government of Missouri had been legally overturned.

While the convention was in session, a man arrived in St. Louis whose job it was to win the West for the Union. He was John C. Frémont, one of the most famous men in the country, recently promoted to major general and given command of all the Union forces in Missouri. Of all the decisions made in Washington during the first year of the Civil War, none appeared to be more perfect than the choice of Frémont for this job.

As an Army officer, Frémont had explored the West and helped open it up for settlement. His reports of these explorations had captured the imagination of the nation. Furthermore, he knew Missouri well and his wife, Jessie Benton Frémont, was the daughter of Missouri's most famous Senator, Thomas H. Benton. Frémont himself had been elected to the United States Senate from California and in 1856 he had been nominated as the first candidate of the Republican Party for the Presidency. He had made a respectable showing, paving the way for the Republican victory in 1860. Frémont appeared to be a rare combination of soldier and politician. As a former Army officer, he was better qualified for promotion to general than many others in 1861. Everything seemed to point to him as the ideal candidate for the job in St. Louis.

But there was another side of Frémont that might have caused some misgivings. He was a handsome man, the bastard son of a French dancing master and a Virginia matron, and he had shown considerable instability during his Army career. He had even been court-martialed for insubordination, an incident which had led to his resignation from the Army. He was cordially hated by most professional Army officers, including General Scott. Several of his explorations had ended in disaster.

More important, he fitted the image of the handsome dreamer more aptly than that of the rough commander of men. He did not dominate his surroundings. In the rough and ready frontier city of St. Louis, this was a very serious handicap.

Frémont and Jessie arrived in St. Louis on July 25 and found the city "shuttered, sullen, and hostile." The streets were half deserted, and knots of unemployed men looked at the soldiers in resentment. The disaster at Bull Run had brought orders to send reinforcements to Washington from all over the West; guns and ammunition, such as there were, had mostly been sent to save the capital. Within a few days of his arrival, Frémont was sending desperate appeals to Washington for help. He got off a long letter to Lincoln saying that he was "sorely pressed for want of arms. Our troops have not been paid and some regiments are in a state of mutiny."

But, unfortunately, in addition to being short of arms, Frémont was making some bad mistakes. He surrounded himself with a staff composed largely of foreign officers, something greatly resented by the Missourians he had been sent to lead. He brought in a Hungarian as his chief of staff, and elevated another Hungarian to the important position of chief engineer. He adopted the European practice of having his own personal cavalry unit as a bodyguard, and this was headed by yet another Hungarian. Even his judge advocate was a lawyer he had brought from Ohio. This entire court was established in the palatial Brandt Mansion in St. Louis and as this group of foreign-speaking officers closed in about him, they effectively insulated Frémont from the public. Rumor soon had it that the general was unapproachable to any native American.

Behind this protective barrier, Frémont prepared for war. His first responsibility was to General Lyon, off in the southwestern part of the state chasing General Price. But when Frémont received a note from Washington that President Lincoln wished to know of the situation in Cairo, on the Mississippi directly south of St. Louis, Frémont loaded his retinue into a boat and sailed southward to find out. He had an enjoyable holiday and succeeded in reinforcing the area, meanwhile sending orders to Lyon to retreat if necessary.

By this time, Lyon and his German troops were far from their base in St. Louis, and facing an opponent who outnumbered them, as Confederate units were brought in to support General Price. Lyon had been a rare type in the United States Army for many years — an officer who hated slavery. He had personally taken part in the campaign on the southwest frontier in which Southern politicians and the United States Army had combined to defeat free soil efforts in the territories. Within him there had been built up a tremendous desire to pay back the Southern aristocracy for all the humiliations he had suffered and the impending battle with General Price was to represent this payment. There could be no retreat.

Lyon and Price met on August 10, at a place called Wilson's Creek in southwest Missouri. In a decisive battle, the Union forces were routed, Lyon was killed in action, and the entire western anchor of the Union thrown into danger. It was the second real battle of the war and it went just as the first one had, with complete victory for the Confederacy. Panic seized the Union men in St. Louis as they found themselves in the same position that Washington had been in only three weeks before. The secessionists in St. Louis went wild with joy. As they poured into the streets, the Union authorities suddenly realized that they had a very slim hold on the city. Most of the municipal officials were opposed to the Union cause, the Police Board had been appointed by the secessionist Governor Jackson, and the mayor, judges, clerks and many other city officials were secessionist-minded.

As this Southern sentiment threatened to burst into flame with the news of Wilson's Creek, the Union officers hurriedly took over the police power in the city. Major McKinstry was appointed Provost Marshal of St. Louis by Frémont. During the first night after news of the disaster reached the city, there

were no riots, but the next day Major McKinstry issued a proclamation of martial law. In the wave of fear that swept the
city, he issued orders to the police commissioners to suppress
all the secessionist newspapers in the city and arrest their editors. The police commissioners having refused, he ordered
Colonel McNeil of his own staff to do the job.

There were three newspapers which the Union men hated.
The worst was the *War Bulletin,* which had been published by
the same printer who had put out the *State Journal* before it
was suppressed. The others were the *Missourian,* an evening
newspaper, and the *Morning Herald.* Colonel McNeil personally visited these newspapers and took possession of the offices.
Then he arrested all three editors and took them to Turner's
Hall where they were held for about a week. Within a few days
after the defeat at Wilson's Creek, every important secessionist
paper in St. Louis had been silenced.

The refusal of the police commissioners to carry out the arrests was something Major McKinstry could not forget. So he
ordered the arrest of John Brownlee, President of the Police
Board, on the charge of treason. Colonel McNeil made the arrest and the elderly Brownlee was taken to the arsenal where a
comfortable apartment was found for him. He was freed a week
later when he agreed to resign his position and leave the state of
Missouri permanently.

The other members of the Police Board promptly elected
Basil Duke as President, in a defiant move against Major
McKinstry. Duke was a firebrand secessionist who had nearly
precipitated a riot on March 4, the day Lincoln was inaugurated, by raising a Confederate flag in the heart of St.
Louis. This was the same Basil Duke who was to serve as second
in command later in the war to General John Hunt Morgan
during Morgan's famous cavalry raids into Kentucky and Ohio.
But McKinstry did not tangle with Duke; he just ignored the
Police Board and dealt directly with the chief of police, who was
willing to take his orders. Special squads of police were formed

to prevent any mobs from assembling in the city and the sale of firearms was prohibited.

A real sense of urgency developed in Washington over Frémont's position after Wilson's Creek. St. Louis became the most critical post on the Northern line. President Lincoln wrote Frémont that "the War Department has notified all Governors you designate to forward all available troops." Frémont asked the governors of Illinois, Indiana, Ohio, Iowa and Wisconsin to "send forthwith all disposable forces you have, arming them as you best can for the moment. Use utmost dispatch." Soon St. Louis was crowded with soldiers from the neighboring states. Money, which had been denied to Missouri since the beginning of the war, was suddenly forthcoming in large amounts from Washington and laborers were hired to build fortifications around the city. Some of the unemployed were put to work, thus partially alleviating one of the most pressing local problems. Gunboats were rushed to completion along the wharves. Railroad tracks were laid in the city so that railroad cars could be shuttled between the various stations and used in whichever direction they were most needed. The chain of forts around St. Louis was strengthened and several new redoubts added. Each fort was on an elevated spot where artillery could command the surrounding countryside.

As usually happened at such times, political arrests became more frequent as the fear grew. Two men in St. Louis were arrested for using insulting language to a Union soldier and held in prison for several days. Some teamsters who had been hired to work on the fortifications struck for higher wages and all twenty-three of them were arrested by Major McKinstry and put in Turner's Hall where they were held for several days. Speaker McAfee of the Missouri house of delegates was arrested in North Missouri and sent to a military camp where he was held for several days until a peremptory order came through from General Pope to release him.

General Pope was very busy during this period. He had been

assigned to command in North Missouri, where a major secessionist revolt had broken out, complete with bridge burning,
firing on trains, and explusion of Union sympathizers. Pope
decided that a severe policy of repression was necessary. He
set up his headquarters in St. Charles, just above St. Louis, and
began making arrests. He threw the editor of the St. Charles
Reveille into jail for treason. He issued a proclamation stating
that the citizens of North Missouri could prevent the burning
of bridges if they wanted to, so he would assess the nearest
town for any damages done to them. He set up Committees of
Public Safety in each county, with the responsibility for keeping the peace. As members of the committees, he selected the
wealthiest persons in town, and made them responsible for all
the property. In many instances, they were secessionists, who
promptly ordered all the Union men out each night to guard
the railroads. This angered the Union men and only made matters worse.

After a passenger train had been fired on in the vicinity of
Palmyra, Missouri, Pope, in his first test case, levied a $10,000
fine on the county in which it had occurred and $5,000 on the
city of Palmyra, to be paid if they did not come up with the
guilty parties within six days. But he was completely unsuccess-
ful in finding the guilty parties, and both Governor Gamble
and Frank Blair were entirely opposed to the levy. So on August
30, Pope, having failed to collect anything from anybody, was
forced to cancel his plan.

Many newspapers throughout the state were suppressed as
the Union forces moved out to meet General Price. West of
Jefferson City, General Grant ordered that the Boonville *Patriot* be suppressed. "Bring all the printing material, type, etc.,
with you," he wrote the local commander. "Arrest J. L. Stevens
and bring him with you and some copies of the paper he edits."
Near the western border of the state some federal troops went
to Savannah, Missouri, and took possession of a paper called
the *Northwest Democrat*. This paper had bold headlines ad-

vocating Jeff Davis for President and Claiborne Jackson for Vice President.

Martial law was declared over the entire state of Missouri on August 30. General Frémont issued a proclamation in which he fully described the condition of the state:

> Its disorganized condition, the helplessness of the civil authorities, the total insecurity of life, and the devastation of property by bands of murderers and marauders who infest nearly every county of the State, and avail themselves of the public misfortunes and the vicinity of a hostile force, to gratify private and neighborhood vengeance, and who find an enemy wherever they find plunder, finally demand the severest measures to repress the daily increasing crimes and outrages which are driving off the inhabitants and ruining the State. . . .
>
> In order therefore to suppress disorders, to maintain as far as now practicable the public peace, and to give security and protection to the persons and property of loyal citizens, I do hereby extend and declare Martial Law throughout the State of Missouri.
>
> All persons who shall be taken with arms in their hands within these lines shall be tried by court martial, and if found guilty, will be shot.

Had Frémont ended his proclamation at this point, he might have saved himself a considerable amount of trouble. But he decided to go one step further and set forth clearly what would happen to secessionists:

> The property, real and personal, of all persons in the State of Missouri, who shall take up arms against the United States, and who shall be directly proven to have taken active part with their enemies in the field, is declared to be confiscated to the public use, and their slaves, if any they have, are hereby declared free men.

In this document, Frémont was issuing his own emancipation proclamation for Missouri, without so much as asking President Lincoln's permission. With Kentucky still hanging in the balance, Lincoln was not yet prepared to go so far. And so the stage was set for a dispute that was to linger for nearly two months while Frémont's fate was being decided in Washington. All of the pent-up emotions of the state were let loose as opinion was divided sharply into Frémont and anti-Frémont factions. The pathfinder of the West was to prove once again that he could inspire loyalty and hatred in a measure far beyond that of most men.

While Frémont's future was being debated during September and October, 1861, arrests reached a high point in St. Louis, just as they did everywhere else in the North. And they were accompanied by other bizarre attempts to control the population of St. Louis, one of which was the closing of all the saloons in this frontier city, teeming with confirmed German, Irish, and American drinkers who considered themselves among the best in the world.

CHAPTER 20

ARRESTS IN ST. LOUIS

During the Civil War, the major place of entertainment was the saloon. In St. Louis, the Germans, the Irish, and the home-bred Americans all loved to drink and it was one of the few methods of relaxation available to them. In every neighborhood, each group had a saloon where it gathered to discuss the news of the day and seek diversion. In the city that stretched some six miles along the Mississippi River, there were nearly six hundred saloons. Most of them were hotbeds of political discussion and reflected the sentiments of the neighborhood in which they were located. And they attracted soldiers like flies to honey.

The Union authorities were greatly concerned that the saloons were luring soldiers away from their duty and their Union sympathies. A major barroom brawl occurred one day between some troops who had just returned from their defeat at Wilson's Creek and some civilians. Word of the brawl came to Major McKinstry who used it as an excuse to close nearly all the saloons in the city. His order stated that:

> From and after this date, until further orders, all Saloons and Bar-rooms, and other places kept for the retailing of spirituous and intoxicating liquors in the City and County of St. Louis, except the Saloons connected with the principal Hotels, and such others as may after due investigation, receive special permission to open, be and remain closed; and the sale . . . of any intoxi-

cating liquors or beverages, at retail . . . is hereby expressly forbidden.

With a dull thud, nearly six hundred saloons closed their doors, and one of the principal industries of St. Louis was stopped. The continued existence of both the beer companies and the saloonkeepers was threatened. Furthermore, the large proportion of the saloonkeepers were Germans and so were their clientele; and the Germans formed the backbone of Union sentiment in St. Louis.

Tremendous pressure was applied to get the saloons open once again. Many appeals were made to the authorities, indicating the untold suffering of the population. About a week after the closing, Major McKinstry set up a commission consisting of three honorable Union men to handle applications for re-opening. The rules were simple. All the saloonkeeper had to do was get two reliable Union men to vouch for his loyalty and then subscribe to an oath which was to be conspicuously posted in his saloon:

> It is understood that the undersigned accepts this permit or licence on his word of honor, that he is and will be ever loyal to the United States, and if hereafter found in arms against the Union or in any way aiding her enemies the penalty will be death.

Although the death penalty was rather extreme, the saloonkeepers were willing to chance it, and cheerfully signed the oath in order to get back into business.

Within twenty-four hours permits were being issued in wholesale lots. The first day 115 were granted, and the next, 246 more. Soon nearly all the saloons were open once again and the Germans were back in their beer halls, gulping beer at the usual rate. Thus, the loyalty of the most important group in St. Louis was assured.

While the beer halls were closed, several other actions were taken to get better control of the city. The secessionist police commissioners in St. Louis were finally fired and replaced with Union men. A system of exit permits was established, so that no one could leave the city without the approval of the authorities, a move which greatly irritated many people. And to prepare for any additional political arrests which might be required, it was decided to set up a special prison.

The need for a prison in St. Louis had been apparent for some time since the arsenal was already filled. The provost marshal, casting about for another place to put prisoners, discovered a slave mart which had just opened. This building had been constructed with large pens for holding slaves prior to their sale. It was admirably suited to the purpose of holding political prisoners and was immediately purchased by the federal authorities. It was known locally as the prison at Fifth and Myrtle and many Southern sympathizers were destined to spend time there during the coming months.

The first prisoner to be confined here was James W. McDonald, a well-known sculptor who had made a famous bust of Thomas Benton. He had frequently expressed his opposition to the war and to the Union Army and on August 19th, he was picked up by federal authorities and sent to the prison at Fifth and Myrtle. Being the first one there, he had a kind of proprietary interest in it and took his imprisonment in excellent spirits. As the prison became the home of some of his compatriots, he helped while away the hours by drawing burlesque cartoons of fellow prisoners. McDonald soon became quite a favorite with everyone. Fortunately for him and the other St. Louis political prisoners, their terms were quite short. The long terms of the Maryland prisoners were almost completely unknown in St. Louis and the seventeen days that McDonald spent in prison were quite typical.

Another of the early prisoners was George Negus, a young man who had been employed in the office of the *State Journal* before it was suppressed. He had taken a job running a stationery and newspaper store in Planters' House. When it was discovered that he was violating an order forbidding the sale of maps in the city, several federal detectives visited the store and carted off Negus to the new prison. Major McKinstry, the provost marshal, ordered his release during an inspection of the prison two days later.

Maps were causing quite a bit of trouble during these times in St. Louis. James Clark, a well-known local publisher, issued a map with all the flags of the world on it. Included among them was the Confederate flag, and Mr. Clark was summarily arrested and sent to prison by order of the provost marshal. He was confined for five days in September, but didn't seem to learn any sense of restraint from his experience. In October, he applied for permission to make prints of the secessionist flag, so he was arrested again and sent to prison for several more days. He finally took the oath and was released for good.

As always, lawyers were particularly susceptible to imprisonment. Henry Hart was a young St. Louis lawyer who had been an active figure at Camp Jackson. He had subsequently been indicted by a grand jury for treason and remained free on $30,000 bail until September when he was arrested and sent to the prison at Fifth and Myrtle. A week later he was released and ordered before the United States district court to be tried for treason. But his case, like so many others, never came to trial.

Mr. Hudgins, a member of the state convention, had been elected as a Conditional Union man but was considered by many to be an unconditional secessionist by the middle of September. He was arrested one day by a company of Union troops scouting in the neighborhood of his home town, St. Joseph, in the northwestern part of the state. He was brought by steamboat to St. Louis, where a great deal of excitement developed over the arrest of so eminent a man. He was taken to the arsenal and imprisoned temporarily, but General Frémont, unwilling to alienate the members of the state convention who might still be wavering, ordered Hudgins' release and sent him back home.

Two other members of the state convention were arrested

by the provost marshal in St. Louis. The first was Samuel B. Churchill, one of the leading legal lights in the city. He was a member of the state legislature and had supported Governor Jackson in his efforts to take the state out of the Union. He was arrested in October and spent ten days in the prison at Fifth and Myrtle. After his release, he became an agent in St. Louis for General Price, handling exchanges of prisoners of war.

Perhaps the most celebrated arrest in the city occurred on October 19, when Uriel Wright was sent to the prison at Fifth and Myrtle. Born and raised in Virginia, Wright had moved to St. Louis where he became a member of the state legislature and St. Louis' outstanding criminal lawyer, as one biographer put it, "saving the lives of many hardened criminals by his ardent eloquence." Early in 1861 he was elected to the state convention as an Unconditional Union man and fought secession until the capture of Camp Jackson. This incident shocked him as it did many others and that night from the steps of Planters' House he had shouted that as a result of the "atrocious deeds" he had witnessed that day he "was no longer a Union man." He turned his brilliant oratory and scathing invective against the Union and became a leader of the opposition in the state convention. His arrest occurred while he was transacting business as a lawyer in the United States District Court. He spent ten days in the prison and upon his release joined the Confederate forces as a staff officer and served out the war with the South.

In the middle of October, the Reverend Dr. McAnally, editor of the *Christian Advocate*, a religious tract published in the city, was arrested. The good clergyman had frequently taken exception to some of the actions of the authorities and had printed a very sarcastic account of the capture of Camp Jackson "in which 600 young men and boys, some of whom were without arms, and the remainder without ammunition, were captured by a small force of seven thousand, well armed and with a good park of artillery. The killed and wounded were men, women and children who were curious enough to be lookers on." For publishing such sentiments, he was arrested and taken to the office of the provost marshal for a review of his case. However, he pleaded that he was a sick man and his friends guaranteed that there would be no more such articles in his paper, so he was released.

Occasionally, chance remarks were enough to bring about an arrest if they reflected on the good judgment of the authorities. A horse trader named Barry appeared in St. Louis one day and at the completion of his visit went to the provost marshal's office to see about a permit to leave the city. When he read the conditions on the pass, he gave a sour look and said he would be "damned if he'd sign that." The clerk called an officer and Barry was sent to prison. He remained there a few days, finally signed an oath and was set free. But when he next applied for a permit to leave the city, he was more careful with his language.

One of the biggest fish caught in the net of Union loyalty drives was James O. Edwards, a former President of the North Missouri Railroad. Mr. Edwards lived in St. Louis County about fifteen miles north of the city, and was arrested one day while staying at Planters' House. The charge was that he had been in traitorous correspondence with the enemy in southwest Missouri, having offered to raise a troop of 100 men for the support of the rebel cause. It was claimed that a letter had been intercepted in which he had made this offer. He was released after spending a week in the prison at Fifth and Myrtle Streets.

Most of these arrests appear to have been relatively harmless, almost as though someone were play-acting. The prisoners seemed to march in and out of jail almost at random, with most of them remaining but a few days. While this comic opera was being played at the prison at Fifth and Myrtle, an entirely different scene was being enacted across the city at the arsenal. For it was at the arsenal that the prisoners were held who had been brought in from the state. They were being given formal trials before a tribunal unknown to the laws of the United

States, the military commission. And in these trials, men were being sentenced to death rather than a few days behind bars.

The military commission was a kind of bastard organization, half civil and half military. The civil processes were obviously failing in handling the treason cases, due mainly to the severe restrictions in the Constitution, which required that "no person shall be convicted of Treason unless on the Testimony of two Witnesses to the same overt Act, or on Confession in open Court." The enormous number of indictments for treason and the complete failure to convict caused the federal authorities to lose confidence in civil justice. So they turned to the military, and the court-martial concept. Without any justification in law, they simply brought civilians to trial before boards of military officers, acting much like a court-martial, but with greatly expanded powers and with much wider jurisdiction. Thus, the military commission was born.

At the St. Louis Arsenal, military commissions began sitting in early September, as the city was being flooded with prisoners from out in the state and some method of disposing of their cases had to be developed. One of the first prisoners to be tried was Joseph Aubuchon, charged with treason against the United States Government. His home was in Ironton, Missouri, and it was claimed that he had been in open rebellion against the federal government and had become a lieutenant in the Confederate army.

Aubuchon was a handsome young man, with a cavalier manner and winning ways. In the regular manner of court-martials, he was tried under a set of special orders which listed the "charges" and "specifications" and he was granted regular military procedures. The commission found him guilty of treason and he was sentenced to imprisonment at hard labor during the remainder of the war. However, the court recommended that his sentence be remitted. General Frémont concurred and Aubuchon was released. He was only one of many civilians convicted of treason before military commissions in St. Louis in 1861.

Another man brought up for trial was William Hearst, a farmer living in Jefferson County south of St. Louis. He was tried on the charge of violating the laws of war by burning a bridge. He pleaded not guilty but was convicted and the commission sentenced him to be shot to death. Again, however, the commission recommended clemency as it "had reason to believe that the prisoner is an unusually stupid and ignorant man," and his sentence was commuted to imprisonment during the war.

Many men brought before the military commissions were released outright because there was no evidence against them. As soon as the first military commission had heard a few cases, it complained to General Frémont that "many of the prisoners . . . were found without any charge whatever lodged against them; others had but trivial charges. . . . [The commission found] many persons charged with being spies and traitors. These charges were not sustained by any evidence whatever. The persons taking them prisoners did in most cases send no names of witnesses along. . . . Some were sent here prisoners because one Union man considered them dangerous. The commission has felt itself obliged to release most of these prisoners."

Nevertheless, by the end of September, 1861, military commissions had sprung up all over the Union-occupied areas of Missouri, and sentences, including many death sentences, were being meted out. The helter-skelter manner in which the military commissions developed, and the almost complete lack of understanding of the constitutional provisions concerning treason, made for a great deal of chaos. Many of the decisions of the military commissions were later reversed, and few, if any, men were actually executed as a result of these sentences. Whenever a Union commander seriously threatened to shoot someone, the rebels in the state would arrest a Union man and threaten to execute him in retaliation. The result was that no one was shot.

But the military commissions did succeed in providing a

method of handling the mass of civilian prisoners who were pouring into St. Louis and other cities of the state.They were at least capable of making decisions as to the guilt or innocence of the prisoner, and one case had a profound impact on the policy of repression in the free states.

Out in Columbia, Missouri, a military commission tried the case of Edmund J. Ellis, editor and proprietor of the Boone County *Standard*. He was charged with publishing incendiary articles under such titles as "Root, Abe, or Die," and "The U.S. Flag — Rebellion." He also had the obnoxious habit of printing such things as the message of President Jefferson Davis to the Confederate Congress. All of these articles were included in the "charges" and "specifications" under which he was tried and he was found guilty of every one of them. The commission sentenced Ellis to be exiled from the state of Missouri, and recommended confiscation of all of the press, type, furniture and materials of the printing office of the Boone County *Standard*.

When the details of this particular case were forwarded to the Secretary of War for review, the Secretary was very pleased and said that he would order this form of procedure to be followed in all the other army departments. This led directly to the grand hoopla that surrounded the development of military commissions in free states later in the war, and it eventually culminated in the disastrous Vallandigham case in Ohio. The Administration in Washington found in the end that there was simply no way to make such activities palatable.

During the entire period of Frémont's command in Missouri, arrests were made and newspapers suppressed. Just as in Maryland and the free states of the North, opposition to official policies was not tolerated. Yet, because St. Louis was so far away from Washington and the wrath of William E. Seward, most political prisoners were released quickly. Perhaps this was also caused in part by the great cloud that was hanging over Frémont, McKinstry and the entire Union headquarters in St.

Louis. In his lifetime, Frémont was to know great triumph and great failure. Yet never did he go through a more trying period than the two months of September and October, 1861. His every act was reviewed and investigated as the man in the White House eight hundred miles away tried to make up his mind amidst a thousand clamoring voices on the burning question of the day — should Frémont be dismissed?

CHAPTER 21

FRÉMONT'S AGONY

GENERAL FRÉMONT, an important national figure long before he was sent to St. Louis, found nothing but trouble when he arrived there. Frank Blair considered himself to be the political boss of Missouri. His influence had earlier in the year twice brought about the dismissal of the old professional, General Harney. He had helped lead the attack on Camp Jackson and had represented St. Louis in Congress during the summer session in Washington. His brother was Postmaster General and his father was the unofficial sage of the Administration, with easy access to the ear of President Lincoln. When Frank Blair returned to Missouri in mid-August after Congress adjourned, he expected to be recognized as the leading politician in the state.

But instead he found himself ignored. Money was being spent at a prodigious rate in Missouri for horses, feed, rifles, ammunition, and everything else the Army needed. Frank Blair had friends whom he felt should get many of these contracts, but nobody paid any attention to his recommendations. And while Frémont was making an enemy of Blair, he made no effort to form alliances with other politicians in the state. He fought with Governor Gamble as readily as with Frank Blair. Isolated behind his foreign staff, Frémont exercised none of the political tact that the situation required. As the anti-Frémont feeling built up, letters began pouring into Washington, urging that he be replaced. One letter written from St. Louis in August noted: "Oh, how badly have we been disappointed. We have got instead of a General an Egotist and ass. . . . Save us and remove Frémont." James Broadhead, one of the leading Union men in the city, reported that although Frémont was a gallant soldier, in time of public peril, "a blunder is worse than a crime. Frémont," he said, "does not keep himself advised of the facts from which he must form a correct judgment." It was not long before Lincoln was commenting that Frémont was "losing the confidence of men near him, whose support any man in his position must have to be successful. His cardinal mistake is that he isolates himself and allows nobody to see him."

Frémont did nothing to remedy the situation. Not only was most of his military staff foreign but his political advisers were from other states. One of them was Owen Lovejoy, an ardent abolitionist whose brother Elijah had been killed by an anti-abolitionist mob several years before. Slowly Frémont was won over to the school of thought which held that the war could be won with a stroke of the pen. According to this theory, the key to the South lay in its slaves. Without them, the men serving in the Army would have to remain at home to till the soil and protect their families. If the slaves were freed, it would deprive the South of its ability to carry on the fight. The idea of issuing his own emancipation proclamation began to take form in Frémont's mind.

At the same time, Frank Blair and many other leaders in the state, who were excluded from Frémont's deliberations, became convinced that Frémont was incompetent. The point of explosion was reached at the end of August when two events occurred which split the Union elements in the state wide apart and from which Missouri never fully recovered during the entire war.

The first of these events occurred on August 30, when Frémont issued his emancipation proclamation, as already noted. The General was in deadly earnest in this matter. He set up a commission to administer the proclamation and it began issuing deeds of manumission to slaves. Within a few days several deeds had been issued, including two which freed the slaves of Thomas L. Snead, one of the leading rebels in the state, on the grounds that he had been "taking an active part with the enemies of the United States, in the present insurrectionary movement against the government."

The reaction in the North to Frémont's freeing the slaves was enthusiastic. One member of Congress wrote that "it stirred and united the people of the loyal States . . . far more than any other event of the war." The fire-eaters in the Republican party were enthusiastic and the abolitionists jubilant. But men in Kentucky felt very strongly that the state could well be lost by the emancipation. James Speed, a man to whom Lincoln turned repeatedly for advice, wrote on September 2 that it would be "condemned by a large majority of the Legislature and people of Kentucky." General Anderson, the man who just a few months before, as a major, had led the defense of Fort Sumter, and was now in command in Kentucky, wrote that the proclamation and manumissions were "producing most disastrous results" there and added that if it was not disavowed "Kentucky will be lost to the Union." And from a group of Kentucky Unionists came the warning, "There is not a day to lose in disavowing the emancipation or Kentucky is gone over the mill dam."

Three days after the proclamation, Lincoln wrote Frémont a very conciliatory letter "in a spirit of caution, and not of censure." He said that the emancipation proclamation would "perhaps ruin our rather fair prospects for Kentucky." And without giving any formal order, he added: "Allow me, therefore, to ask that you will, as of your own motion, modify that paragraph." Frémont replied with a long letter in which he defended his action and said that if Lincoln considered him wrong in the proclamation, "I have to ask that you will openly direct me to make the correction." Lincoln therefore sent him a formal order to modify the clause and Frémont made the necessary change.

The second major event in the Missouri explosion occurred

two days after Frémont's proclamation was issued. On that day, Frank Blair wrote a letter to his brother, Montgomery, in which he declared war on Frémont. He set forth in detail Frémont's incompetence and accused him of splitting Union sentiment in St. Louis into two widely separated camps. "Oh, for an hour of our dead Lyon," he wrote, adding that men who came to St. Louis to inform Frémont of the true state of affairs were "not allowed to approach Frémont, and go away in disgust." He went on:

> I have felt it my duty to tell him what they say, and he throws himself behind the reports of his officers, who are trying to prevaricate and shield themselves from neglect of duty; and he still clings to them and refuses to see for himself. . . .
>
> My decided opinion is that he should be relieved of his command and a man of ability put in his place. The sooner it is done the better.

Montgomery Blair forwarded the letter to President Lincoln and its existence soon became common knowledge in Washington. Frémont's enemies seemed to be gathering momentum and it appeared that he would soon be dismissed unless drastic action were taken to save him. And so Jessie Frémont, with her usual direct approach, decided to take a dramatic step.

Jessie Frémont was one of the most remarkable women in American history. Her father, Senator Thomas Hart Benton of Missouri, had fought his share of battles on the Senate floor and elsewhere, and had raised his daughter to love the atmosphere and infighting of Washington. But when a romantic Frémont appeared in the capital as an Army lieutenant who had been on the exciting expeditions into the unknown West, she had fallen in love with him. She married him against her father's wishes and it took some time for the old Senator to become reconciled to the match. Jessie had done much to help her husband, and had been in the foreground of everything he did. She was the one who had actually drafted the fascinating reports of his western explorations which caught the imagination of the country. Her part in the 1856 Presidential campaign was reflected in the Republican motto, "Frémont and Jessie." And when her husband was sent to St. Louis, she became known as General Jessie. As one unfriendly newspaper put it, "Mrs. General Jessie Benton Frémont is now in command of the United States troops in Missouri, with her husband, John C., attached."

As Frémont's enemies combined against him, Jessie conceived the idea that she could straighten everything out if only she could see the President personally. So she climbed onto a train on September 8, and started out on the long trip to Washington. After two days and nights she arrived in the capital and sent word to the President that she would like to see him. He replied that he would see her immediately.

Unfortunately for her, Lincoln was not the kind of a man to be won over by the importunings of an aggressive female. He reacted against her instinctively. Without asking her to be seated, he said "Well?" in a manner which she later recalled as "hard" and "repelling." She immediately began talking about the troubles confronting Frémont in Missouri and the problems he was facing. Lincoln later said that she "tasked me so violently with so many things, that I had to exercise all the awkward tact I have to avoid quarreling with her." They had an intense conversation which ended inconclusively. But it was clear that she had done nothing to help her husband and she returned to St. Louis in low spirits.

The day after Jessie got back to St. Louis, Frémont ordered the arrest of Frank Blair. Blair was confined to his quarters at the arsenal for nearly two weeks until General Scott personally ordered his release. While Blair was under arrest, a catastrophe struck Frémont which sealed his fate.

In the retreat from Wilson's Creek, Union forces had retired to the eastern and central portions of the state before the advancing rebel army. Colonel Mulligan and some 3,000 troops reached Lexington, on the Missouri River, where they dug in to stop the rebel advance. Reinforcements in ample number were within a few days' march of them and it appeared that they were in no danger .Frémont ordered troops to relieve Mulligan in Lexington, but somehow they never got there. After a week of maneuvering around Lexington, General Price stopped the water supply of the Union forces and forced the surrender of the entire contingent. This incident was the crowning disaster for the Union and fully avenged the ignominious surrender by the state troops at Camp Jackson. And Frémont could be held directly responsible for it.

The story of the lone rider from Lexington who had tried to inform Frémont of the situation there and had been refused an audience received wide circulation. When the city fell to Price, it was clearly the end for Frémont unless he could redeem himself with a dramatic victory. He had been in Missouri just two months and during this time he had lost two disastrous battles, tried to emancipate the slaves without authorization, and arrested the leading Republican hero of Missouri. It is almost unbelievable that anyone could get himself into so much difficulty in such a short time. Yet he still had an aura about him that made it difficult to fire him summarily. He was the hero of the radical Republicans and the Germans loved him. There was talk of an insurrection against Lincoln if he should fire Frémont.

Three days after the fall of Lexington, another macabre incident occurred in St. Louis. The *Evening News*, a strong Union newpaper, published an article on the fall of Lexington which referred to the defeat as "easily avoidable." It said that the thought never occurred to Mulligan that "with 40,000 friendly National troops within a few days march of him, he could be neglected and left to the mercy of a besieging force for a whole week. . . . But the heroic officer calculated too largely on the cooperation of the authorities in St. Louis." As soon as this article was published, Frémont's headquarters issued an order for the suppression of the newspaper and the arrest of the proprietor and editor. The newspaper was seized and the two men brought to headquarters for questioning. The next day, however, they gave guarantees that their paper would no longer contain articles "of a character calculated to impede the operations of the government and impair the efficiency of the operations of the army of the West." So they were released and the order suppressing their newspaper was revoked.

By this time, Frémont fully realized that only a military victory could save him. He sent word to the War Department, "I am taking the field myself and hope to destroy the enemy." A week after the fall of Lexington, he started off into the western regions of Missouri while the rest of the country debated his fate. Lincoln was besieged with letters from all sources giving him advice on Frémont. From Cincinnati came the warning: "Don't remove him! If you do — Missouri is lost." From Governor Kirkwood of Iowa: "The removal of Gen. Frémont at this time would be . . . disastrous to our cause." And from another westerner, "Let Frémont alone."

But Senator Trumbull of Illinois reported that he had "found a most deplorable state of things" in St. Louis. James Broadhead said Frémont was "incompetent" and added "What excuse is there for the fall of Lexington?" General Curtis, on Frémont's staff, felt that the only way to save Missouri was to remove Frémont. Secretary Cameron was sent to Missouri to review the situation. He was given a letter of dismissal with the understanding that he should deliver it to Frémont if he felt it necessary. But Fremont impressed him. Cameron showed Frémont the letter but did not deliver it, offering to let the general remain in command until he had had an opportunity to report to Washington. Ward Lamon was sent to look the situation over and was equally impressed. Lamon reported, "Doubt the policy of his removal."

Amidst all this turmoil, Frémont was subjected to attack

from still another source. Many men felt that if they could prove Frémont had defrauded the government, he could be dismissed without any political repercussions. And so hordes of investigators descended on St. Louis to find just such proof. Lorenzo Thomas, the adjutant general, reviewed the situation while he was there and Congressman E. B. Washburne convened a Congressional investigating committee in St. Louis and took testimony for many days on Frémont's procurement policies. Every man who had been unable to get a contract was glad to appear and denounce anyone else who had been successful. It wasn't long before they found ample evidence of questionable practices. It is likely that a detailed investigation of any state in the Union would have produced as much evidence of wrong-doing. Decisions had to be made quickly and in Missouri this was especially true. So there was plenty to find.

To make matters worse, the Congressional investigators sent daily dispatches back to Washington giving their impressions of the proceedings. On October 19, E. B. Washburne wired, "Committee directs me telegraph you that examination discloses the most stupendous frauds." And two days later, "The disclosures of corruption, extravagance and peculation are utterly astounding. We think the evidence will satisfy the public that a most formidable conspiracy has existed here to plunder the Government." The actual testimony was particularly directed against McKinstry, who had been Frémont's quartermaster general as well as his provost marshal. There were luscious stories of the Hall carbines, originally purchased for $3.50, sold to a broker for $12.50, who sold them to Frémont and McKinstry for $22. A Mississippi gunboat was being built with an engine worth $40,000 which was sold to McKinstry for $48,000. Frank Blair testified that Frémont was letting contracts to New Yorkers and Californians whom he knew and that the loyal Missourians Blair recommended were ignored. Another story was published that McKinstry's wife

was presented with a silver service worth $3,000 by some fa-
vored contractors. And so it went on and on.

Adding to all of this were Frank Blair's howls. When he was
released from his arrest, he said he would not serve under
Frémont, and made a great fuss over the fact that he had been
arrested and released without any charges having been made
against him. So Frémont decided to prefer charges. He had
Blair arrested again and issued a special order directing his
court-martial. This special order was given wide publicity and
the entire country was fascinated to read about Frank Blair's
having assaulted the personal and official character of his superior officer while acting as a colonel in the Army. Frémont
also accused Blair of writing a letter to his brother Montgomery, "thus using his family relations with the Cabinet to
get secret, insidious, unsustained and ungentlemanly charges
against said Commanding General before the President of
the United States . . . for the purpose of effecting the removal of the said Commanding General."

Frank Blair, of course, was not one to avoid a fight. So he
set about preparing his own set of charges and specifications
for the court-martial of General Frémont, and forwarded
them to the adjutant general in Washington. He charged
Frémont with "neglect of duty and unofficer-like conduct
. . . in establishing about his headquarters in the city of St.
Louis a barricade, whereby information absolutely indispen-
sable to the public service was repelled and shut out from his
mind." He also charged Frémont with gross extravagance,
waste, mismanagement, misapplication of the public funds,
and despotic and tyrannical conduct. In one of his specifications he cited the fact that Frémont had "ordered a public
journal in the city of St. Louis, known as the Evening News,
to be suppressed, and its proprietor to be arrested and imprisoned for a fair and just criticism upon his conduct, although
he well knew that said newspaper had always given a fair and
loyal support to the Government of the United States."

To provide the capstone of Frémont's agony, Secretary Cameron, despite his reluctance to fire Frémont on the spot in Missouri, gave a very adverse report of affairs in the state and concluded that Frémont's "mind is incapable of fixed attention or strong concentration — that by his mismanagement of affairs since his arrival in Missouri, the State has almost been lost — and that if he is continued in command, the worst results may be anticipated."

Frémont was never to be given the opportunity to win a decisive victory in the field. But he was able to work out an agreement with General Price which he hoped would stop the continued harassment of Union men in Missouri. Frémont and Price, each in his own camp, signed an agreement which was dated November 1, 1861. It was one of the many efforts that had been made since the Harney-Price agreement earlier in the year to prevent the illegal harassment of men for the voicing of political sentiments. It held that:

Future arrests or forcible interference by armed or unarmed parties of citizens . . . for the mere entertainment or expression of political opinions shall hereafter cease . . . and that the war now progressing shall be exclusively confined to armies in the field. . . .

No arrests whatever on account of political opinion, or for the merely private expression of the same, shall hereafter be made within the limits of the State of Missouri, and all persons who may have been arrested . . . shall be forthwith released.

This joint proclamation had the same effect on events that most other such proclamations have had since the beginning of time — practically none.

Before he signed this proclamation, however, Frémont's fate had finally been decided in Washington. A definite order was prepared on October 24, relieving him of his command and requesting that he report to Washington immediately. The only problem that remained was getting the order to Frémont. Some of the New York newspapers had reported that Frémont was being dismissed, and the General had a record of disobedience to the orders of his superiors which went back twenty years. Coupled with this was the fanatical devotion he seemed to inspire in his followers. Every step in the process of delivering the order had to be carefully laid out in advance.

The order was hand-carried to St. Louis from Washington by one of Lincoln's closest advisers. In St. Louis, it was decided to use an anonymous messenger to deliver the document to Frémont, someone who would have a good excuse for being within the Union lines. They found their man in Captain J. C. McKinney, who was in St. Louis on leave from one of the Iowa regiments. He was informed of the decision to remove Frémont and told not to deliver the order if a battle was in process or imminent. McKinney rode on horseback for two days and two nights to Frémont's camp, arriving there at 5 o'clock on the morning of November 2. He strolled about the camp for five hours, striking up conversations with the men. He soon learned that no battle was imminent and at 10 A.M. went to Frémont's headquarters and asked to be admitted. He was asked what his business was but said he must see the General and would talk to no one else. After some argument among Frémont's staff, he was admitted and delivered the order. Frémont read it over hurriedly and asked him abruptly: "Sir, how did you get through my lines?" McKinney replied, "I came through with an express messenger." Frémont replied, "Did you have a pass, sir?" "None, sir, except a general pass from General Curtis." Frémont paused a moment and said, "You can retire, sir, for the present."

At least, this was the story that was circulated widely at the time of Frémont's dismissal, and it suited the Administration because it seemed to indicate that Frémont had indeed tried to stop the order from getting to him. Frémont was one of the first great names to be broken by the Lincoln Administration during the Civil War. The experience was humiliating. Frémont had lasted one hundred days on the job (shades of Napoleon once again) and now he was through. But as time went on the burden became lighter. Others were disgraced and humiliated, and as the number grew, Frémont became less conspicuous. A Congressional committee which was oriented toward radical Republicanism investigated his conduct in Missouri and not unexpectedly gave him a clean bill of health. The General was given a minor command in West Virginia and finally moved gently aside so that he exerted no further influence on the Civil War. In 1864, he was considered for nomination to the Presidency as a radical candidate against Lincoln but declined to run. Jessie, whose hair had turned grey from the agony of waiting out Frémont's final military campaign against Price, had settled down to become a wife and mother, rather than "General Jessie."

After the war, Frémont became a multimillionaire when gold was discovered on his estate in California. But within a few years his entire fortune was lost in his vain attempt to build a railroad to the Pacific. Slowly the Frémonts descended to a level of abject poverty so complete that they were forced at one time to separate and live with friends for several months because they did not have enough money to maintain even a flat of their own. Frémont was eventually given a territorial governorship by Congress, but was always troubled with financial problems. So ended the saga of the first Republican candidate for the Presidency and the daughter of Senator Thomas Hart Benton.

The man picked to replace Frémont in St. Louis was General Henry W. Halleck, and unlike Frémont, whose reputation was ruined in Missouri, Halleck's was made there. With his rare sense of timing, Halleck was able to work effectively in the same political wonderland that had completely baffled and wrecked his predecessor.

CHAPTER 22

HALLECK AND THE SECESH LEVY

BY COMPARISON with Frémont's, General Halleck's command in St. Louis was tame almost to the point of boredom. There were no more disastrous defeats, no more emancipation proclamations, no more arrests of Frank Blair, no more wives chasing off to Washington to save their husbands. The Hungarian officers disappeared, the body guard was disbanded, and the rumors that nobody could get to see the commanding general died out. Many of the same problems remained but whereas Frémont had tended to irritate everyone he dealt with, Halleck soothed them. The job really needed a politician and in Halleck it found one. Instead of watching everything go wrong in Missouri, the North enjoyed watching everything go right.

Halleck went through many of the motions of an efficient commander. Shortly after arriving he discovered that although martial law had been declared in St. Louis, there was no authority from Washington to do so. Halleck pointed this out to his superior, General McClellan, and asked for the authority. It was immediately forthcoming. The problems of prisoners pouring into St. Louis from all over the state troubled him as much as it had Frémont, and he issued a special order in an attempt to stop it:

> In all cases where prisoners taken at other posts or in the field are sent to St. Louis, they will be accompanied with a written statement of the charges against them and the evidence

upon which the arrest was based. Otherwise prisoners so sent will be released on their arrival here.

No person will be hereafter arrested without good and substantial reasons, and officers making arrests without sufficient cause, or without authority, will be held to account and punished. And officers sending prisoners to St. Louis without charges, proofs, or proper explanations, will be charged with the expenses of their transportation.

This order, like all the others that had gone before, had little effect on events.

The number of men arrested in St. Louis on such charges as making treasonable remarks, acting as a spy, general disloyalty, and publishing treasonable articles, reached a high point in September, as it did all over the country. It dropped off in October and following Halleck's arrival in mid-November, it continued to drop. Through the end of February, the numbers never again reached the level that had been customary before he took over the command.

The general purpose of the arrests, however, and the length of time spent in prison, remained about the same. One young man living in St. Louis was arrested on December 17 for hurrahing for Jeff Davis. He spent two days in prison and was released under oath. About two weeks later, a doctor was arrested for using "treasonable language," and sent to the prison at Fifth and Myrtle, where he spent seventeen days before being released. A notary public in the city was arrested for expressing disloyal sentiments and released after a few days in prison. The following month he was again arrested and this time held several weeks as a second offender.

Two young men, sons of wealthy families, decided to express their sympathy for the South by printing tracts poking fun at the Union. They got hold of a hand press, some compositors' cases and set up shop in an attic. When their tracts began to circulate throughout the city, the military police found and arrested them. Their style was not deathless, but it annoyed the authorities. One of their doggerels read:

> O General Frémont thought he'd fix them,
> When he marched from St. Louis away.
> He thought he'd make brave Price surrender,
> But he was fooled and called away.

When they were arrested their parents interceded for them and they were released under oath.

During January, General Halleck and the city of St. Louis went on an oath-taking spree. All of the city officials, from the mayor down to the lowest clerk, were required to take the oath. As The Mercantile Library Association, a very exclusive club of wealthy men, was thought to have secessionist officers, Halleck ordered its president, secretary, and directors to take the oath. He also required that all officers of the Chamber of Commerce do so. The order added rather ominously:

> Any of the above named officers who shall neglect to file in the office of the Provost Marshal General within ten days of the date of this order, the oath so subscribed, will be deemed to have resigned, and any one who after neglecting so to file his oath of allegiance, within the time prescribed, shall attempt to exercise the functions of such office, will be arrested for contempt of this order, and punished according to the laws of war.

As soon as these organizations had been cleaned up, a drive was launched to get all the lawyers in the city to sign the oath. Then all the clergymen. Then all the doctors. Thousands trooped to the office of the Provost Marshal, duly signed the document and went on record as being loyal. Seldom have so many people placed so much confidence in a single document. Nobody could get out of prison without signing the oath. Nobody could vote without taking it. Nobody could get a contract with the military or a job with the government without signing, and there were precious few other jobs available, with trade disrupted and business confidence shattered. The oath became a part of the daily lives of the people.

Just as the issuance of too much paper money debases its value, so the repeated taking of the oath of allegiance reduced its significance. Among those swaying between the Union and Confederate side, it was treated lightly. General Pope, who was operating in central Missouri, wrote that "one-half the men in this section of the country have been sworn by one side or the other but there are few of them who observe such oaths."

In January an election was held in St. Louis to fill a vacancy in the national House of Representatives created by the expulsion of one of the Congressmen from St. Louis. But the city was so firmly under federal control by this time that only Unconditional Union men even considered running in the election. Needless to say, an Unconditional Union man won.

Politics in Missouri had been greatly scrambled by the events of 1861, and by the end of the year each side had its legislature and its governor. The Union element had its state convention and Governor Gamble to give legal trimmings to its activities. After the defeat at Wilson's Creek, the secessionists overran a good share of the state, and it was deemed advisable not to risk a Union election in 1861, so the state convention was called together in October and deferred elections until 1862, with Provisional Governor Gamble remaining in office in the interim.

Also needing an aura of legality for their activities, a handful of secessionists in the state legislature who had retreated with the militia met at the town of Neosho in the southwest corner of Missouri on November 2, 1861. Here they went through the formality of appointing proxies for the absent majority and passed an ordinance of secession. Then they adjourned and fled the state with General Price. As winter came on, many of Price's troops went home and the rest withdrew within the protective cover of Confederate Arkansas.

In St. Louis, Halleck was busy working out a novel method of humiliating the leading secessionists in the city. Every week scores of Union men were arriving in St. Louis from the outlying areas of the state. They told agonizing stories of being visited in the middle of the night by armed bodies of secessionists and threatened with their lives if they didn't flee. Many had been given only a few hours to get out of the county in which they had settled and made their homes. They arrived in St. Louis without money, friends, jobs or hopes.

Taking care of these refugees was a major problem in the city. Some contributions came from the federal government and some from private sources, but the refugees still went hungry while many Southern sympathizers were living in luxury. And, of course, the secessionists in St. Louis never contributed anything for the support of the refugees. General Halleck conceived the idea of forcing them to contribute. On December 12, 1861, he issued General Order #24 which struck the city dumb with amazement:

> The suffering families, driven by rebels from Southwestern Missouri, . . . have been supplied by voluntary contributions made by Union men. Others are on the way, to arrive in a few days. These must be supplied by the charity of men known to be hostile to the Union. A list will be prepared of the names of persons of this class, who do not voluntarily furnish their quota, and a contribution will be levied on them of ten thousand dollars, in clothing, provisions and quarters, or money in lieu thereof. This levy will be upon the following classes of persons, in proportion to the guilt and property of each individual; 1st, those in arms with the enemy, who have property in this city; 2nd, those who have furnished pecuniary or other aid to the enemy, or to persons in the enemy's service; 3d, those who have verbally, in writing, or by publication, given encouragement to insurgents and rebels. . . .

Any one who shall resist or attempt to resist the execution of these orders, will be immediately arrested and imprisoned, and will be tried by a military commission.

It was almost as though Frémont were back. But Halleck, in his canny wisdom, had something more in mind than just the $10,000. Nothing had been done to strike at the hard core of wealthy first families in St. Louis who were sympathetic toward the South. Only a few had been arrested and they had been released almost immediately. There had been no attempt in St. Louis, as there had been in Baltimore, to send the cream of society and politics to prison and keep them there. So the more subtle act of the forced levy for charitable purposes was devised. In the popular parlance of the day, it soon became known as the "Secesh levy."

A list was drawn up consisting of some three hundred names of people who were to be subject to the levy. They were the first families, the bon ton of Southern society, the leaders of those opposing the war. Each man on the list was to be forced to contribute to a cause he despised. And it was to be done without recourse to courts, judges, lawyers, or any legal forms. In the first assessment, sixty names were selected from the list and a form letter was sent to each:

You are hereby notified that . . . you have been assessed a sum of ———— hundred dollars. . . .
You will therefore pay the amount so assessed, or . . . execution will be issued against your property for sufficient to satisfy the assessments, costs, and 25% penalty in addition.

The assessments varied from $100 to $800 and by the end of December, all the notices had been delivered to the persons assessed. A period of five days was provided for payment, and by the time it had expired a fairly substantial number had made the necessary contributions.

However, the day after Christmas, 1861, twenty-three men

and two women sent a note to General Halleck refusing to pay the levy. They protested that it violated the fundamental law of the land which provided that no person should be deprived of his property without due process of law. They pointed out that at a time when Congress was in session, the courts in operation, and civil officers exercising authority, they had been tried "before a secret inquisitorial tribunal," and condemned to pay a forced contribution "for alleged charitable purposes." They added that they realized they were defenseless, and that resistance would be idle, but they could not give to Halleck's levy "even such recognition as might be implied from our voluntary payment of the sums required of us." Their refusal led to what was probably the most famous auction in the history of St. Louis.

Samuel Engler, a prominent candlestick merchant in St. Louis, had been assessed $300. He did not pay and on January 21, several policemen drew up in front of his store with a furniture wagon. They removed eighty boxes of candles, over his protests. Mr. Engler immediately sued out a writ of replevin to recover his property. The clerk of the court issued the writ authorizing the sheriff to demand return of the property; if it were not returned the sheriff was authorized to seize the property by "summoning a posse of citizens to assist him, if necessary." The clerk also commanded the sheriff to summon General Halleck to appear before the Court of Common Pleas to answer the complaint of Engler.

The sheriff of the County of St. Louis found himself in an unenviable position, but he set out unflinchingly to perform his duty. First he visited the office of the Provost Marshal and handed him a copy of the summons, demanding the surrender of Engler's candles. The Provost Marshal politely refused to do so, and the sheriff announced that it became his duty to take the property in question by force. He proceeded to the government storeroom where the candles were being held and demanded admittance. A squad of United States soldiers was guarding the storeroom and the officer in charge inquired by what authority the demand was made. "By the authority of the Court of Common Pleas," responded the sheriff with all the dignity he could muster. The federal officers refused to admit him, and the sheriff replied that he should then be under the disagreeable necessity of forcing an entrance. He summoned six or eight bystanders to act as his posse in liberating the candles but the posse found it could not advance against the bayonets and loaded muskets in the hands of the troops.

At this point, the sheriff concluded that he had done his duty and retired. The next move was up to General Halleck and it was not long in coming. First, he ordered that Engler be arrested. Next, Engler's lawyer and the man who had given security on the replevin bond were also arrested. All three of them were sent to the prison at Fifth and Myrtle and later in the day, Halleck issued a special order directing the exile of Engler from the state. Engler, he said, had resisted the federal authority by seeking to recover his candles, and was not to return to St. Louis without the permission of the commanding general. For good measure, Halleck added that the "Provost Marshal General will arrest each and every person, of whatever rank or office, who attempts in any way to prevent or interfere with the execution of any Order issued from these Headquarters."

Two days later, Engler was taken on the train to Cincinnati and left there. He was told he could go anywhere in the world except the Department of the Missouri and the Confederacy. The other two men who had been arrested with him were released after two days in prison.

Halleck's positive action in the Engler case ended the legal attacks on the levy. But there were still many prominent citizens who refused to pay their assessment. One of these was Dr. William McPheeters, a leading physician in St. Louis. McPheeters had been born in North Carolina, the son of one of the leading Presbyterian clergymen of the day, and he had studied at the University of North Carolina. He came to St. Louis, where he helped found the first public dispensary west of the Mississippi and became a medical professor at St. Louis University. He was a former president of the Missouri Medical Association, editor of the *St. Louis Medical and Surgical Journal*, a ruling elder of the Pine Street Presbyterian Church and president of the St. Louis Branch of the Western Society for the Suppression of Vice.

All in all, Dr. McPheeters was an outstanding man and physician. He had, however, one flaw, in the eyes of General Halleck. He was part of the Southern-minded aristocracy of St. Louis and he was opposed to the war. An assessment of $300 was levied on him and he not only refused to pay it, but also sold his more easily negotiable property, including his horses. But this did not stop Halleck's men. They visited his home in January and took a buggy, a set of harnesses, two damask-covered rosewood sofas, six rosewood chairs, one center table, with Egyptian marble top, and a rosewood piano. As it turned out, these goods did not bring enough in the auction to cover the amount McPheeters owed, so a few days later another furniture wagon visited his house and carted away a cooking stove, a sheet iron stove, a black walnut bureau, a black walnut bedstead, two mattresses, a lithograph picture, a bust of the Reverend Mr. Potts, D.D., an office table, a sofa, an easy chair, and a hat rack. These items were sold at the second auction. When it was over Dr. McPheeters' home didn't have much left in the way of furniture. McPheeters was so outraged that he left St. Louis and joined Price's army as medical director. He continued to serve as a surgeon in the Confederate Army during the entire war and after it was over he returned to St. Louis and resumed the practice of medicine.

Trusten Polk was a United States Senator from Missouri who went south when the war began and was expelled from the Senate. An assessment of $500 was levied against his goods and when his wife refused to pay, the police visited his home with the furniture wagons. They took one oak hat rack, two oak chairs, two sofas, one center table, four sofa-bottomed chairs, two easy chairs, one carriage, one "what-not," one hair-bottomed sofa, two cane-seat chairs, two hotel chairs, four hair-bottomed chairs, one imitation rosewood meddler, one piano and two parlor carpets. There were very few places left to sit in the house.

Another person who felt the humiliation of the levy was Rebecca Sire, one of the dominant, socially minded women in the Southern elite of St. Louis. Her husband had been a leading fur trader in the city and she was also related to the prominent Chouteau family, after whom one of the main avenues of St. Louis was named. When she refused to pay her assessment of $100, the police visited her home and made off with a piano, a mahogany sofa and a rosewood "what-not." At the auction, the piano sold for enough to satisfy the assessment and all penalties and the remainder of the furniture were returned to her.

Another secessionist was John Kennard, who with his son ran one of the largest carpet businesses west of New York City. The elder Kennard had emigrated to St. Louis from Maryland and although his business prospered, it was said that he made it his goal never to be worth more than $50,000. He gave away any money in excess of this, but his charity did not extend to the Union refugees streaming into St. Louis. A levy of $300 each was made against the two Kennards. When they refused to pay, they were visited by the police and some $800 worth of carpets was seized from their store.

William Clark, another of the men picked for the levy, was a prominent lumber merchant, with his own steam sawmill on the banks of the Mississippi River, and in addition, he was a bank director and a ruling elder in the Pine Street Presbyterian Church, which numbered many of the Southern elite among its members. Clark was assessed $400 and when he failed to pay, the 25 per cent penalty raised the figure to

$500. Late in January, the van appeared at his doorstep and relieved him of a portion of his possessions. This was auctioned but did not satisfy his account so the police made off with more of his furniture. Mr. Clark was quite outspoken on the subject and as a result was arrested and sent to prison. He spent two weeks there before he was allowed to return to his furnitureless home.

Many other well-known men had their goods seized. The president of one of the major banks in the city, and the judge of the probate court were both subjected to seizure of goods. General Frost, who had surrendered Camp Jackson and had now gone south, was given a large assessment and his home raided for enough furniture to satisfy it. The owner of one of the largest manufacturing plants in the West had some of his furniture seized. A former police commissioner was also included in the round-up.

Finally, the day that most of St. Louis had been waiting for arrived. On February 3, 1862, probably the liveliest and most exciting auction ever held in Missouri took place as the best furniture of the wealthiest people in the city was auctioned off like that of ordinary tax-delinquents. The auction was scheduled to begin at 1 P.M., but by 9 o'clock in the morning the rooms were filled. The bidding proved to be lively, although articles sold for much less than their true value. The auction lasted all afternoon and another was held the following week. The second sale didn't draw quite the crowd that the first one did, but the goods went well and the federal authorities were satisfied. Later in the month, a third auction was held and by the time it was over, the magic goal of $10,000 had been reached. General Halleck, after two months of strenuous effort, had finally succeeded. He breathed a sigh of relief, and immediately ordered that "no further assessment will be levied or collected from any one who will now take the prescribed oath of allegiance." He had had his fill of secesh levies.

But his idea lived after him. Like Frémont's military commission, Halleck's secesh levy was copied throughout the states of the North and was used increasingly in St. Louis after Halleck left for Washington. Under General Curtis, the field commander whose brilliant victory over the Confederate forces eventually earned him Halleck's job, the relatively restrained levy turned into outright exile and confiscation of all the property of Southern sympathizers. But this was to come later. Under Halleck, the secesh levy was a rather successful venture into the unknown. He got the money, humiliated the secessionists, and his reputation came through the ordeal untarnished.

Halleck's drive against disloyalty in St. Louis reached its climax on February 14, 1862, when he ordered that all men who had actively aided the rebellion "by word or deed" were to be arrested. This order was followed by a small flurry of arrests and several businessmen, politicians, and printers who had escaped the earlier dragnets, found themselves in the prison at Fifth and Myrtle for short periods of time. One outspoken man, a steamboat captain, remarked aloud one day that some Confederate prisoners had more friends than they realized as they were being escorted through the city. He added: "It's not safe for a man to speak his mind now-a-days." He was right because one of the federal police overheard him and the steamboat captain spent several weeks in prison.

In general, however, even Halleck's proclamation did not have much effect on arrests and the prison at Fifth and Myrtle had about as many political inmates before it as after. For the only real determining factors were the fears in the minds of the men who were out making the arrests. When there was real fear, as occurred after the Battle of Wilson's Creek, the arrests increased. As the fears subsided, the arrests subsided with them.

The most important business that concerned Halleck during this entire period, of course, was the attack on the Confederate forces in Missouri. In this matter, Halleck's judgment was further vindicated. He selected General Curtis to lead the

Union forces and at the Battle of Pea Ridge, in northern Arkansas, Curtis won a resounding victory. Fought in early March, 1862, this battle reaffirmed the Union hold on Missouri and secured the western end of the Northern line. Though bushwhacking, raiding, and occasional armed invasions of the state occurred throughout the war, Missouri was never again seriously threatened by the Confederate forces. However, the political fighting between radical and conservative Union elements continued to plague the state. The lines that had solidified during Frémont's one hundred days were destined to remain firm and cause untold difficulties.

But the main arena in the struggle between North and South could not be Missouri. It was too far west. Geography dictated that the main arena would be Kentucky. So it was in Kentucky that the political stakes were the highest and the waiting policy of President Lincoln was given its most severe test.

CHAPTER 23

KENTUCKY JOINS THE NORTH

K ENTUCKY, the center of the old Union and the key to the new one, was slowly making up its mind during the summer of 1861. When the news of Bull Run reached Louisville, it touched off a typical border state reaction. Secessionists crowded in front of the office of the Louisville *Courier*, and cheered when news of the Confederate victory was posted. As one man put it, "they cracked their parched and shriveled throats with frantic cries, and then went off to moisten them with whiskey." The glorious news was sent off into the surrounding countryside by a horseman carrying a little secession flag. Then the secessionists began to demonstrate all over the city. During this celebration some tempers were aroused and a member of the Union police force shot and killed one of the demonstrators. The coroner, a Southern man, said he was shot without sufficient cause, but the Union judge who heard the case said the killing was justified and the policeman was freed.

After Bull Run, the pace began to quicken in Kentucky. Simon Buckner, commander of the Kentucky militia, resigned his office and went to Tennessee to join his fortunes with those of the Confederacy. The Knights of the Golden Circle, a secessionist organization, began swearing in members at a fast rate. But most important of all, the Union men in the state decided the time had come to set up a Union camp. They waited, however, until after the regular election of the new state legislature on August 5. The secessionists had already lost one important contest, when the Congressional election in June resulted in a Union victory. But they hoped that with the war actually being fought they would now do better. The issue in the August election was whether Kentucky would go North or South.

When the votes were counted, the Union men had won another overwhelming victory. One hundred and three Unionists were elected to the state legislature against 38 of the opposition. This was a crushing defeat for the secessionists and for the Confederacy. Kentucky, with its strategic position, and its 1,150,000 people, would be a crucial factor thrown into the balance against the South.

But this vote did not mean that the struggle for the state was over. The Union men knew they must be prepared for war. So they went ahead with their plans to establish a camp on the farm of Dick Robinson. This farm was located in Garrard County, in the central part of the state where Union sentiment was strong. The Lincoln guns that had been shipped into this region in May had paid handsome dividends. The main turnpike from Lexington turned southeast for the Cumberland Gap at Dick Robinson's farm and the camp was well situated to receive refugees from East Tennessee as well as to oppose any invasion.

The day after the August election, the camp was established and men began pouring into it. Most of them were without arms so more Lincoln guns had to be shipped in. The Union authorities put some on a train at Covington and started them on their way to Lexington. But the trip lay through some rabid secessionist country, including the town of Cynthiana, from which one company had already mustered into the Confederate Army. As the railroad train with the guns drew near Cynthiana, the conductor saw a large crowd at the station, so he ordered the train into reverse and took the guns back to Covington. The guns were then shipped by boat to Louisville, where they arrived at the wharf at 2 o'clock in the morning of August 20. Union men hurriedly put them into wagons and transported them across the city to the railroad station. And from there they were shipped through Union country to Lexington.

Word of the anticipated arrival of the guns at Lexington reached both the Union and the secessionist elements of the town at about the same time. There were two companies of troops organized in the city. The captain of the Union men was Dr. Ethelbert Dudley, the leading physician of the city. The Southern element was under Captain John H. Morgan, who later became a Confederate general and conducted some of the most famous cavalry raids of the war. Dr. Dudley knew that Morgan might try to intercept the guns so he sent word to Camp Dick Robinson for reinforcements.

Just before daybreak the guns arrived in Lexington and the situation became very tense. Morgan's signal to his men to gather for an attack was to be a bugle blown from the roof of the company's armory. Dr. Dudley's signal to rally his company to defend the guns was to be the ringing of the courthouse bell. Suddenly, everything happened at once. The bugle sounded, the bell rang, and at the same moment 200 cavalry rode into town from Camp Dick Robinson. The first battle of the war in Kentucky was about to start on this rainy August morning. But somehow bloodshed was avoided. With the reinforcements from Camp Dick Robinson, the Union men greatly outnumbered the secessionists. Senator Breckinridge was in Lexington this day and he prevailed on Morgan to hold off, so the attack was not carried out. The guns were loaded into wagons and started on their slow trip to Camp Dick Robinson under heavy escort. There were no further incidents. By this time many battles had been fought in Maryland, tidewater Virginia, western Virginia, and Missouri. Kentucky was literally surrounded with Union and Confederate camps just across its northern and southern borders. Yet, within the state peace was still being preserved.

Kentucky, of course, was the great loophole in the North's blockade of the South. It was entirely devoid of either United States or Confederate troops, and there were no real restrictions on trade with Tennessee. Goods in enormous quantities were consigned to Bowling Green or some other point near the Tennessee border and then shipped across to Nashville. Many a Louisville merchant was growing rich on this trade. Even in its most prosperous days, the city had never seen such trade. Bacon, coffee, pork, beef — everything possible and impossible, from a lady's glove to terra cotta was being sent south.

The city was a beehive of activity. Several of the main streets were completely blocked with goods which overflowed the depot and the wharves. As one man described it, "Drays, black drivers with long whips, singing amidst the tumult, and laughing at the universal fun, and white drivers, swearing and pushing forward, were being formed." Off the wagons went to Nashville and God help any man who tried to stop them. The blockade had officially been declared by the North and the United States Marshal made minor attempts to stop the trade, but all in vain. As was pointed out, he "might as well station himself at the foot of the rapids opposite our city, and strive with a lady's fan to sweep back the descending waters of the majestic Ohio." Whenever Union men talked of banding together to stop the traffic, the local Knights of the Golden Circle would call out its members to protect it. Most of the Northern papers got their news of the Confederacy by way of Louisville. With peace at hand, with trade booming, with prosperity on the land, Kentucky seemed to have the best of all worlds as August drew to a close. Yet, it was in September that events began to move the state into the vortex of the war. Within a few short weeks neighbor would be pitted in mortal combat against neighbor and before the war was over Kentucky would be dragged into an abyss which would be compared with the condition of Germany after the Thirty Years War.

The immediate reason why war came to Kentucky was the August election. The legislature which had been sitting at Frankfort in early 1861 had been fairly evenly split between Northern and Southern elements. Most of the men holding office in Kentucky, as well as the other border states, had been elected on issues almost entirely unrelated to secession; even after ten years of argument and dispute the issue of slavery and secession had descended upon the American people with awful suddenness in 1860. The fact that such a large proportion of elected officials in the border states were Southern-minded reflected mainly the Southern orientation of the aristocracy. But when the August election resulted in an overwhelming victory for the Union and when Camp Dick Robinson set up, the rebels knew that the state would have to be won by force.

On September 2, the new Union legislature met in Frankfort, with a 3 to 1 majority, enough to override any veto that the southern-inclined governor, Beriah Magoffin, might make. Magoffin's message to the legislature ignored this fact, however, and recounted the wrongs that the federal government had committed in Kentucky. He pointed out that the formation of Camp Dick Robinson had been carried out without any consultation with the state authorities. Furthermore, he felt that the "continued introduction of Federal guns into the State . . . unwarranted by law, is another source of constant irritation," which the legislature would do well to correct. He said that the real object of the President was "the prosecution of an unconstitutional war of coercion against the South. . . . I protest against all and every one of the President's usurpations and unconstitutional and illegal acts."

But this was mere window dressing. Kentucky had been lost to the South and plans were already in motion in the Confederacy for a three-pronged attack on the state. War came on September 3, 1861, when General Leonidas Polk (Bishop Polk, as he was frequently called — he had left the Army some years before, entered the ministry and become bishop of Louisiana) moved into the western tip of Kentucky and occupied the two towns of Hickman and Columbus. General Grant, from his position at Cairo, Illinois, immediately requested permission from General Frémont to occupy Paducah, Kentucky but before he received a reply, he decided the situation was too critical to wait, and made the move on his own responsibility. He was reported to have said that he would "take Paducah, and save Kentucky, if it costs me my commission." He then issued a proclamation saying that the enemy had "planted its guns upon the soil of Kentucky and fired upon our flag." Polk did not advance further and for a time this front remained quiet.

A few days after Polk's invasion, the Confederate General Felix Zollicoffer came through the mountains from the Cumberland Gap and occupied some Kentucky territory in the southeastern part of the state. Camp Dick Robinson had been established to counter this threat and some troops moved out immediately toward Zollicoffer. But here, also, except for a few minor skirmishes there was little fighting at this time.

And then, suddenly, on September 17, Louisville found itself threatened. General Simon Buckner had organized his troops into camps just across the Tennessee border and had prepared for an invasion of the rich Green River valley in the southern part of Kentucky. Buckner advanced to Bowling Green and sent scouting parties on ahead to Elizabethtown. One party came within thirty-three miles of Louisville and burned a bridge over the Rolling Fork of the Salt River.

As Buckner moved toward Louisville, that city went through the same panic that Washington had experienced after Bull Run and St. Louis after Wilson's Creek. The first indication of Buckner's advance came when the through train from the Tennessee border failed to arrive in Louisville on the afternoon of September 18. At first it was thought that perhaps there had been an accident, but by 8 o'clock that night it was apparent that something was up. The telegraph lines had been cut and all communication with southern Kentucky was ended. Word of the advance of scouting parties to Elizabethtown was magnified into rumors of an attack by 7,000 troops directly on Louisville. It was said that they had occupied Muldraugh's Hill, only twenty-eight miles south of the city and the next day they would enter it.

General Robert Anderson, of Fort Sumter, was in command in Louisville. His situation was critical if indeed Buckner did plan an all-out attack on the city. For he had almost no troops. Definite word of the attack arrived at 8 P.M.; by 9 o'clock the captains of all the companies in Louisville had been called together and General Anderson asked how long it would take to call up the militia. He was told that it could be done in two hours and the call went out immediately. By 11 P.M., some 1,800 troops had been organized and rail transportation was being arranged southward. The troops were without uniforms and almost without training, but they climbed into trains immediately and headed for Muldraugh's Hill under the command of General William T. Sherman. At the same time a request for reinforcement was sent across the river to General Lovell Rousseau at Camp Jo Holt. Rousseau acted quickly and by 1 A.M. his troops had arrived in Louisville. They were ordered south to join Sherman the next day.

Sherman, meanwhile, had arrived at the Rolling Fork of the Salt River and found the bridge burned. He concluded that Buckner was not planning any advance, so he forded the river and occupied Muldraugh's Hill himself. This hill was one of a chain that neatly divided the Louisville area from the Green River area further south. It was a natural defensive position and was considered vital to the defense of the city.

For several days after Buckner's advance, Louisville was a bundle of nerves. Stores were closed at 4 P.M. every afternoon so that the men could drill. General Anderson issued a proclamation designed to reassure the city, "Let us trust in God and do our duty, as did our fathers." Soon Indiana, Ohio, and Illinois troops were pouring through on their way to the front lines.

While the invasion of Kentucky was going on, the new Union legislature formally declared war on the Confederacy and joined the North. Resolutions were passed by both houses declaring that Generals Polk and Zollicoffer had invaded Kentucky soil and proclaiming: "The invaders must be expelled." General Anderson, a federal officer, was appointed to take control of the Kentucky militia. These "War Resolutions" passed the legislature by a vote of approximately 3 to 1 and Kentucky was in the war, her neutrality at an end. For over five months, Kentucky alone had remained aloof from the passions of the day. But slowly Abraham Lincoln, who had received fewer votes in Kentucky than he did in Virginia, had won the state that had to be won. And by the end of September, Kentuckians were mourning sorrowfully, "The war is in our state."

CHAPTER 24

COERCION IN KENTUCKY

POLITICALLY, Kentucky's declaration of war on September 18 was one of the most important events of the entire war. The long struggle that led up to it, the slow erosion of the position of the Southern elite in the state, the cautious policy of the Lincoln Administration, all occurred without any really dramatic incidents. Yet, they were conclusive. When the war in Kentucky actually began in September, there was a rush of volunteers to both the Union and Confederate forces. But far more joined the Union Army and the state as a whole was firmly anchored to the North. A base existed now for preserving the Union and launching an invasion of the Confederacy. During the next three years, the military professionals operating from Kentucky would destroy much of the South.

While Louisville was in a state of near panic at the approach of General Buckner, the most celebrated Kentucky arrest of the entire war occurred, that of ex-Governor Charles S. Morehead. Morehead was a man of commanding appearance, courtly manners, and was a very impressive stump speaker. He had been elected governor of Kentucky on the Know-Nothing ticket, served out his term and was later elected to Congress. In the 1860 election, he had been for Bell and Everett who carried Kentucky under the slogan "The Union, the Constitution, and the Enforcement of the Laws," in a contest in which Lincoln had been ignored. Morehead had even traveled through Louisiana and Mississippi during the 1860 campaign to make Union speeches.

As the spring of 1861 arrived, Morehead was elected to the Border State Convention as a Union delegate. But he was a wealthy landowner who had an estate in Mississippi reputed to be worth $400,000, worked by 180 Negro slaves. Morehead's economic interest lay in a peaceable separation, if separation must come, and by June he was saying that if the country were ever to be reunited, there was no better way to bring it about "than a prompt recognition" of the Confederacy. He made a trip to Mississippi during the summer and returned even more convinced that the South must be allowed to go in peace. Furthermore, he made several speeches attacking the suspension of the writ of habeas corpus by the federal government. He was fair game to anyone who felt some arrests should be made.

On the day after General Buckner's advance, the young Governor Oliver P. Morton of Indiana, a Republican firebrand who took special interest in affairs of Kentucky, was in Louisville. He conferred with the United States Marshal for Kentucky, A. H. Sneed, and Sneed started a move that was to have repercussions all over the state. He went before the local justice of the peace in Louisville and, in a very unusual procedure, stated that he had proof of Morehead's aiding and abetting the enemies of the United States. The justice made out a warrant for Morehead's arrest for treason, and directed Sneed to arrest him and "take him to the court having jurisdiction of the offense." That night, shortly after midnight, Marshal Sneed appeared with a posse before Morehead's home, knocked on the door and announced that he was under arrest. Morehead was escorted from his house and taken across the Ohio River to Jeffersonville, Indiana, where he was held until the next day.

A writ of habeas corpus was immediately sued for Morehead before Judge Catron, an associate judge of the United States Supreme Court, who was sitting as a circuit judge in Louisville. It was his court, of course, that had jurisdiction of the offense. As soon as Sneed heard about the writ, he frantically sent a telegram to President Lincoln asking "What action shall I take. Four thousand rebels are within 75 miles of here advancing on this place. . . . The effect of these arrests has been beneficial and it would be disastrous to have them released." The reply was received from Simon Cameron, "Send Governor Morehead, of Kentucky, immediately to Ft. Lafayette." Morehead was soon on his way east.

Along with Morehead, Marshal Sneed arrested two other men. One was a secessionist named Reuben Durrett who wrote for the Louisville *Courier*, a newspaper violently opposed to the war. In one article, Durrett had said that Kentucky was on the verge of civil war and the only way to avert this calamity was "by separating from the Northern Union. . . . We therefore deliberately pronounce the assumption of any authority over Kentucky by the Lincoln Government . . . as a usurpation and revolutionary and which no citizen of Kentucky is bound to obey."

For voicing such opinions, Durrett was visited the same night as ex-Governor Morehead, with a similar warrant from the local justice of the peace, and taken on the long trip to Fort Lafayette. Durrett later claimed that Marshal Sneed "took me from my residence in summer clothes and without a cent of money and in this condition I was conveyed to New York . . . without clothes warm enough to protect me against the cold days and nights which came upon us. My suffering was intense." After arresting Durrett, the marshal visited the office of the Louisville *Courier* and suppressed the paper.

Also arrested that same night was a telegraph operator who had been sending Southern-oriented articles to newspapers in New Orleans. His name was M. R. Barr and he was swept along with the other two more important men to the great prisons in the East.

The next morning the city of Louisville was dumbstruck. One of its leading newspapers had been suppressed and three of its citizens had been arrested and spirited out of the city. Kentuckians had believed that they were somehow above such shenanigans, which they had read about so long in Maryland, Missouri and the free states of the North. But now they found that they, too, were losing their citizens and their newspapers in the excitement of war.

The entire country was a witness to the strange journey of these three men from far-off Kentucky to Fort Lafayette. Their progress was reported daily and the story of the habeas corpus which was vainly pursuing them was recounted. Ex-Governor Morehead soon became one of the most well-known prisoners in the fort and as he was the first man arrested in Kentucky, his position was unique.

The arrests shook Kentucky from end to end and set off a loud clamor over the fate of the men. Foremost of those who came to Morehead's defense was the editor of the Louisville *Journal*, George D. Prentice, the man whom one secessionist newspaper called the real governor of Kentucky. His Union newspaper circulated widely throughout the state and wielded great influence. Five days after the triple arrest in Louisville, he wrote a letter to President Lincoln recommending that Morehead be released. He said that Morehead "has been one of the dearest of my personal friends for nearly thirty years. I do not believe his arrest was necessary or expedient."

Once again Abraham Lincoln emerges from the background briefly and we see him clearly in his role of arbiter, the man above the battle, who did no more than make suggestions to his subordinates. He forwarded the letter to Seward with the comment that Morehead was "sent to Ft. Lafayette by the military authorities of Kentucky and it would be improper for me to intervene without further knowledge of the facts than I now possess." This comment was dutifully forwarded to Prentice by Seward and no further action taken. Unfortunately for Morehead, the letter reached the White House in late September, 1861, when the fears caused by the phantom invasion of the North were at their height. Arrests were occurring daily throughout the North and the Maryland legislature had just been seized. It is small wonder that the Prentice letter should have received so little attention.

Some time later, Morehead's son-in-law came to Washington to see Lincoln and plead for the former governor's release. Lincoln requested Seward to see the man, and added: "I understand the Kentucky arrests were not made by special direction from here, and I am willing if you are that any of the parties may be released when James Guthrie and James Speed think they should be." Morehead might have been released quickly had there not been other participants in the struggle over his fate. One particularly important one was the bitter Leslie Coombs, who wrote that Morehead was the most "dangerous of all our Kentucky traitors. A traitor to his country, his native State, his party and his confiding friends." Lincoln simply sent the letter to Seward without comment. While the battle was raging, Morehead, with all the dignity he possessed, refused to become a supplicant for Republican clemency himself. He wrote no letters, made no complaints, and suffered his fate with dignity and reserve.

For three months Morehead remained in prison, until the venerable Kentucky citizen, John J. Crittenden, entered the lists on his behalf. Crittenden pointed out to Seward that Morehead could not sign an oath without losing his estate in Mississippi. Then he raised a question that rarely failed to get action out of Seward. He said that further imprisonment would be "peculiarly calamitous" since Morehead required a delicate surgical operation. Seward had no desire to watch a former governor of Kentucky die as a political prisoner and immediately ordered his release.

The same battle arose over the fate of Reuben Durrett, the secessionist writer who was arrested with Morehead. One man claimed that his release would "be a fatal mistake." Others suggested that he be released immediately, mainly on the ground that his wife was on the edge of delirium over him. Many of these letters were written to Lincoln who forwarded them to Seward without comment. But no action was taken. Then, two months after his arrest, Reuben Durrett wrote a letter directly to Seward from his prison cell. In this letter he displayed the virtuosity of writing which had made him a power in the Louisville press. The letter alternated between well-documented outrage, concern over the health of his wife, penitence, and slim hope. It was a masterpiece. The most poignant paragraphs dealt with the desperate condition of his wife:

> I myself can bear all that has been imposed upon me without writing you a letter of complaint, but I cannot bear the sufferings which these wrongs to me inflict upon my wife and children who are dearer to me than I am to myself. It is for them and not for myself that this appeal is made. . . .
>
> I am now I fear a bankrupt, and my wife and children are thrown upon the charity of friends. But worst of all the peculiar disposition of my wife renders her incapable of bearing these troubles. I am advised that she is breaking down with her load of grief and is now prostrate upon a sick bed. To add an overflowing drop to my cup of bitterness it has been published in the papers at home that my wife has lost her mind, but I have been assured this is not true. I was informed by last night's mail, however, that she is very ill and threatened with brain fever. . . .

This story impressed even the cold-hearted Seward. As soon as he read the letter, he ordered Durrett's release.

The third man arrested, Martin W. Barr, worked in Louisville for the New Orleans newspapers. He naturally selected stories to send to his readers which would interest them, and these were mostly rumors and articles with a Southern slant. After Barr was sent to Fort Lafayette, Marshal Sneed claimed that he had been arrested because he had written treasonable letters giving advice and counsel to the governor of Tennessee. To all who sought to find what evidence he had, Sneed merely said that the United States court in Frankfort would be looking into the case on the 21st of October and it would be given the evidence which, he said, "was overwhelming."

But when the court met after Barr had been in prison for over a month, not a witness stepped forward to accuse him or present any evidence. And so Barr was left to his own devices and those of his friends, in order to get out of prison. George Prentice requested Barr's release and several others from Kentucky joined him. Finally, Seward relented and ordered the release if Barr would take the oath, but he refused. He said he wished to go south and would, if necessary, arrange for the exchange of a Union telegrapher from the South. In the meantime, his friends in New Orleans wrote to the Confederate Secretary of War requesting that he use his influence to obtain the release of Barr on the grounds that "his usefulness to the press of the Confederate States as a telegraphic operator cannot be exaggerated." Barr was finally released on parole in March, 1862, after spending six months in prison.

Some time later, President Lincoln was requested by the United States Senate in a formal resolution, to transmit all the information available in regard to the arrest of Morehead, Durrett and Barr. Lincoln replied that it was "not deemed compatible with the public interest at this juncture to furnish the information desired." In fact the information was never provided.

These three arrests were the first of hundreds in Kentucky. The state was thrown into turmoil by the triple-pronged invasion from Tennessee and the threat to Louisville. Secessionists in small groups began drifting south to join the Confederacy, many of them convinced that they would share the fate of Morehead if they remained in Kentucky. Any man who was away from his home was suspect, and if he was headed in a southerly direction, he was considered a traitor. Orders were sent out to the Home Guard units in the towns and villages to stop these men.

One of the first such men arrested was James B. Clay, the

son of Henry Clay, and master of the Clay estate, Ashland, just outside Lexington. Clay was arrested forty miles from his home on the road to Zollicoffer's army, which was invading the state from eastern Tennessee. The circumstances were highly suspicious. The first word of his arrest came from a major in the volunteers, who reported with an air of surprise: "Just now the boys brought in James B. Clay."

Clay was taken to Louisville and a writ of habeas corpus was issued by Judge Catron, who had just missed catching Morehead. But this writ was more successful. It was issued against General Anderson, who sat down and talked the whole problem over with Judge Catron and James Guthrie, a leading lawyer in Louisville who had been Secretary of the Treasury under President Pierce. They recommended that Anderson turn Clay over to the judge in accordance with the writ. General Anderson wrote to President Lincoln that he would "not resist in thinking that this course and his being placed under heavy bail for conspiracy if not for treason will produce a good effect." But Lincoln and Seward were not disposed to be so lenient. Seward replied the same day that by direction of the President, Anderson was to disregard the writ and send the prisoners to Fort Lafayette unless James Guthrie or James Speed felt that they should be released. Anderson made a quick reply that he had already consulted Guthrie and that the course of action he recommended had been approved. Clay was brought up before Judge Catron, released on $10,000 bail and bound over to be tried before the court in January on the charge of conspiracy and treason. The case never came to trial.

One man who had been arrested with Clay, named William Grubbs, was spirited out of Louisville before dawn of the day he was supposed to have been brought before Judge Catron. Across the river in Jeffersonville, he was put on a train and sent to Fort Lafayette. Grubbs was a very unimportant man and no high officials wrote any letters on his behalf, but he sat down and wrote Seward that he would be willing to take the oath. Seward checked on him with several Kentuckians and got differing opinions as to whether Grubbs should be released. The general consensus was that the prisoner was "worthless" and had "little intelligence" so he was released after two months in prison. Grubbs was so poor he was hardly able to get back to Kentucky.

Several other men who were arrested near Camp Dick Robinson were sent to Louisville and ordered to be brought before Judge Catron on a writ of habeas corpus. When General Anderson wired President Lincoln, asking what to do with them, Seward replied that they should all be sent to Fort Lafayette. General Anderson, however, who was following a very lenient policy, informed Seward that his telegram had come too late and that he had ordered the men discharged. "Their rearrest (now impracticable as they have left the city) would have a very injurious effect. Many men lately prominent against us are being won to our side by the course we have adopted." Seward did not intervene further in the case.

During this same period a number of other Kentucky prisoners were sent to Fort Lafayette. Many of them were very poor men trying to get to Tennessee to join the Confederate Army. One man got drunk one night and agreed with some friends to go south. He woke up the next morning, thought better of it, and returned home, only to be arrested. Seth Hawley, who was appointed by Seward as a commissioner to look into the cases of the prisoners and recommend what to do with them, thought most of the Kentucky prisoners were not worth holding. After talking with them and looking into their cases, he pointed out to Seward that they were mostly impoverished farmhands and unskilled workers. He referred to each of them in turn with such phrases as "has little intelligence," "very common man," "no intelligence," and "very stupid." He summed it all up by saying, "I think we can fill all our forts with much better men who are much more dangerous than they," and his recommendation that most of them be released was accepted.

After Kentucky joined the war, General William Nelson

had been transferred to the eastern part of the state to set up a camp on the banks of the Ohio River in order to operate against the Confederate armies which were gathering in the area. In early October, he got word that there was a nest of secessionists in the town of Maysville, led by a former Congressman, Richard Stanton, who was collecting money to outfit and drill men for the Southern army. Nelson, who had a temper like a tornado, arrested Stanton and six other men in the town and sent a letter to Washington saying that Stanton was too dangerous to keep in a jail near his home. Seward ordered the whole group to Fort Lafayette where they were sent just ahead of some habeas corpus writs.

Stanton spent nearly three months in prison writing letters trying to find out what he had been arrested for. He admitted that he had opposed the introduction of the Lincoln guns into Kentucky and that he had been "in favor of Kentucky maintaining a neutral position in the contest," but he said that when he and his friends were arrested "we were engaged in our usual and ordinary occupations." He added that they had never contributed money or advised men to go south. Those who wrote letters on his behalf included General Sherman, James Speed, the local Congressman, and most of the Kentucky legislature. Stanton was finally released the day after Christmas.

The other six men arrested with him were merchants from Maysville, including the editor of the Maysville paper, a local plow manufacturer, and two liquor dealers. They all suffered the same fate as Stanton. After the storm this case kicked up, General Sherman issued an order that the removal of prisoners from Kentucky without giving them an opportunity for trial "does not meet with the approval of the commanding general." In the future all such cases were to be taken immediately before a judge or United States commissioner "to be examined and dealt with according to law." However, there is no evidence that this order had any effect on events.

Once the mania for accusing people of treason had gotten going in Kentucky, it spread quickly. The chief of police in Louisville received twenty to thirty anonymous letters every day which contained accusations of treasonable activity against people in that city. He issued a statement that the writers "might as well save their time, trouble, ink, envelopes and postage stamps, because he does not and will not pay any attention to anonymous communications of any kind."

Among the more important men arrested were three members of the state legislature from the secessionist western part of Kentucky. While the legislature was in session, they left Frankfort and started traveling due south. They got about thirty miles when their conduct aroused some suspicions in Harrodsburg, where they were offering very large amounts of money for a wagon. The Home Guard arrested them and threw them in the local jail. As soon as the legislature heard about the incident, a delegation was sent to Harrodsburg and managed to get them released. Later, the incident became a *cause célèbre*, as the Kentucky legislature debated whether to condemn the secessionists for heading south or the Home Guard for arresting them. In the end no resolution was passed. But the Louisville *Democrat* said it would not want to "go security" that they had not already joined the Confederate Army.

In the scramble that took place in September, many important men in Kentucky did go south. But nothing quite shook the state as much as the defection of John C. Breckinridge. Breckinridge was a brilliant man, born with a silver spoon in his mouth, with every advantage of birth and training to aid him on his way. Before reaching the age of forty, he had been twice elected a member of the House of Representatives, had been a Senator and Vice-President of the United States, and a candidate for the Presidency in 1860. Breckinridge believed in armed neutrality during the spring and summer of 1861, along with the rest of Kentucky. He attended the special session of Congress in Washington that began on July 4, making speeches throughout the country opposing the war, but it was unclear for a long time exactly which way he would jump when the time of decision arrived. After Morehead was arrested, however, Breckinridge feared for his own safety and fled the state. Later he became Secretary of War for the Confederacy. His defection was a political blow of major proportions to the Union.

Newspapers were among the first victims of the war in Kentucky as elsewhere. Many of the local printers could not get enough advertising to pay for the paper, and it was sometimes difficult to tell whether they stopped publishing because of bad business conditions or because of official action. The Henderson *Reporter*, a four-page weekly newspaper published on the banks of the Ohio River was strongly secessionist. It had blazing pro-South editorials all summer long. "The South will never submit," its editor wrote. "One-tenth of the usurpations of President Lincoln would have created revolution in the most despotic government in Europe. . . . While you are sleeping and hugging to your bosoms the dead corpse of the Union, your State sovereignty and individual liberties are being lost. Better ten thousand times ten thousand the Federal Government should sink to rise no more, than your State sovereignty should be lost, and you, as individuals, subjected to the arbitrary and dictatorial behest of King Lincoln."

The Henderson *Reporter* ceased publication with the issue of September 26 as war swept the state into the Union. It remained silent for five months. Then the printer in Henderson once again began issuing his weekly paper, with an entirely different tone. The first page had a four-column story, "The Nurses' Revenge" and a long poem called "True Sympathy," by Kate Boyd. There were no editorials. The paper, it announced, had assumed an attitude of neutrality in the war.

Several other newspapers died quick deaths. The Lexington *Statesman*, which reflected the views of John C. Breckinridge,

ment in Washington. But whenever anyone tried to sell it in the Union areas of the state, he was arrested.

There were some Confederate camps in Union areas of Kentucky during September and October. Humphrey Marshall, a lawyer who had served as Kentucky Congressman and United States Minister to China, was in charge of one camp in Owen County, not far from Frankfort, where, by early October, he had collected several hundred secessionists. General Anderson tried to get them to disband, and agreed to make no arrests if the camp were dissolved, but Marshall replied that he had left his home "only because I was apprehensive of an arrest . . . I was informed the business of arresting gentlemen who belonged to the Southern Rights party had been commenced and that my name was certainly inclosed in a warrant already in an officer's hands." He refused to disband his camp and later led his men south to the Confederate lines.

Arrests were occurring all over the state of Kentucky during this period. Home Guards, local police, the United States marshal, United States troops, and (it seemed) just about everybody else was making arrests and sending men off to jail. Some of the prisoners were sent to Louisville, some to Cincinnati, some to Camp Chase and others ended up in Fort Lafayette. Some were held many months, others only a few days. One day Marshall Sneed took a train to Danville, Kentucky, and arrested a painter, a tanner, a tinker and a grocer's clerk. A county judge in Campbell County was arrested. Ex-Governor Helm was arrested and released in two days. The Kentucky legislature and all the generals involved tried to stop the arrests, issuing proclamations against them, but to no avail. As long as fear was on the land, the arrests continued.

At this time there was very little fighting going on in Kentucky. Grant's and Polk's troops scarcely met in the western part of the state. Buckner in southern Kentucky was not attacked and did not attempt any further advance. In the east there were a few skirmishes with Zollicoffer but nothing important developed. Meanwhile the United States command went through some rapid changes, with General Anderson being relieved by General Sherman in October and Sherman by Don Carlos Buell in November. Sherman had told Cameron that 200,000 men were needed to defend Kentucky and that Kentuckians would not fight for their state. One wag wrote, after he was replaced by Buell, that "this is an economical movement, a General being much cheaper than 200,-000 men."

In November, a special convention of secessionists was held in Russellville, in southern Kentucky, under the shadow of Confederate guns. Delegates from the various counties of the state of Kentucky met in a rump convention and passed resolutions stating that the United States President and Congress "have substituted for national liberty a centralized despotism founded upon the ignorant prejudices of the masses of Northern society. . . . [They] have turned loose . . . the unrestrained and raging passions of mobs and fanatics." The secessionist conference then formally seceded from the Union, declaring "Kentucky to be a free and independent state."

Despite this token action, Kentucky remained with the Union and served as the launching platform from which the South was eventually destroyed. As the year 1861 drew to a close, it seemed to many that the first year of the war had meant only disaster for the Union. Militarily, one defeat had followed another. Bull Run, Wilson's Creek and Lexington had all been lost. But these battles would not affect the outcome of the war. The mainstream lay in the political sympathies of the border states and in this struggle the Union had won. The tides were already running strongly against the Confederacy which could not maintain its position without strength in people, resources, and land. When the Confederacy lost Kentucky, it lost the one chance it might have had to win a long war.

By the end of 1861 the only hope of a Confederate victory

lay in making the war so costly that the Northern will to win would be sapped. The first year of the war had proven decisive. Two great nations, with the same culture, the same language and the same history were now pitted against each other in a life-and-death struggle. The first of the great modern wars had arrived, in which all the resources of both sides would be devoted to victory at any cost, with no mercy from the winner and no surrender from the loser. The industrial revolution had made this type of war possible and the age of the common man had made it inevitable. The war would grind on and on, until the side with the most men and factories would slowly win the victory. Surrender would come only after the weaker nation had died. Victory would be total, and defeat overwhelming.

CHAPTER 25

FORT LAFAYETTE

ALL THE PRISONERS from the border and free states who were sent to Fort Lafayette knew that life there would be very unpleasant. As each was rowed across the water of New York harbor to his new home, he looked out fearfully to see what it was like. Slowly it took form in front of him, rising forbiddingly above the small island on which it was situated. The walls of the fort rose from the water's edge to a height of 60 feet. They formed a hollow enclosure on the island which was in the Narrows, between Long Island and Staten Island. The first view was always disheartening to the prisoner; the fort was old and small, and appeared unfit for human habitation.

The first shock was only the beginning, however. After the prisoner had been herded onto the island, and the proper receipts made out and signed, acknowledging his delivery, he was assigned a casemate with anywhere from ten to forty other men, depending on its size and the number of guns that had to be squeezed in. The prisoner was given an iron bed, a mattress of either moss or straw, two sheets, a blanket and a pillow. This was to be his home, and as one prisoner expressed it, "a gloomier place than Fort LaFayette, both within and without, would be hard to find."

The regular prison food was terrible. Breakfast, according to an inmate, consisted of "some discolored beverage, dignified by the name of coffee, a piece of fat pork, sometimes raw and sometimes half cooked, and coarse bread cut in large thick slices." At noontime the fare was bean soup, although there was some doubt about the number of beans included. One prisoner said that "from actual experiments with unmitigated labor for a space of 3 minutes, assisted by a pair of 'Pike's' dollar spectacles, I have succeeded, after a tedious operation, in fishing up one bean from my pint of soup, and so overcome have I been at the discovery that, with instinctive reverence for the propagator of that bean, I have universally uncovered my head during the process of mastication." Supper was described as consisting of "tea or coffee, in the inevitable greasy tin cups, and slices of bakers' bread." Although the federal officers in charge at the fort claimed that the food was regular soldiers' fare, the prisoners considered it abominable.

Even the water was bad. On some days a glass of water would contain a dozen tadpoles "from one-quarter to one-half inch long without counting the smaller fish." In addition, the guards at the fort were insolent and the commanding officer took no apparent interest in the comfort of his prisoners.

Into these primitive conditions, a substantial number of the elite of Maryland and Kentucky were thrown, together with some of the wealthier citizens of the free states. But these were vigorous and resourceful men and as soon as they got over the initial shock, they started rearranging things more to their liking. Their most pressing problem was to disassociate themselves from some of the lower classes that were being thrown into prison with them. Common traders and impoverished farmers from Kentucky were not appreciated by these leaders of society. The upper classes soon formed themselves into a clique and excluded all others. They managed to get the rooms rearranged so that most of them lived together. Then, taking advantage of one of the customs of the day, they formed an exclusive eating club, which they referred to as their mess, and had their food especially prepared by someone outside the prison and brought to them each day. The fee of $1 per day prevented many of the poorer prisoners from joining, but in addition a special invitation was required to gain membership. Soon the upper classes were having scarcely any contact with the other groups.

How the excluded prisoners reacted to this is not recorded, as none of them wrote of their experiences. There was undoubtedly some resentment, however, as they watched the others enjoy good food while they were forced to rely on lowly prison fare. It was commonly noted in the newspapers that several social classes had developed at the fort. At the top of the pinnacle were men like ex-Governor Morehead of Kentucky, Mayor Brown, Marshal Kane, Frank Key Howard and the police commissioners of Baltimore. Next under them came the sturdy farmers and small-town lawyers who made up most of the Maryland legislature, "respectable men, but not moving in higher circles."

The third class consisted of the traders, men who had been trying to make money supplying arms and munitions to the rebels and had been caught. "These are purely mercenary. . . . Gentlemen do not like to associate with such men on terms of familiarity." At the bottom of the ladder were the impoverished Kentucky farmhands. One prisoner said that all grades of society were represented, "even to the idiot — one of the latter having been sent hither from Kentucky as a 'prisoner of state'!!! instead of being sent to a lunatic asylum."

The prisoners whiled away the time in many ways. All were convinced of the justice of the Southern cause and lively conversations developed among them, each vying with another in the attempt to support the South and condemn Lincoln and Seward. They claimed that Fort Lafayette was the only place in the country where a man could speak freely. They also spent much time writing and receiving letters, although visitors were rarely allowed. They played chess, whist and backgammon. Sometimes they enlivened the evenings by organizing burlesques giving humorous representations of the events of the day. New arrivals were greeted fondly as they sometimes brought news from home. One prisoner wrote: "Another arrival today, Mr. Carter, of Baltimore, an old friend; surprised to see him here." He took Carter around and introduced him to friends to "make him feel as much at home as possible." He also invited Carter to join the mess, for which the Baltimorean was very grateful. Newspapermen visiting the fort were invited one day to "see the Maryland legislature at dinner" and found them eating "bread without butter, and coffee without milk. Each man had a tin cup but no other table service."

How each individual fared under these conditions depended a great deal upon his ability to adjust and the bitterness in his soul. F. Key Howard, the fiery editor of the Baltimore *Exchange,* was one of the most bitter. He was outraged at his arrest and refused to reconcile himself to his imprisonment. As he would not compromise his principles and refused to take the oath, he remained in prison some fourteen months. When he got out, he wrote a book *Fourteen Months in American Bastiles* which was full of bitterness. He described his small quarters with minute accuracy, and recounted every insult and order from the guards. Daily life in Fort Lafayette was depicted as a constant agony, the jailors as modified monsters and the government as an unfeeling persecutor which took delight in abusing its political prisoners. There were many like Howard, for whom the imprisonment was a crusade with no quarter given. For them, it probably was.

But there were others who were not so bitter. One was Lawrence Sangston of Baltimore, who kept a diary while he was in prison and after his release published it under the title *Personal Journal of a Prisoner of State.* Sangston was a rich Baltimore merchant who had been nominated by the Southern Rights Party for a seat in the Maryland legislature during the insurrection in Baltimore. He was elected, attended three sessions of the legislature during the spring and summer and then was arrested in September and sent to Fort Lafayette.

Sangston was one of the upper class, belonged to the mess and generally kept himself vigorous and active. He left a good day-to-day picture of events in the fort. He referred to the privates on duty as "the most villainous looking set of miscreants I ever laid eyes on." The doors were locked every night at dark, he said, and only a few candles were allowed, making it impossible to read. "Played cards in the evening with Governor Morehead and Mr. Barr on the top of the washstand, find it better for that purpose than the gun carriage." On Sunday there was usually a religious service, led by one of the prisoners. Governor Morgan of New York offered to send them a clergyman but they declined. "We did not want any religious advisor of his choosing," Sangston wrote.

The doctor at the fort was of little help to the prisoners. But fortunately, there were always doctors among the prisoners. Dr. McGill of Hagerstown, Maryland, treated the sick prisoners for many months, although he didn't have a very adequate supply of medicines. There was one man that the doctors could not help, however, named James M. Haig. Haig was a young man of thirty-five, with a wife and family, who belonged to the lowly class of "traders" in the fort. He had been arrested through the activities of Lafayette C. Baker, who posed as a Confederate secret agent in Baltimore and asked Haig to buy some $200,000 worth of primers, cartridges and other equipment, for which Baker told Haig he would give him a profit of $50,000. As soon as Haig agreed to the deal, Baker had him arrested. Haig was sent to Fort Lafayette and when his letters to Seward asking to be released went unanswered, he went mad. As another prisoner put it, "during the evening his shrieks could be heard all over the Fort; he was put in double irons and gagged." The guards put Haig in isolation and wouldn't let anyone see him, in the belief that he was faking. The next morning the prisoners were aroused once again "about daylight by the shrieks of Haig, who is now raving mad; could discover by the suppressed stifle, that the guards were again gagging him." Finally, the authorities requested that he be removed from Fort Lafayette, "as he is a perfect maniac." After spending about a month in prison, Haig was released in the custody of his friends in Baltimore. This, however, did not satisfy one of his enemies in the city who wrote to Seward that he had read that Haig had been released because of insanity. Haig, he said, was "a consummate rascal . . . and a scheming artful villain, and I have no doubt whatever that his insanity is altogether feigned. Take care now that he don't cheat you." Haig was not returned to Fort Lafayette but he spent several months in the insane asylum at Mount Hope, Baltimore and eventually recovered to return to his family.

Another prisoner who caused some excitement was Daniel Lowber of New Orleans, who had been arrested on his return from England in August and sent to Fort Lafayette. After spending two months in the dreary prison, he conceived a plan for escape. Somehow he contrived to get hold of a wash-tub and a life preserver. At 2 A.M. on the stormy morning of October 27, he opened the shutters to his casemate with a key that he had had made and began lowering his equipment to the ground on the outside of the fortress wall. First came the bathtub, then the life preserver, and then Mr. Lowber himself came down the rope. A guard happened to hear the noise of the tub being lowered against the wall of the fort, waited patiently while Lowber lowered himself to the ground and then seized him. Lowber was put back into his cell and finally released three months later, on his parole to go to England and remain there during the war.

One story went the rounds concerning a prisoner who was brought in and introduced to his companions as Mr. Bacon of Delaware. One of the prisoners took his hand; and with much solemnity inquired, "Did I understand that your name is Bacon?" "Yes," said the newcomer, "my name is Bacon." "Then," said the other, "I am sorry to inform you that you will be very well cooked before you get out." The other prisoners, to whom the condition of bacon had become a rather comical matter, thought this uproarious, but the newcomer didn't think it funny at all.

As the main prison for political inmates, Fort Lafayette lasted scarcely three months. Yet, these months were the crucial period from August to October, 1861, when the phantom invasion of the North threatened, and men from all over the country were being sent to prison. During this time, this small piece of forgotten rock in New York harbor cast its shadow over the entire North. It became a kind of American Bastile, its name on everyone's lips. As such, it was a weapon in the hands of the Lincoln Administration, a weapon that was used to dominate the North, and to establish the fact that the federal government was the greatest power in the nation.

But Fort Lafayette was bleak, dreary, and damp, and in the middle of the winter it would be dangerous to leave so many elderly men there. In early October, a petition signed by nearly every prisoner in the fort was sent to President Lincoln. It listed many complaints including the crowded conditions, the dampness, the stench, the lack of water and the bad food. "Many of the prisoners are men advanced in life; many more are of infirm health or delicate constitutions. . . . They cannot believe that it is the purpose of the Government to destroy their health or sacrifice their lives by visiting them with such cruel hardship." After a few official inspections had been made, it was decided to send the prisoners to Fort Warren in Boston harbor.

At the end of October they all made the journey, jammed into a small ship. Upon arrival, they were confronted with another old fort turned into a prison, but it was a decided improvement over Fort Lafayette. Perhaps most important of all they had a humane warden in Colonel Dimick, the commander of the fort. Even the bitter F. Key Howard had kind words for him.*

In Boston the prisoners aroused great curiosity. Reporters

---

* After the war Colonel Dimick made a visit to Baltimore as the honored guest of one of his former prisoners, and was given a warm and hearty reception by the prisoners from Baltimore.

were allowed to visit the fort and described some of the better-known men. Marshal Kane, of Baltimore, they reported, was the most noticeable man in the fort. "A fine-looking, well-dressed gentleman . . . he bustles about, in a Scotch cap, with his pant legs within his boots, and by a stranger might be mistaken for the principal person in the garrison." Mayor Brown of Baltimore was "a quiet, tidy gentleman, evidently does not like his position." Ex-Governor Morehead of Kentucky was described as a fine-looking man, tall and portly, who "does not hesitate to express his contempt for the 'cobbling Yankees.'" It was noted that the prisoners "nearly all take to smoking, and talk to something like excess. One would judge at first glance, by their manner, that they are as jubilant as though at a summer water-place." All kinds of ways were thought up for passing away the endless time. On a typical day, "Mr. Wallis would deliver a brief treatise upon the elements of jurisprudence, Mr. Warfield was poring over the last edition of Price Current, Mr. William G. Harrison busily engaged in making a pot of tea, and Mr. Charles Howard at the wash-tub cleaning his linen."

At Fort Warren, Lawrence Sangston's diary waxed pleasantly. Although the routine remained very dull, it was not hard. Sickness almost disappeared and the wealthy men who participated in the mess made it an even more exclusive club. Sangston mentions that on November 10, the mess had a special Sunday dinner, "roast turkies, roast and boiled mutton, roast beef and lobster salad, and dessert of nuts of several kinds, fresh peaches in cans, honey and coffee." Said Sangston: "Our mess continues to improve; fare now equal to any of the hotels." The charitable ladies of Boston sent presents to the prisoners, including some secondhand Testaments and Sunday school hymn books, several jars of jelly, and quite a number of "calico comforts."

The biggest event during the stay at Fort Warren was the arrival of Mason and Slidell, the Southern commissioners who had been taken from the British vessel *Trent* on the high seas. Their seizure caused a major international incident and threatened to bring England into the war on the side of the Confederacy. While the fate of Mason and Slidell was being debated in Washington, orders were sent to Fort Warren to prepare quarters suitable to their rank. Nine men were turned out of their rooms to accommodate them, the floor was carpeted and the rooms were made comfortable with good beds, tables and chairs. Mason and Slidell arrived in a most cheerful manner, "a stranger might have supposed they were visitors instead of prisoners," said Sangston. They fitted very nicely into the highest social circles at the fort and Morehead, Brown, Howard and the others had long conversations with them. Sangston played a few games of whist with the new arrivals but found "they were too scientific for me" and "were not disposed to be at all complimentary in their comments on my skill as a player." Mason and Slidell continued to be treated royally until their release a few weeks later on orders from President Lincoln. They were turned over to the British and war was avoided.

As Christmas approached, preparations went forward for an enjoyable holiday. The prisoners received many boxes from home containing food for the holidays. Mutton, hams, terrapins, oysters, turkeys, geese, and fruitcakes arrived in abundance. Christmas day, said Sangston, was spent "pretty much as I would have done at home." He visited all the rooms, "taking a glass of egg-nog here and of apple toddy there. Had the best dinner of the season, but no one appeared disposed to eat it, the egg-nog having supplanted the dinner." The visiting continued until 11 at night, under special permission from Colonel Dimick. During the evening, the prisoners were in a high humor and held a trial and execution of William E. Seward on the charge of high treason, for having abolished the Constitution and the laws and usurped the government:

About 50 of the prisoners were present and participated in it; a stuffed figure had been made, representing the culprit, who was seated in the criminal box; a judge was selected, twelve jurymen drawn, the prisoner was assigned counsel, the prosecuting attorney opened the case, and the examination of witnesses went on in due form; speeches were made by counsel on both sides, and the case given to the jury, who after some deliberation (I fear they were biased) found the prisoner at the bar guilty; the judge, after making the usual preliminary speech on the enormity of his crimes and the justness of his condemnation, pronounced the sentence and he was immediately executed. One of the garrison officers was present, and between the trial and a bucket of egg-nog on the table in the corner of the room where he stood, seemed to enjoy it very much.

The next morning Sangston awoke with a severe hangover, much as he would have at home, and spent most of the day in bed.

Sangston, who was released soon after Christmas, had a special reason for celebrating. Most of the other prisoners were released before spring, although a few of the Marylanders remained longer. Never again during the war were the forts to be filled with political prisoners as they were in 1861. Never again was one man to seize the reigns of government as Seward did in 1861 under the permissive guidance of President Lincoln, and carry his personal will into every city and state in the North. During this period Seward wielded more arbitrary power over American citizens than any other man ever has. The apparatus of the federal government as it extended into the North in 1861 was the apparatus of Seward. For this was his program and he carried it out almost without interference. He established largely by illegal means the fact that the federal government had the will and the power to act against those opposed to the war.

And so it was entirely fitting that on Christmas day, fifty prisoners in Fort Warren should hold a mock trial and execution of the Secretary of State for his unconstitutional acts, while the egg-nog bucket was being emptied. No political pris-

oner was put to death and none died in prison as a result of
Seward's acts. Enough freedom was allowed in prison to permit the pretended execution of William E. Seward, and enough
freedom was allowed in the land so that anti-Administration
newspapers plagued the government during the entire war.
But an example had been set and the will of the federal government had been asserted. When 1862 dawned on the nation,
the North was ready for a real war.

CHAPTER 26

OPTIMISM AND
THE GENERAL AMNESTY

O F THE ENORMOUS waves of emotion that swept the North during the war, none was more complete than the optimism that set in during the first months of 1862. Several minor battles in January set the stage. The victory at Logan's Cross Roads in Kentucky gave hope in the central regions. Far to the west, General Curtis was chasing General Price out of Missouri. Nearer Washington, George B. McClellan, the little Napoleon, had whipped the Northern armies into shape and was now planning to move on Richmond.

President Lincoln helped things along in January when he suddenly removed Simon Cameron from office as Secretary of War. Cameron had been appointed as a political reward for swinging his support to Lincoln in the Republican convention in 1860. The War Department had been used many times before and was to be used many times afterwards as a good place to put a man who needed paying off. But in 1861, the job of Secretary of War suddenly became crucial and Cameron simply didn't measure up to it. All sorts of shady dealings were coming to light in the Department and something had to be done.

As Lincoln was casting about for a man of great ability to replace Cameron, he kept bumping into the name of Edwin Stanton. Stanton had been born in Ohio forty-seven years before and had become a practicing lawyer in Steubenville. His biographer, Fletcher Pratt, says "there is hardly a case of the period in the counties of Harrison, Jefferson, Carroll, Colum-

biana, Belmont, or Tuscarawas in which he does not appear."
He so terrified witnesses that his opponents had difficulty getting anyone to testify. He was known as "the King of Steubenville," and had the largest house in town. He even bought a
glass factory that obstructed his view of the river and had the
building torn down.

In 1855, Stanton was one of four lawyers chosen to handle
the famous McCormick Reaper Case as a representative of the
Manny interests, who were defending themselves against a pat-
ent infringement claim by McCormick. Cast alongside Stanton
was another lawyer, Abraham Lincoln. Lincoln, however, was
no match for the man from Steubenville. Various comments
are attributed to Stanton during this case, such as "Where did
that long-armed baboon come from?" and "If that giraffe appears in the case, I will throw up my brief and leave." Lincoln
had originally been invited to give the final argument for the
defense, but when the time came, a choice had to be made between him and Stanton, and Stanton was chosen. The disappointed Lincoln sat on the sidelines and listened as Stanton
gave an impressive argument and won the case.

Stanton's fame spread rapidly and he soon became one of
the leading lawyers before the United States Supreme Court.
During the last days of the Buchanan Administration, after the
defection of several of Buchanan's Southern cabinet members,
Stanton was appointed Attorney General. Although he had
been a Breckinridge Democrat, Stanton was an ardent Union
man and became a pillar of strength for the Union in the last
days of the Buchanan Administration. When Lincoln was inaugurated, Stanton, of course, was replaced, but he continued
to live in Washington.

During the early months of the Lincoln Administration,
Stanton's opinion of Lincoln remained low. He once, in a letter
to a friend, referred to the "painful imbecility of Lincoln." But
he carefully cultivated many of the important figures in Washington, including Seward, Chase, and McClellan. Pratt says

that Stanton and McClellan "were in perfect agreement on the subject of the President, whom Stanton referred to as 'the original gorilla,' remarking that if DuChaillu had known his business, he would have gone to Springfield, Illinois, instead of to Africa to conduct his researches in anthropology." Whether or not Lincoln was aware of these remarks, he certainly knew that Stanton would be a difficult man to deal with. But he needed a man of great administrative ability and overrode any personal feelings he may have had on the matter. On January 15, he sent Stanton's name to the Senate for confirmation as Secretary of War.

And so there came to the War Department an administrative genius, who converted a department full of corruption into one without scandal. Stanton was to make mistakes, and some of his actions after the war cast his name under a permanent cloud. During January and February of 1862, however, he was considered a gift from the gods. Seward referred to him as "Stanton the Divine." Chase and McClellan were both happy to have the new Secretary in the job and even the outgoing Simon Cameron was pleased. The newspapers reflected the "almost universal satisfaction" in the appointment and one remarked that "the Secesh call him an Abolitionist, and the Abolitionists call him a pro-slavery Democrat. Pretty good evidence that he is all right." Fernando Wood, the mayor of New York who came closer to being arrested than he knew, wrote Lincoln that the Stanton appointment "has given the best proof of your own ability to govern." The Senate confirmed him 38 to 2 in a remarkable show of near unanimity. The war, at last, would get under way.

Stanton went to work with his usual vigor in the new job. He issued an order that the Department would be closed on Tuesdays, Wednesdays, Thursdays and Fridays against all business except that relating to active operations in the field. On Saturdays, he announced, he would devote himself to the business of Senators and Representatives and on Mondays to the business of the public. He saw applicants at 11 A.M. and these morning hours became famous. A line of applicants would trail past him, and he would dispose of their cases in a few moments each. Even President Lincoln enjoyed going over to Stanton's office and watching his Secretary of War handle the passing parade. Stanton completely dominated the show and he had the administrative genius to make such a system work.

Shortly after he took office, as if by a miracle, the war actually did begin to move. The hard work of Frémont and Halleck in the west was beginning to pay off. Grant started moving south along the Tennessee River and took Fort Henry. On February 7, General Halleck sent a jubilant message to Washington, "Fort Henry is ours. The flag of the Union is re-established on the soil of Tennessee. It will never be removed." Next came wonderful news from Cape Hatteras. The capture of Roanoke Island, Elizabeth City and New Bern followed each other in rapid succession. A large share of North Carolina's seacoast was brought under Union control and General Ambrose Burnside's reputation was made. From out in Missouri came the news that Springfield, in the southwestern part of the state, had been reoccupied and Confederate forces driven from the state.

As though this were not enough, on February 17 came Grant's smashing victory at Fort Donelson. This victory sent the North into ecstasy. In Baltimore, it was reported that the "streets are crowded with Union men, who in the drenching rain, are exchanging congratulations. . . . Secesh is overwhelmed with their Waterloo defeat." In Philadelphia, there was "great public rejoicing. . . . Flags are being recklessly thrown out in every direction." In Cincinnati, a newspaper reported "intense excitement and joy" and in Boston, a "perfect furor of patriotic jubilation." For this was an entirely unexpected victory, coming so quickly after Fort Henry, and both Grant and Halleck were getting reputations as men able to accomplish things. General Buckner, the former commander of

the Kentucky militia who had gone south, was captured at Fort
Donelson, much to the delight of Union men in the state.
Bowling Green was evacuated by Confederate troops and later
in February came the culminating news that Nashville had been
taken without a fight. Tennessee itself was crumbling before
the might of the Union armies. Unable to win in 1861,
the Union armies had, it seemed, been trained, armed, equipped
and were now easily the superior of their Southern enemies.
Good generals had been found and bad ones discarded. The
New York *Tribune* noted "the marvelous change a few days
have wrought. . . . Joy sparkles in every eye, and there is a
glow of pride on every cheek."

Edwin Stanton reaped the full harvest of these advances. In
fact, Horace Greeley decided that everything that had happened since Stanton took office was the result of his conduct
of affairs. He editorialized that just "the other day all was
doubt, distrust and uncertainty." Now all was changed. "We
seem to have passed into another state of existence. . . . It is
by the impassioned soul, sleepless will, and the great practical
talents of the Secretary of War that the vast power of the
United States has now been hurled upon their treacherous and
perjured enemies to crush them to powder." Stanton modestly
replied that undue merit should not be ascribed to him, but
rather to the gallant troops who fought the battles. There was
plenty of glory for everybody.

Amidst all this glory, the idea that one good battle would
win the war was resurrected. The fatal lure of Richmond, less
than one hundred miles away, so near and yet so far, began to
dominate everything. If the capital of the Confederacy could
be captured, all would be over. Stanton would be the victorious
War Secretary, McClellan the victorious general and Lincoln
the victorious President. No delay could be allowed and a long
war was out of the question. Rapidly the magic word spread
throughout the country that a year from the date of Fort
Sumter the war would be won. April would be the month of

victory. Nothing could stop the Union armies. And so the optimism of the day fed on itself, reaching incredible proportions.

The policy of repression, which had been so significant during the dark days of September, soon became pointless. There is no spur to tolerance as certain as optimism and confidence. And the mood of the Lincoln Administration and of the entire country during February, 1862, was one of unbounded optimism. The danger was over, it seemed, and the war nearly won.

In the middle of February, therefore, President Lincoln decided on a general amnesty for political prisoners. He issued Executive Order No. 1, which shows evidence of having been written by Stanton. This order pointed out that at the beginning of the war there was "great confusion and perplexity of the public mind. Disloyalty before unsuspected suddenly became bold, and treason astonished the world by bringing at once into the field military forces superior in number to the standing Army of the United States. . . . Every department of the Government was paralyzed by treason. Defection appeared in the Senate, in the House of Representatives, in the Cabinet, in the Federal Courts." In these circumstances, the President was forced to suspend the writ of habeas corpus and have men arrested who had or were about to engage in treasonable practices.

Recently, the order went on, a favorable change of public opinion had occurred. The line between loyalty and disloyalty had become plainly defined. The whole structure of the Government had become firm and stable. "The insurrection is believed to have culminated and to be declining. . . . The President, in view of these facts and anxious to favor a return to the normal course of the administration . . . directs that all political prisoners now held in military custody be released on their subscribing to a parole engaging them to render no aid or comfort to the enemies in hostility to the United States. . . . To all persons who shall be so released and who shall keep their parole the President grants an amnesty for any past offenses of treason or disloyalty which they may have committed."

This was a wholesale order to empty the prisons. Within a few days, nearly all the political prisoners were streaming back to their homes. Newspapers which had been suppressed began to reappear. The New York *Daily News* was reported to be preparing for republication the day after the order. In far-off Henderson, Kentucky, the *Reporter*, which had last been published in September, was soon back in business.

In addition to declaring the general amnesty, this order provided that "extraordinary arrests will hereafter be made under the direction of the military authorities alone." With a sweep of the pen, the entire program was transferred from the State Department, where the unpopular Seward had presided over it for six months, to the War Department, where the new hero of Washington, Edwin Stanton, was in charge. And in a day when most orders were disobeyed (indeed, an age not unlike our own), this last one was carried out to the letter. Never again in the entire war did Seward order a man to prison. Stanton had begun his drive for power.

The general amnesty was greeted with delight throughout the North. Nearly every important newspaper noted the general satisfaction. Horace Greeley welcomed the document as announcing "that the reign of lawless despotism is ended." Another newspaper noted that "neither the Secretary of State nor the Secretary of War can make arbitrary arrests hereafter in the loyal states." But this was overly optimistic. The arrests continued throughout the country after the amnesty. But unlike the period of panic in 1861, they were made infrequently, reluctantly, and usually by local commanders rather than by the authorities in Washington. By February, 1862, the deliberate policy of repression was being brought to a halt.

CHAPTER 27

LINCOLN, THE HUMANITARIAN

THE YEAR 1861 was perhaps the most exciting in American history. Not only did it witness such dramatic events as the firing on Fort Sumter and the emergence of two great American nations at war, but it also saw a political cloud descend over the North, causing the temporary obliteration of the traditional American system of due process of law. In handling the problem of loyalty, the entire judicial system was set aside. The laws were silent, indictments were not found, testimony was not taken, judges did not sit, juries were not empaneled, convictions were not obtained and sentences were not pronounced. The Anglo-Saxon concept of due process, perhaps the greatest political triumph of the ages and the best guardian of freedom, was abandoned.

The constitutional safeguards against convictions for treason seemed to be too stringent. As one federal judge in New York told a grand jury in November, 1861: "Words, oral, written or printed, however treasonable, seditious or criminal by themselves, do not constitute an overt act of treason, within the definition of the crime." Many indictments were brought in the federal courts, but usually the cases were continued from one term to the next and eventually dismissed by the government. One authority who studied this matter concluded that "in the midst of . . . disloyalty . . . the tribunals of civil justice failed, in the large sense, to function as agencies for the suppression and punishment of treason." The problem was so new and the necessary alteration in the balance of power between the states and federal government so great, that it could be made only through summary action.

And so, the political steps necessary to preserve the American nation were taken by the Lincoln Administration. For Abraham Lincoln, who seemed so frequently to let his subordinates run the government, never allowed them to stray far from his major goals. He was prepared to make every sacrifice to save the Union and the arbitrary arrests were, in his opinion, part of the necessary sacrifice.

During 1861, two great political events occurred which preserved the Union. The first was the detachment of three slave states from the Confederacy and their firm anchoring to the Union. Without success in this effort, the war could not have been won. These three states, Maryland, Missouri and Kentucky, not only occupied highly strategic positions, but they had a combined population of approximately three million people. Without them the population advantage of the North over the South would have been only 3-to-2, which probably would not have been enough to support the massive Union campaigns of brute force by which the South was eventually destroyed. With them, however, the proportion was 5-to-2, and made possible almost any human attrition without seriously jeopardizing the North's position. The South was in such a serious situation by the end of 1861 that it must lose the war unless the North's will could be blunted.

The second major political achievement in 1861 was the unification of the free states by the federal government. No war could be fought and won by a weak executive against the odds that faced the North. And so States Rights, which prior to 1860 had been as important a part of northern political beliefs as southern, were overturned to meet the crisis. The North would be more than an alliance of independent states. By the end of 1861, a radical transformation in the balance of political power within the North had occurred. This was accomplished through the policy of repression more than by any other action and it was Lincoln's success here which insured that the North's will to win would not be blunted.

In carrying out the policy of repression, President Lincoln was a man caught in an agony. The first comments that he wrote on the subject epitomized his attitude: "Unless the necessity for these arbitrary arrests is *manifest*, and *urgent*, I prefer they should cease." He was forced to do something that he hated to do, since he felt it was necessary for the preservation of the Union. Nevertheless, his personal intercession again and again was in the direction of leniency. When the question of arresting the Maryland legislature first came up in April, 1861, he decided against it. When it was reported that one of the prisoners was in bad health, he ordered that his confinement be "mitigated so far as it can be consistently with his safe detention." When he heard that conditions were bad in Fort Lafayette, he directed the United States marshal in the vicinity of the forts to "supply decent lodgings and subsistence for such prisoners."

When Senator William M. Gwin and two others from California were arrested and brought to Washington for an interview, the President decided that "they might go their several ways, they to ask no questions nor any questions to be asked of them and the pending affairs . . . to be thus entirely disposed of and ended." When James W. Wall was in prison, he wrote to Lincoln: "Permit me to lay before you how deeply I am impressed with your exceeding great kindness in extending to my wife and little ones your unrestricted permission to visit me at this place. . . . An act of kindness like that you have just performed touches the generous sympathies of my heart with great power."

"Mr. Lincoln doesn't believe in hanging," said the New York *Times*. A later writer said that "Lincoln used this power with discretion and forbearance. . . . He was the most humane man that ever wielded such authority. He had no taste for tyranny."

Despite his great leniency, he was a man of iron who was willing to see hundreds of thousands of young men die for the sake of the Union and not above sending a few hundred to prison for opposing the war. Repeatedly, whenever Congress asked for information on the arrests, he replied that it was not in the public interest to furnish the information. Furthermore, he formally suspended the writ of habeas corpus in progressively larger areas as the war continued. This fact, plus a few highly publicized cases, such as the arrest of Vallandigham, which occurred later in the war, made it appear that the policy of repression was being enlarged. But such was not the case. Had Vallandigham been arrested in September, 1861, when he was a member of Congress, the occurrence would have rated scarcely a paragraph in the newspapers. When he was actually arrested two years later, after he had lost his seat in Congress, he became a national celebrity. By this time, the famous knock on the door at midnight had become a rare event.

The desire of President Lincoln to avoid the arrests, and the agony they caused him, never changed. But in 1861 he believed them necessary to preserve the Union. After a few months of experience in sending men to Fort Lafayette, however, he became convinced that this power could safely be used sparingly. During the rest of the war, he never changed his opinion. For President Lincoln had gone through the valley of the shadow during 1861 and had emerged a stronger man and the nation a stronger nation. Great disasters and terrible defeats lay ahead as the war moved toward a climax, but the President was never again thrown into a panic such as the one he lived through in 1861. With his slow, sure tread, he moved away from the policy of repression and the North was spared the omnipresent shadow of Fort Lafayette.

The ultimate legal question of arbitrary arrest and imprisonment was settled the year after the war in the case of *Ex parte Milligan*, in which the Supreme Court held that in the absence of actual invasion such actions were illegal while civil processes were unobstructed and the courts in session. In language which has echoed to our own time, the Court held that "the Constitution of the United States is a law for rulers and people, equally in war and in peace, and covers with the shield of its protection all classes of men, at all times, and under all circumstances."

It is not difficult to imagine Abraham Lincoln nodding in agreement, had he lived, when the Court added that "during the late wicked Rebellion, the temper of the times did not allow that calmness in deliberation and discussion so necessary to a correct conclusion" on this question. For no one had regretted the acts more than he, and when the war was over and the Union saved, the prairie lawyer who became President would probably have sought, with the Court, to prevent his successors from following this dangerous precedent.

NOTES

INDEX

Page
11 Kane telegram to Johnson, Baltimore *Clipper*, May 2, 1861.
12-13 "Hordes" and "through breaches in the walls," Radcliffe, p. 67.
13 "Civil War in Baltimore," See Baltimore newspapers, April 20, 1861.
13 "For the defense of the city," Baltimore *Sun*, April 22, 1861.
13 "Great patriotism," Baltimore *Sun*, July 12, 1861.
14 "Stout hearts and strong arms," Baltimore *Sun*, April 22, 1861.
14 "As a unit in defense," Baltimore *Sun*, April 22, 1861.
16 "Those Carolinians," Radcliffe, p. 68.

CHAPTER 2. The Occupation of Maryland

Benjamin Butler, *Autobiography and Personal Reminiscences of Maj-Gen'l Benj. F. Butler* (Boston, 1892); Theodore Winthrop, *Life in the Open Air, and other papers* (Boston, 1863); George Nason, *Minute Men of '61* (Boston, 1910); William Swinton, *History of the Seventh Regiment, National Guard* (New York, 1870); William Seabrook, *Maryland's Great Part in Saving the Union* (1913); Thomas Scharf, *History of Baltimore City and County* (Philadelphia, 1881).

Page
18 "Very glad the oldest general," Butler, p. 127.
19 "Commanded a larger body of troops," Butler, p. 127.
19 "Minute Men of '61," see Nason.
19-20 "Called to prepare troops" and "remains unfinished," Butler, p. 170.
20 "Has not been equalled," Boston *Post*, April 17, 1861.
21 Butler proclamation, Butler, p. 195.
22 "It was worth a life" and trip through New Jersey, Winthrop, p. 219.
23 "Uniforms all grimy," Winthrop, p. 229.
23 "It was a parade," Winthrop, p. 230.
23 "Do not let them come," Baltimore *Sun*, April 29, 1861.
23 Hicks "has turned traitor," New York *Tribune*, April 25, 1861.
24 "Peaceably, quickly and civilly," Baltimore *Sun*, April 29, 1861.
25 Privilege of writ suspended, *Official Record*, Ser. 2, I, 567.
26 "Are our few insane enemies," Scharf, p. 313.
26 "Poisoner General," Frankfort (Ky.) *Yeoman*, May 16, 1861.
27 Arrest of Spencer, Baltimore *Clipper*, May 9, 1861.
27 Release of Spencer, Baltimore *American*, May 16, 1861.

CHAPTER 3. Baltimore Rejoins the Union

Thomas Scharf, *History of Baltimore City and County* (Philadelphia, 1881); George Brown, *Baltimore and the Nineteenth of April, 1861*

(Baltimore, 1887); George Radcliffe, "Governor Thomas H. Hicks of Maryland and the Civil War," *Johns Hopkins University Studies in Historical and Political Science* (Baltimore, 1902); *Ex parte Merryman*, 17 Fed. Case 144; Francis Beirne, *Baltimore—A Picture History* (New York, 1957); Maryland House of Delegates, *Report of the Committee on Federal Relations—Upon the Messages of the Governor in Regard to Arbitrary Proceedings of the United States Government* (Frederick, 1861); Maryland House of Delegates, *Resolutions of the Committee on Federal Relations*, May 14, 1861 (Frederick, 1861).

Page

29 "Devoted to the South," Scharf, p. 635.

31 "Should the hour ever arrive," Radcliffe, p. 16.

31 Lincoln opinion on arrest of Maryland legislature, Lincoln to Scott, April 25, 1861, Lincoln Papers.

32 "Which the Federal Government has declared," Maryland House of Delegates, *Resolutions of the Committee on Federal Relations*.

32 "We know we have no constitutional authority," Baltimore *Sun*, April 29, 1861.

32 "Safety Bill," Radcliffe, p. 76.

33 "Where no less than $1 million," Baltimore *Clipper*, April 30, 1861.

34 "The authorities of the city," Radcliffe, p. 86.

35-36 Butler's proclamation, Baltimore *Sun*, May 14, 1861.

36 "Wade in at them," Baltimore *American*, May 15, 1861.

37 "Tom Thumb," Beirne, p. 29.

38 "I also thought that if such a man," Butler, p. 228.

38 Dispatch from Scott to Butler, Butler, p. 235.

40 "The body of John Merryman" and "high and delicate trust," *Official Record*, Ser. 2, I, 575.

40 "To answer for his contempt," *Official Record*, Ser. 2, I, 577.

41-42 *Ex parte Merryman*, 17 Fed. Case 144.

42-43 Conversation between Brown and Taney, Brown, p. 88.

43 Greeley's comment, New York *Tribune*, June 2, 1861.

43-44 Indictment, Baltimore *Sun*, July 11, 1861.

CHAPTER 4. A City on Trial

Thomas Scharf, *History of Baltimore City and County* (Philadelphia, 1881).

Page

45-46 W. G. Snethen, see letter from Snethen to Cameron, Dec. 7, 1861, Lincoln Papers.

46 "Only served to madden," New York *Tribune*, May 26, 1861.

46 "Not less than a dozen," New York *Tribune*, June 4, 1861.

47 "There is a decided purpose," New York *Tribune*, June 13, 1861.

Page
48 "Fight to the death," and other quotations in this paragraph, New York *Tribune*, June 11, 1861.
48 "I must tell you," New York *Tribune*, June 30, 1861.
49 "I learned through a lady," New York *Tribune*, June 12, 1861.
49 "Grossly insulted," New York *Tribune*, June 21, 1861.
49 "According to the best Secession authority," New York *Tribune*, June 22, 1861.
50 "Seize at once," *Official Record*, Ser. 2, I, 64.
50 "Need only have sent," Baltimore *Sun*, June 28, 1861.
51 "I hear Marshal Kane," Baltimore *Clipper*, June 28, 1861.
51 "By direction or indirection," Baltimore *Sun*, June 28, 1861.
51 "For distinguished gallantry," Scharf, p. 133.
52 "Off duty for the present," *Official Record*, Ser. 2, I, 626.
52 "Enough money," Baltimore *Sun*, June 29, 1861.
52 "Concealed arsenal," Baltimore *Sun*, July 2, 1861.
53 "There is no telling," Snethen to Scott, June 29, 1861, Lincoln Papers.
53 Banks "warrant," Baltimore *American*, July 2, 1861.
54 Banks proclamation, Baltimore *Sun*, July 2, 1861.
55 "His death in prison," *Official Record*, Ser. 2, I, 627.
55 "There is no fear," and "I think the government," Banks to Seward, July 9, 1861, Lincoln Papers.
56 "General Banks has struck," and "is virtually placed," New York *Tribune*, June 28, 1861.
56 "Its bloodlessness," New York *Tribune*, July 7, 1861.

CHAPTER 5. Battle of St. Louis

Robert Rombauer, *The Union Cause in St. Louis in 1861* (St. Louis, 1909); Thomas Scharf, *History of St. Louis City and County* (Philadelphia, 1883); William Sherman, *Memoirs of General Wm. T. Sherman* (New York, 1875); Thomas Snead, *The Fight for Missouri* (New York, 1888); Burton Hendrick, *Lincoln's War Cabinet* (Boston, 1946).
Page
59 "I am constantly," Missouri *Democrat*, May 13, 1861.
60 "Immediate surrender," St. Louis *Republican*, May 11, 1861.
60 "Irrepressible conflict," a popular phrase used by Seward in a speech delivered on Oct. 25, 1958. See Hendrick, p. 34.
61 "Inhuman and diabolical," Scharf, p. 490.
61 "Ready, willing and anxious," Scharf, p. 491.
62 "All sexes, ages, classes," Scharf, p. 492.
63 "Wholly unprepared," Missouri *Democrat*, May 13, 1861.

ceased publication a few days after he went south; the editor of Cynthiana *News* was arrested and sent to Cincinnati. The Frankfort *Yeoman*, a newspaper which had been supported by political advertising from the Democratic legislature, had been full of anti-war and anti-Lincoln editorials until mid-September, but with the Confederate invasion and the widespread closing of newspapers, it fell silent editorially and avoided suppression.

The most famous paper to be suppressed in Kentucky was the Louisville *Courier*. The *Courier* had fought against the war and the Lincoln Administration for many months and its columns had been filled with political invective. As the state moved closer and closer toward the Union, the tone of the newspaper became more strident. One day in mid-September, a copy of the *Courier* was sent to Seward who forwarded it to Montgomery Blair in the Post Office Department, suggesting that it be prohibited from circulating by mail. Blair was only too happy to oblige and on September 18 ordered that "the Louisville Courier, found to be an advocate of treason . . . be excluded from the mails and post offices of the United States." This order was received by Marshal Sneed in Louisville during the panic caused by General Buckner's approach and it fitted in well with his plans for cleaning up the city of Louisville. Instead of excluding the paper from the mails, Sneed closed it down, arrested Reuben Durrett and tried to arrest the owners of the paper. One of them, a man named Haldeman, who lived a few miles from Louisville, was on his way to the city when he heard the news that the *Courier* had been suppressed and Durrett arrested. He got off the train at a small station outside Louisville and without ado headed south. At Bowling Green, under the protection of General Buckner and the Tennessee troops, he found a more congenial atmosphere and started publishing the *Courier* in that town, as a newspaper of the Peace Party. The Louisville *Courier* was now a Southern newspaper, beyond the reach of the govern-

Page
63 "Damn the Dutch," Rombauer, p. 233.
64 "This clapped the demon," New York *Times*, May 15, 1861.
64 "Had in his hand," Sherman, p. 173.
65 "We went over the grove," St. Louis *Republican*, May 11, 1861.
67 "Preferred total annihilation," Scharf, p. 498.

CHAPTER 6. Missouri in Turmoil

Robert Rombauer, *The Union Cause in St. Louis in 1861* (St. Louis, 1909); Thomas Scharf, *History of St. Louis City and County* (Philadelphia, 1883).

Page
69 "Would all be prisoners," Missouri *Democrat*, May 13, 1861.
71 "To Hell with," Missouri *Democrat*, May 13, 1861.
72 "Like wild Beasts," Missouri *Democrat*, May 13, 1861.
73-74 "I know the stinker," Rombauer, p. 245.
74 Harney proclamation, Missouri *Democrat*, May 13, 1861.
74 "White-livered cowards," Missouri *Democrat*, May 13, 1861.
75 "Walnut Street Tragedy," Missouri *Democrat*, May 16, 1861.
75 "The force of these," Scharf, p. 508.
76-77 McDonald case, see daily issues of Missouri *Democrat*, May 15-June 10, 1861, and *Official Record*, Ser. 2, I, 114.

CHAPTER 7. The Harney-Price Agreement

John McElroy, *The Struggle for Missouri* (Washington, 1909); Robert Rombauer, *The Union Cause in St. Louis in 1861* (St. Louis, 1909); John Nicolay and John Hay, *Complete Works of Abraham Lincoln* (New York, 1894).

Page
79 "The market was so insignificant," Missouri *Democrat*, May 16, 1861.
79 Harney proclamation, Missouri *Democrat*, May 15, 1861.
80 Arrest of John Dean, Missouri *Democrat*, May 17, 1861.
80-81 Lincoln's letter to Blair, Nicolay and Hay, VI, 275.
81 "Slaughter of the people," McElroy, p. 93.
82-83 Potosi incident, Missouri *Democrat*, May 17, 1861.
83 "The U.S. American Volunteer," Missouri *Democrat*, May 22, 1861.
83 Harney-Price agreement, McElroy, p. 97; Missouri *Democrat*, May 21, 1861.
84 "Return with your friends," Missouri *Democrat*, May 23, 1861.
84 Harney dismissed, McElroy, p. 102; Rombauer, p. 252.

CHAPTER 8. War Comes to Missouri

John McElroy, *The Struggle for Missouri* (Washington, 1909); Robert Rombauer, *The Union Cause in St. Louis in 1861* (St. Louis, 1909); Thomas Scharf, *The History of St. Louis City and County* (Philadelphia, 1883); Thomas Snead, *The Fight for Missouri* (New York, 1888).

Page

85 Price's proclamation, Missouri *Democrat*, June 5, 1861.

86-87 Meeting at Planter's House, Snead, p. 198; Rombauer, p. 262; McElroy, p. 117; Missouri *Democrat*, June 12, 1861.

86 "Rather than concede," Rombauer, p. 262.

87 "We want two passenger cars," Missouri *Democrat*, June 17, 1861.

87 Jackson proclamation, Missouri *Democrat*, June 14, 1861.

88-89 Lyon's advance, Missouri *Democrat*, June 17, 1861.

89 Lyon's proclamation, Missouri *Democrat*, June 18, 1861.

89 Tucker arrest, Missouri *Democrat*, June 15, 1861.

89 Barrett arrest, New York *Tribune*, June 14, 1861; Missouri *Democrat*, June 14, 1861.

90 Dimick incident, Missouri *Democrat*, June 14, 1861; June 17, 1861.

90-91 Incident at Seventh and Olive, Missouri *Democrat*, June 18-29, 1861.

91 "Fire" and "My God," Missouri *Democrat*, June 20, 1861.

93 Suppression of *State Journal*, Scharf, p. 958; New York *Times*, July 18, 1861; New York *Tribune*, July 17, 1861; Rombauer, p. 287; Missouri *Democrat*, July 13, 1861.

94 "By fraud, by deception," Missouri *Democrat*, July 13, 1861.

CHAPTER 9. The Lincoln Guns

Reverend Daniel Stevenson, "General Nelson, Kentucky, and the Lincoln Guns," *Magazine of American History*, Vol. X, 1883; Thomas Speed, *The Union Cause in Kentucky* (New York, 1907).

Page

96-97 Visit of Lieutenant Nelson to Joshua Speed, Stevenson, p. 122.

97 "Cast your eyes," Stevenson, p. 118.

98 "I do not wish," Stevenson, p. 120.

98 Meeting in Frankfort, Stevenson, p. 121.

98-99 Shipment of guns, Frankfort *Yeoman*, May 20, 1861; Stevenson, p. 123.

99 "Was the signal," Frankfort *Yeoman*, May 20, 1861.

99 Number of arms in hands of militia, Louisville *Democrat*, Jan. 24, 1861.

99-100 "Have received information," Stevenson, p. 126; Frankfort *Yeoman*, May 25, 1861.

Page
100 "Knights of the Golden Circle," Stevenson, p. 126.
100-102 Shipment of guns to Danville, Stevenson, pp. 127-132.
101 "Do not go into," and "they hadn't better take," Stevenson, p. 129.
101 "If I was a man," Stevenson, p. 130.
102 "It would be impossible," Stevenson, p. 131.
102 Unionists encouraged, Letter from Joshua Speed to Lincoln, May 29, 1861, Lincoln Papers.
103-104 Magoffin refusal to furnish troops, Stevenson, p. 116.
104 Union victory in May election, Speed, p. 87.

CHAPTER 10. Peace in Kentucky

Robert Rombauer, *The Union Cause in St. Louis in 1861* (St. Louis, 1909); Thomas Speed, *The Union Cause in Kentucky* (New York, 1907); James Hall, "Free Speech in War Times," *Columbia Law Review*, Vol. XXI, 1921; John Nicolay and John Hay, *Complete Works of Abraham Lincoln* (New York, 1894).
Page
105 "Lie so low," Frankfort *Yeoman*, May 30, 1861.
105 "Rather than concede," Rombauer, p. 262.
105 "Kentucky looks to the West," Henderson *Reporter*, June 20, 1861.
106 "Military board," Speed, p. 33.
106 Magoffin proclamation, Speed, pp. 47-49.
106 Rousseau speech in senate, Speed, p. 127.
107 Description of Camp Jo Holt, New York *Tribune*, July 16, 1861.
107 "During the summer," Speed, p. 117.
107 "At the hotel breakfast-table," New York *Tribune*, July 14, 1861.
107 "It is wonderful," New York *Tribune*, July 14, 1861.
108 "Oh, Lord," Hall, p. 526.
108 Election of June 20, Speed, p. 88.
108 "With the least possible," Nicolay and Hay, VI, 325.

CHAPTER 11. Washington at Bay

U.S. Congress, *Congressional Globe*, 37th Cong. 1st Sess.; John Nicolay and John Hay, *Complete Works of Abraham Lincoln* (New York, 1894); Burton Hendrick, *Lincoln's War Cabinet* (Boston, 1946); Fletcher Pratt, *Stanton, Lincoln's Secretary of War* (New York, 1953); William Roehrenbeck, *The Regiment That Saved the Capital* (New York, 1961); Frederick Seward, *Reminiscences of a War-Time Statesman and Diplomat* (New York, 1916).

Page
112 Strength of troops, statement of Lorenzo Thomas, April 5, 1861, Lincoln Papers.
112 "Would it impose," Nicolay and Hay, VI, 238.
112 Seward wrote Scott's acceptance speech, Hendrick, p. 204.
113 "The disgusting subject," Scott to Cameron, Aug. 12, 1861, Lincoln Papers.
113 "I have but little," Scott to Lincoln, April 15, 1861, Lincoln Papers.
113 "These, I think," Scott to Lincoln, April 16, 1861, Lincoln Papers.
114 Stanton's comments, Pratt, p. 123.
114 Frederick Seward's comments, Seward, p. 157.
114 "Capture of Washington City," Roehrenbeck, p. 123.
114 "We are in advance," Scott to Lincoln, April 20, 1861, Lincoln Papers.
115 "I feel confident," Scott to Lincoln, April 22, 1861, Lincoln Papers.
115 "Release the troops hemmed in," Scott to Lincoln, April 24, 1861, Lincoln Papers.
115 "Through very respectable channels," Scott to Lincoln, April 26, 1861, Lincoln Papers.
115 "Not a gun," Scott to Lincoln, April 30, 1861, Lincoln Papers.
116 Arrests in Washington, New York *Herald*, May 18, 1861.
116 "Unless the necessity," Nicolay and Hay, IV, 372.
116 Suspension of habeas corpus, *Official Record*, Ser. 2, II, 18.
116-117 Lincoln's habeas corpus statement to Congress, *Official Record*, Ser. 2, II, 15.
117-118 Bates' opinion, *Official Record*, Ser. 2, II, 26.
119 "I am not disposed," *Congressional Globe*, p. 392.
119 "So far as the violation," *Congressional Globe*, Appendix, p. 19.
119 "Not believe the President," *Congressional Globe*, p. 393.

CHAPTER 12. Bull Run and McClellan

H. J. Eckenrode and Bryan Conrad, *The Man Who Saved the Union* (Chapel Hill, 1941); William Myers, *General George Brinton McClellan* (New York, 1934); William Hale, *Horace Greeley: Voice of the People* (New York, 1950); J. F. C. Fuller, *The Conduct of War* (New Brunswick, 1961); George McClellan, *McClellan's Own Story* (New York, 1887); Seward Papers, University of Rochester.

Page
120-121 For information on McClellan's life, see Eckenrode and Conrad, pp. 2-15.
121 "Annihilated two armies," *Official Record*, Ser. 1, II, 205
122-123 Power of defense, Fuller, pp. 103-106.
123 "Can the rebels be beaten," Hale, p. 258.

Page
123 "Will be the crowning," Frankfort *Yeoman*, July 23, 1861.
124 "I find myself," and "I went to the Senate," McClellan, p. 82.
124 "All was chaos," Myers, p. 199.
125 "I receive letter," McClellan, p. 85.
125-126 McClellan's letter to Scott, April 8, 1861, Lincoln Papers.
126 McClellan sends copy to Lincoln, letter from McClellan to Lincoln, Aug. 8, 1861, Seward Papers.
126 Scott's letter to Cameron, August 9, 1861, Lincoln Papers.
126-127 McClellan's letter to Lincoln, August 10, 1861, Lincoln Papers.
127 Scott's letter refusing to withdraw resignation, Scott to Cameron, August 12, 1861, Lincoln Papers.
127 Rumors of attack into Maryland, New York *Times*, Aug. 18, 1861; New York *Tribune*, July 31, 1861; unsigned, undated note included in August letters, Lincoln Papers.

CHAPTER 13. Riots in the North

William Hale, *Horace Greeley: Voice of the People* (New York, 1950); Roy Abrams, "The Jeffersonian, A Copperhead Newspaper," *Bill of Rights Review*, Vol. II, 1942; John Marshall, *American Bastile* (Philadelphia, 1870).
Page
130 "There is no longer," Shuman to Seward, Aug. 9, 1861, Lincoln Papers.
130 For discussion of Greeley, see Hale.
131 "A certain Northern" and "our Southern papers," New York *Times*, Aug. 11, 1861.
131 "Fire, you traitor," New York *Times*, Aug. 11, 1861.
133 "Lynch them" and "Doom of Traitors," New York *Times*, Aug. 11, 1861. See also *Journal of Commerce*, Aug. 22, 1861.
133-134 Bangor Democrat incident, *Journal of Commerce*, Aug. 22, 1861; New York *Tribune*, Aug. 13, 1861.
134 Peace meeting at Old Saybrook, New York *Tribune*, Aug 19, 1861; *Journal of Commerce*, Aug. 22, 1861.
134 Meeting in Danbury, *Journal of Commerce*, Aug. 1, 1861.
135 Incident of Ambrose Kimball, New York *Times*, Aug. 22, 1861.
136 Easton mob, New York *Times*, August 24, 1861.
136-137 *Jeffersonian* incident, Abrams, p. 284.
137 Stark County *Democrat* incident, Marshall, p. 119.
137-139 Bridgeport *Farmer* incident, New York *Herald*, Aug. 25, 1861; New York *Times*, Aug. 28, 1861; New York *Tribune*, Aug. 25, 1861; *Journal of Commerce*, Aug. 22, 1861.
139-140 Peace meeting at Newton, New York *Tribune*, Aug. 31, 1861.

Page
140 "There can be no justification," New York *Herald*, Aug. 24, 1861.
140 "If these newspapers," New York *Times*, Aug. 28, 1861.

CHAPTER 14. The Policy of Repression

George Hull, "The Rights of the People," *American Law Review*, LIX 1925; George Nason, *Minute Men of '61* (Boston, 1910); Edward Mc-Pherson, *The Political History of the United States of America during the Great Rebellion* (Washington, 1882); Roy Abrams, "The Jeffersonian, A Copperhead Newspaper," *Bill of Rights Review*, II, 1942; Allan Pinkerton, *The Spy of the Rebellion* (New York, 1883); Richard Rowan, *The Pinkertons* (Boston, 1931).

Page
141 "The extension of the federal power," Hull, p. 807.
142 Uniforms of Sixth Massachusetts, Nason, p. 193.
143-144 Grand jury presentment, New York *Herald*, Aug. 17, 1861.
144 Blair excludes newspapers, McPherson, p. 188.
144-145 *Journal of Commerce* incident, *Journal of Commerce*, Sept. 5, 1861; New York *Tribune*, Aug. 29, 1861.
145 Quotations from *Daily News*, New York *Herald*, July 23, 1861.
145-146 *Daily News* incident, New York *Times*, Sept. 15, 1861; New York *Tribune*, Sept. 15, 1861.
146-147 *DayBook* incident, letter from Van Evrie to Lincoln, Jan. 23, 1862, Lincoln Papers.
147-149 McMasters incident, New York *Times*, Sept. 2, 1861; New York *Herald*, Sept. 18, 1861; *Official Record*, Ser. 2, II, 53; New York *Tribune*, Sept. 17, 1861; *Journal of Commerce*, Sept. 18, 1861.
148 *Courier des Etats-Unis* incident, New York *Times*, Sept. 3, 1861.
148-149 *National Zeitung* incident, New York *Times*, Sept. 3, 1861; New York *Tribune*, Sept. 9, 1861; *Official Record*, Ser. 2, II, 496.
149 "There is now," *Journal of Commerce*, Sept. 5, 1861.
149 Henry Reeves incident, New York *Tribune*, Sept. 4, 1861, Sept. 9, 1861; New York *Herald*, Oct. 6, 1861; *Official Record*, Ser. 2, II, 665, 670.
150-151 Flanders brothers, *Official Record*, Ser. 2, II, 66, 938.
151 Pierce Butler incident, New York *Herald*, Aug. 21, 1861; New York *Herald*, Sept. 25, 1861; *Official Record*, Ser. 2, II, 508.
151-152 Seizure of *Daily News*, New York *Times*, Aug. 23, 1861.
152 *Christian Observer* incident, New York *Tribune*, Aug. 24, 1861; Letter from Amasa Converse to his son, Aug. 23, 1861, Lincoln Papers.
152-153 *Jeffersonian* incident, Abrams, p. 287.
153 "Helped public confidence," New York *Tribune*, Aug. 30, 1861.

Page
153-154 Greenhow arrest, Pinkerton, p. 252; Rowan, p. 141.
154-155 Berrett incident, New York *Tribune*, Aug. 27, 1861.
155-156 Potter Committee hearings, New York *Tribune*, Jan. 28, 1862.

CHAPTER 15. Seward and Lincoln Control the North

George Brown, *Baltimore and the Nineteenth of April, 1861* (Baltimore, 1887); Lawrence Sangston, *Personal Journal of a Prisoner of State* (Baltimore, 1863); John Marshall, *American Bastile* (Philadelphia, 1870); Bruce Catton, *Mr. Lincoln's Army* (New York, 1951).

Page
158 Arrest of Faulkner, *Official Record*, Ser. 2, II, 463-484.
159 "My lord," Brown, p. 91.
160 "At a sugar-broker's office," New York *Tribune*, Aug. 27, 1861.
160 Mayor Wood, *Official Record*, Ser. 2, II, 1267-75.
161 Police order restricting information, New York *Herald*, Sept. 18, 1861.
161-163 Marcus Stanley arrest, *Official Record*, Ser. 2, II, 766-771; New York *Tribune*, Sept. 13, Sept. 23, 1861; New York *Herald*, Sept. 13, Sept. 23, 1861.
163-164 Thomas Serrill arrest, *Official Record*, Ser. 2, II, 480; New York *Times*, Sept. 12, 1861; New York *Tribune*, Aug. 18, Sept. 10, 1861.
164-166 Gwin and Benham arrests, *Official Record*, Ser. 2, II, 1010, 1011, 1020.
165-167 George L. Bowne arrest, *Official Record*, Ser. 2, II, 703-710.
167 "Hold your prisoners" and "Send him a re-enforcement," *Official Record*, Ser. 2, I, 640.
168 George Hubbell arrest, *Official Record*, Ser. 2, II, 60, 76.
168-169 "Letters de Cachet," New York *Tribune*, Sept. 26, 1861.
169 "Sunning himself," New York *Times*, Sept. 24, 1861.
169-170 Ellis Schnabel arrest, New York *Herald*, Aug. 31, 1861; Sangston, p. 56; *Official Record*, Ser. 2, II, 623.
170 Visit to Stralenberg, New York *Tribune*, Sept. 7, 1861; New York *Herald*, Sept. 7, 1861.
170-172 Wall incident, *Official Record*, Ser. 2, II, 772; Marshall, p. 143; *Journal of Commerce*, Feb. 6, 1862; New York *Times*, Sept. 12, 1861.
172-173 Bob Elliott arrest, *Official Record*, Ser. 2, II, 688; New York *Tribune*, Sept. 9, Sept. 15, 1861.
173-174 Cyrus Sargent case, *Official Record*, Ser. 2, II, 677; New York *Herald*, Sept. 7, 1861.
174-175 Guy Hopkins incident, *Official Record*, Ser. 2, II, 1249, 1250.
176 Senator Bright letter, New York *Tribune*, Aug. 21, 1861; New York *Tribune*, Feb. 6, 1862.

176-177 William Hill incident, *Official Record*, Ser. 2, II, 1321, 1322, 1332.
179 "Father Abraham," a phrase which appears in the soldier's songs later in the war. See Catton, 359.

CHAPTER 16. The Death of the Maryland Legislature

Morgan Dix, *Memoirs of John Adams Dix*, 2 Vols., (New York, 1883); George Brown, *Baltimore and the Nineteenth of April, 1861* (Baltimore, 1887); Frederick Seward, *Reminiscences of a War-Time Statesman and Diplomat—1830-1915* (New York, 1916); Carl Sandburg, *Abraham Lincoln, The War Years*, 4 Vols., (New York, 1939); Frank Howard, *Fourteen Months in American Bastiles* (Baltimore, 1863); Maryland General Assembly, *Report and Resolutions of the Joint Committee of the Senate and House of Delegates upon the Reports and Memorials of the Police Commissioners*, Document M, Aug. 5, 1861; Thomas Scharf, *The Chronicles of Baltimore* (Baltimore, 1874).

Page
181 Rumors of Beauregard advance, New York *Herald*, July 23, 1861.
181 "If anyone attempts," Dix, II, 21.
181 Dix unable to ride, Dix, II, 21.
182 Need for 10,000 troops, Brown, p. 100.
182 Story of columbiad, Brown, p. 100.
182 Prisoners through Baltimore, New York *Herald*, Aug. 24, 1861.
183 "Unless we have evidence," *Official Record*, Ser. 2, I, 589.
183 "Even when there is," *Official Record*, Ser. 2, I, 589.
183 Breckinridge incident, Baltimore *Clipper*, Aug. 9, 1861.
183 "By word or deed," *Official Record*, Ser. 2, I, 591.
183 "Kid glove," New York *Herald*, Sept. 13, 1861.
183 "An obscure editor," New York *Herald*, Sept. 13, 1861.
184 "After the act of secession," unsigned, undated note, included in August letters, Lincoln Papers.
185 "Real Rebel Design," New York *Times*, Aug. 18, 1861.
185 "Legislate the State," New York *Tribune*, July 31, 1861.
185-186 Wallis Resolutions, *Report and Resolutions of the Joint Committee*.
186 "So absurd that it," Brown, p. 103.
186 Seward takes Davis plan, Seward to Lincoln, undated note, Lincoln Papers, included in September 1861 letters.
186-187 Meeting in Rockville, Seward, p. 176.
188 Cameron to Banks, *Official Record*, Ser. 1, V, 193.
188 Cameron to Dix, *Official Record*, Ser. 2, I, 678.
189 "Arrest without an hour's delay," Scharf, p. 617.

Page
189 Arrest of Henry May, Baltimore *Sun*, Sept. 14, 1861; Baltimore *American*, Sept. 14, 1861.
189 Arrest of Ross Winans, Baltimore *American*, Sept. 14, 1861.
189-190 Arrest of Lawrence Sangston, Baltimore *American*, Sept. 14, 1861.
190 Arrest of Mayor Brown, Brown, p. 102.
190-191 John Brune incident, Baltimore *Sun*, Sept. 14, 1861; Scharf, pp. 617 (see penciled note in copy in Library of Congress), 629.
191 "Into anonymous night," Sandburg, I, 329.
191 Arrest of Frank Howard, Howard, p. 9; *Official Record*, Ser. 2, I, 688; Baltimore *Clipper*, Sept. 14, 1861.
192 "To make any arrest," *Official Record*, Ser. 2, II, 779.
192-193 "The most stupendous," Baltimore *Clipper*, Sept. 14, 1861.
193 "Has no connection," Maryland *Times*, Sept. 14, 1861.
193 "He can be depended upon," Seward, 176.
194 Banks dispatch to Ruger, *Official Record*, Ser. 2, I, 681.
195 "There being no quorum," Baltimore *American*, Sept. 19, 1861.
195-197 Frederick arrests, Baltimore *American*, Sept. 19, 1861; Baltimore *Sun*, Sept. 19, 1861; Baltimore *Clipper*, Sept. 19, 1861.
197 Banks dispatch to Washington, *Official Record*, Ser. 1, V, 194.
197 "Approved the action," Baltimore *Sun*, Sept. 19, 1861.
198 "In all cases the Government," Baltimore *American*, Sept. 21, 1861.
198 "Baseless and atrocious lie," Letter from Howard to the Editor of the Baltimore *American*, Sept. 22, 1861, Lincoln Papers.
198 "I have the honor," *Official Record*, Ser. 1, V, 194.

CHAPTER 17. The End of Free Elections

Richard Rowan, *The Pinkertons* (Boston, 1931); U.S. Congress, *Congressional Globe*, 38th Cong., 1st Sess.; George Brown, *Baltimore and the Nineteenth of April, 1861* (Baltimore, 1887).

Page
201 "All persons who have lately," *Official Record*, Ser. 2, I, 613.
201 "Fully approves your course," *Official Record*, Ser. 2, II, 47.
201 Dix investigation of arrest, *Official Record*, Ser. 2, I, 599.
201 "More annoyed by it," *Official Record*, Ser. 2, I, 613.
201-202 Timothy Webster incident, Rowan, 148; Baltimore *American*, Nov. 23, 1861; Baltimore *Sun*, Nov. 21, 1861.
203 "Just rights," *Official Record*, Ser. 2, II, 103.
203 "To protect the Union voters," *Official Record*, Ser. 2, I, 608.
203 "To convert the elective franchise," *Congressional Globe*, Appendix, p. 95.
203 Posters put up at election places, Baltimore *American*, Nov. 7, 1861.

Page

203-204 Arrests on election day, Baltimore *American,* Nov. 7, 1861; Baltimore *Sun,* Nov. 7, 1861.

204 Clinton James arrest, Baltimore *Sun,* Nov. 17, 1861.

204-205 McManus arrest, Baltimore *Sun,* Nov. 8, 1861; Baltimore *American,* Nov. 8, 1861.

205 August Sollers incident, *Official Record,* Ser. 2, I, 612.

205-206 "Spies and informers abounded," Brown, p. 94.

CHAPTER 18. Release of Maryland Prisoners

Page

207-208 Ross Winans case, *Official Record,* Ser. 2, XI, 687; Baltimore *Sun,* Sept. 25, 1861.

208 Henry May case, *Official Record,* Ser. 2, II, 800.

209 "Uneducated, very ignorant," *Official Record,* Ser. 2, I, 708.

209 "Moderate man in talents," *Official Record,* Ser. 2, I, 702.

210 "No sooner is the conspiracy," *Official Record,* Ser. 2, I, 645.

210 "Man of great amiability," *Official Record,* Ser. 2, I, 645.

210 "Mayor Brown was," *Official Record,* Ser. 2, I, 659.

211 "Neither the power," *Official Record,* Ser. 2, II, 115.

211 Brown's parole and return to Baltimore, Baltimore *Sun,* Jan. 13, 1861; Baltimore *Sun,* Dec. 1, 1862.

CHAPTER 19. A Hero Comes to Missouri

Robert Rombauer, *The Union Cause in St. Louis in 1861* (St. Louis, 1909); Allan Nevins, *Frémont, Pathmarker of the West* (New York, 1955); John Nicolay and John Hay, *Complete Works of Abraham Lincoln* (New York, 1894), John McElroy, *The Struggle for Missouri* (Washington, 1909).

Page

213-214 Governor Gamble, Rombauer, p. 291.

214-215 Frémont's life, see Nevins.

215 "Shuttered, sullen, and hostile," Nevins, p. 473.

215 "Sorely pressed for want," Frémont to Lincoln, July 30, 1861, Lincoln Papers.

215 Frémont's staff, McElroy, pp. 148, 218; Nevins, p. 476; Frankfort (Ky.) *Yeoman,* Nov. 8, 1861.

215 Lincoln note on Cairo, Nicolay and Hay, IV, 339.

217 Suppression of newspapers, St. Louis *Democrat,* Aug. 15, 1861; New York *Times,* Aug. 18, 1861.

217 Arrest of Brownlee, Missouri *Democrat,* Aug. 15, 1861; *Official Record,* Ser. 2, I, 128; New York *Herald,* Aug. 23, 1861.

Page
218 "The War Department has notified," Nicolay and Hay, VI, 344.
218 Arrests of teamsters, Missouri *Democrat*, Aug. 23, 1861.
218 Arrest of Speaker McAfee, *Official Record*, Ser. 2, I, 206-210.
219 Pope proclamation and levy on Palmyra, *Official Record*, Ser. 2, I, 195, 202, 206-13.
219 "Bring all the printing," *Official Record*, Ser. 2, I, 217.
220 Frémont proclamation, *Official Record*, Ser. 2, I, 221.

CHAPTER 20. Arrests in St. Louis

Thomas Scharf, *History of St. Louis City and County* (Philadelphia, 1883).

Page
222 Number of saloons, see Missouri *Democrat*, Sept. 4, 6, 7, 12, 1861.
222-223 "From and after this date," Scharf, p. 401.
223 "It is understood," Scharf, p. 403.
224 Exit permits, Scharf, p. 403.
224 Prison at Fifth and Myrtle, Missouri *Democrat*, Sept. 3, 1861; Scharf, p. 404.
224 McDonald incident, Missouri *Democrat*, Sept. 3, 1861; *Official Record*, Ser. 2, II, 251.
224-225 Negus arrest, Missouri *Democrat*, Sept. 7 and Sept. 9, 1861.
225 Clark incident, Missouri *Democrat*, Sept. 11 and Oct. 4, 1861; *Official Record*, Ser. 2, II, 250.
225 Hart incident, Missouri *Democrat*, Sept. 11 and Sept. 24, Dec. 7 and Dec. 11, 1861; *Official Record*, Ser. 2, II, 250.
225 Hudgins incident, Missouri *Democrat*, Sept. 24, 1861.
226 Churchill arrest, Missouri *Democrat*, Oct. 21, 1861; *Official Record*, Ser. 3, II, 250.
226 Wright arrest, Scharf, p. 1485; Missouri *Democrat*, Oct. 21, 1861; *Official Record*, Ser. 2, II, 252.
226-227 McAnally incident, New York *Herald*, Aug. 29, 1861; Missouri *Democrat*, Oct. 16, 1861; Scharf, p. 946.
227 Barry arrest, Missouri *Democrat*, Sept. 5, 1861.
221 Edwards arrest, Missouri *Democrat*, Sept. 7, Sept. 13, 1861; *Official Record*, Ser. 2, II, 250.
228 "No person shall be convicted," *U.S. Constitution*, Article III, Section 3.
228 Aubuchon case, *Official Record*, Ser. 2, I, 283; Missouri *Democrat*, Sept. 10, Sept. 18, 1861.
229 Hearst case, *Official Record*, Ser. 2, I, 285-291.
229 "Many of the prisoners," *Official Record*, Ser. 2, I, 282.
230 Ellis case, *Official Record*, Ser. 2, I, 276, 453-456.

CHAPTER 21. Frémont's Agony

John Nicolay and John Hay, *Complete Works of Abraham Lincoln* (New York, 1894); Allan Nevins, *Frémont, Pathmarker of the West* (New York, 1955); Robert Rombauer, *The Union Cause in St. Louis in 1861* (St. Louis, 1909); John McElroy, *The Struggle for Missouri* (Washington, 1909).

Page

232-233 "Oh, how badly," letter from John Hurd to Montgomery Blair, Aug. 4, 1861, Lincoln Papers.

233 "A blunder is worse," Broadhead to Lincoln, Sept. 3, 1861, Lincoln Papers.

233 "Losing the confidence," Nicolay and Hay, VI, 352.

233 Need to free slaves, Nevins, p. 501.

233-234 Freeing of Snead's slaves, Rombauer, p. 339; Missouri *Democrat*, Sept. 13, 1861; *Official Record*, Ser. 2, I, 769.

234 "It stirred and united," Nevins, p. 504.

234 "Condemned by a large," Speed to Lincoln, Sept. 2, 1861, Lincoln Papers.

234 "Producing the most disastrous," Anderson to Lincoln, Sept. 13, 1861, Lincoln Papers.

234 "There is not a day," Bullet, Ripley and Hughes to Speed and Lincoln, Sept. 13, 1861, Lincoln Papers.

234 "In a spirit," Nicolay and Hay, IV, 224.

234 "I have to ask," *Official Record*, Ser. 1, III, 477.

235 "Oh, for an hour" and "I have felt," Missouri *Democrat*, Oct. 5, 1861.

236 "Mrs. General Jessie," Louisville *Democrat*, Oct. 12, 1861.

236 Jessie's trip to Washington, Nevins, p. 517; Nicolay and Hay, IV, 415.

236 Arrest of Frank Blair, Frémont to Townsend, Sept. 16, 1861 and memo in Judge Advocate's Office, Sept. 27, 1861, Lincoln Papers.

237 Story of the lone rider, Broadhead to Montgomery Blair, Sept. 3, 1861, Lincoln Papers.

237-238 *Evening News* incident, New York *Times*, Sept. 27, 1861; Missouri *Democrat*, New York *Herald*, Sept. 28, 1861.

238 "I am taking," Frémont to Townsend, Sept. 23, 1861, Lincoln Papers.

238 "Don't remove him," Jordan to Lincoln, Oct. 4, 1861, Lincoln Papers.

238 "The removal of Gen. Frémont," Kirkwood to Lincoln, Oct. 9, 1861, Lincoln Papers.

238 "Let Frémont alone," Tracy to Lincoln, Oct. 29, 1861, Lincoln Papers.

Page

238 "Found a most deplorable," Trumbull to Lincoln, Oct. 1, 1861, Lincoln Papers.

238 "Incompetent" and "what excuse," Broadhead to Montgomery Blair, Sept. 30, 1861, Lincoln Papers.

238 Curtis comment, Cameron to Lincoln, Oct. 12, 1861, Lincoln Papers.

238 "Doubt the policy," Lamon to Lincoln, Oct. 26, 1861, Lincoln Papers.

239 "Committee directs me," Washburne to Lincoln, Oct. 21, 1861, Lincoln Papers.

239 "The disclosures of corruption," Washburne to Lincoln, Oct. 21, 1861, Lincoln Papers.

239-240 Account of frauds, undated account of St. Louis testimony, Lincoln Papers, Vol. 64, Item 13703.

240 Frémont charges against Blair, Missouri *Democrat*, Oct. 5, 1861.

240 Blair's charges against Frémont, Missouri *Democrat*, Oct. 9, 1861.

241 Cameron report on Frémont, Missouri *Democrat*, Nov. 4, 1861.

241 Frémont-Price agreement, *Official Record*, Ser. 2, I, 549.

241-242 Frémont's removal, McElroy, 231; Leonard Swett to Lincoln, Nov. 9, 1861, Lincoln Papers; Cincinnati *Enquirer* clipping datelined Nov. 12, 1861, included in Lincoln Papers.

CHAPTER 22. Halleck and the Secesh Levy

Thomas Scharf, *History of St. Louis City and County* (Philadelphia, 1883); Galusha Anderson, *The Story of a Border City during the Civil War* (Boston, 1908).

Page

244 Halleck requests martial law authority, *Official Record*, Ser. 2, I, 230.

244-245 "In all cases," *Official Record*, Ser. 2, I, 137.

245 Number of persons arrested, *Official Record*, Ser. 2, II, 250-252.

245 Arrests in St. Louis, *Official Record*, Ser. 2, II, 250; Missouri *Democrat*, Jan. 29, Feb. 21, 1862.

245-246 Arrest of two men distributing doggerel, Missouri *Democrat*, Dec. 4, 1861.

246-247 Oath-taking spree, Missouri *Democrat*, Dec. 9, 1861, Jan. 27, 1862.

246 "Any of the above," Missouri *Democrat*, Jan. 27, 1862.

246-247 Oath applied widely, Missouri *Democrat*, Feb. 4, 1862.

247 "One-half the men," *Official Record*, Ser. 2, I, 147.

248-249 "The suffering families," *Official Record*, Ser. 2, I, 150.

249 "Secesh levy," a phrase commonly applied, see Missouri *Democrat*, Jan. 23, 1862.

Page
249 "You are hereby notified," Missouri *Democrat*, Dec. 21, 1861.
249-250 Protest against levy, Scharf, p. 422.
250-251 Engler incident, Missouri *Democrat*, Jan. 24, 25, 27, 1862.
251 McPheeters incident, Scharf, p. 1527; Missouri *Democrat*, Jan. 24, Feb. 21, 1862.
251-252 Polk levy, Missouri *Democrat*, Jan. 29, Feb. 4, 1862.
253 Rebecca Sire, Scharf, p. 1251; Missouri *Democrat*, Jan. 29, Feb. 4, 1862.
253 Kennard incident, Scharf, p. 1305; Missouri *Democrat*, Jan. 23, 1862.
253-254 Clark incident, Missouri *Democrat*, Feb. 1, Feb. 19, 1862; *Official Record*, Ser. 2, II, 250; Scharf, p. 1326.
254 Auctions, Scharf, p. 427; Missouri *Democrat*, Feb. 4, Feb. 11, 1862.
254 "No further assessment," Missouri *Democrat*, Feb. 21, 1862.
255 Later use of levy, Anderson, p. 283.
255 "By word or deed," Missouri *Democrat*, Feb. 17, 1862.
255 "It's not safe," Missouri *Democrat*, Feb. 22, 1862.

CHAPTER 23. Kentucky Joins the North

Thomas Speed, *The Union Cause in Kentucky* (New York, 1907); Edward Smith, *The Borderland and the Civil War* (New York, 1927); Robert Johnson and Clarence Buel, ed., *Battles and Leaders of the Civil War* (New York, 1884).

Page
257 "They cracked their parched," New York *Tribune*, July 28, 1861.
257 Shooting incident, New York *Tribune*, July 23, 1861; New York *Times*, July 29, 1861.
257 Buckner joins Confederacy, Frankfort *Yeoman*, July 23, 1861.
258 Union election victory, Speed, p. 90.
258 Camp Dick Robinson, Speed, p. 178.
258-259 Guns sent to Lexington, Speed, pp. 116, 120; *Henderson Reporter*, Aug. 29, 1861; Frankfort *Yeoman*, Aug. 30, 1861; New York *Herald*, Aug. 18, 1861.
260 "Drays, black drivers," Louisville *Democrat*, Sept. 1, 1861.
260 "Might as well," New York *Tribune*, Sept. 10, 1861.
260 Condition of Kentucky after war, Smith, p. 366.
261 Magoffin's message to legislature, Louisville *Democrat*, Sept. 6, 1861.
262 "Take Paducah," Louisville *Democrat*, Oct. 10, 1861.
262 "Planted its guns," Henderson *Reporter*, Sept. 12, 1861.
262 Buckner advance, Johnson and Buel, I, 379.
262-263 Panic in Louisville, Anderson to Lincoln, Sept. 18, Sept. 21, 1861, Lincoln Papers; Louisville *Democrat*, Sept. 18, 19, 20, 1861.
263-264 Events in Louisville for several days, Louisville *Democrat*, Sept. 26, 1861, New York *Times*, Sept. 27, 1861.

Page
263-264 "Let us trust," New York *Times*, Sept. 27, 1861.
264 "The invaders must" and "War Resolutions," Louisville *Democrat*, Sept. 19, 1861.
264 "The war is in our state," Louisville *Democrat*, Oct. 1, 1861.

CHAPTER 24. Coercion in Kentucky

Thomas Speed, *The Union Cause in Kentucky* (New York, 1907).
Page
265 Volunteers to Union and Confederate armies, Speed, p. 139.
265-271 Morehead, Durrett and Barr arrests and releases, *Official Record*, Ser. 2, II, 288, 805-829; Frankfort *Yeoman*, June 6, 1861; New York *Tribune*, July 16, 1861.
271-272 Clay arrest, *Official Record*, Ser. 2, II, 884-5; Speed, p. 73.
272-273 Grubbs arrest, *Official Record*, Ser. 2, II, 892.
273 "Their rearrest," *Official Record*, Ser. 2, II, 886.
273 "Has little intelligence," etc., *Official Record*, Ser. 2, II, 984.
274 Stanton arrest, *Journal of Commerce*, Oct. 10, 1861; *Official Record*, Ser. 2, II, 913-933.
274 Six others arrested, Frankfort *Yeoman*, Oct. 11, 1861.
274 "Does not meet," *Official Record*, Ser. 2, II, 920.
275 "Might as well save," Louisville *Democrat*, Oct. 23, 1861.
275 "Go security," Louisville *Democrat*, Oct. 8, 1861.
276 "The South will never," Henderson *Reporter*, Sept. 12, 1861.
276 "The Nurses' Revenge," Henderson *Reporter*, Feb. 8, 1862.
277 Cynthiana *News*' editor arrested, Louisville *Democrat*, Oct. 2, 1861.
277-278 Haldeman and Louisville *Courier*, *Official Record*, Ser. 2, II, 70; Henderson *Reporter*, Sept. 19, 1861; Louisville *Democrat*, Sept. 20, Oct. 31, 1861.
278 "Only because I was," New York *Tribune*, Oct. 4, 1861.
278 Arrests in Kentucky, Louisville *Democrat*, Oct. 7, 1861; New York *Times*, Oct. 16, 1861.
279 "This is an economical," Frankfort *Yeoman*, Nov. 15, 1861.
279 "Have substituted for," Speed, p. 204.

CHAPTER 25. Fort Lafayette

Frank Howard, *Fourteen Months in American Bastiles* (Baltimore, 1863); John Brewer, *Prison Life* (no city or state of publication given); William Gilchrist, *Two Months in Fort Lafayette* (New York, 1862); Lawrence Sangston, *Personal Journal of a Prisoner of State* (Baltimore, 1863); George Brown, *Baltimore and the Nineteenth of April, 1861* (Baltimore, 1887).

Page
281 "A gloomier place," Howard, p. 17.
281-282 "Some discolored beverage," Brewer, p. 9.
282 "From actual experiments," Frankfort *Yeoman*, Nov. 1, 1861.
282 "Tea or coffee," Gilchrist, p. 18.
282 "From one-quarter," Sangston, p. 39.
283 "Respectable men," Louisville *Democrat*, Oct. 9, 1861.
283 "These are purely," Louisville *Democrat*, Oct. 9, 1861.
283 "Even to the idiot," Sangston, p. 27.
284 "Another arrival today," Sangston, p. 27.
284 "See the Maryland legislature," Louisville *Democrat*, Oct. 9, 1861.
285 "The most villainous," Sangston, p. 36.
285 "Played cards," Sangston, p. 32.
285 "We did not want," Sangston, p. 52.
285 "During the evening," and "about daylight," Sangston, p. 54.
286 "As he is a perfect," *Official Record*, Ser. 2, II, 845.
286 "A consummate rascal," *Official Record*, Ser. 2, II, 846.
286 Haig in Mt. Hope, Brewer, p. 16.
286 Lowber incident, Baltimore *Sun*, Oct. 29, 1861.
286-287 Bacon story, Baltimore *American*, Nov. 30, 1861.
287 Petition to President Lincoln, *Official Record*, Ser. 2, II, 249.
287 Col. Dimick visit to Baltimore, Brown, p. 111.
288 "A fine looking," "a quiet, tidy," and "does not hesitate," Boston *Traveler*, Nov. 5, 1861.
288 "Nearly all take," Missouri *Democrat*, Nov. 14, 1861.
288 "Mr. Wallis would deliver," Baltimore *American*, Dec. 27, 1861.
288 "Roast turkies," "our mess," and "calico comports," Sangston, pp. 78, 96, 82.
289 "A stranger might," and "they were too," Sangston, pp. 94, 113.
289 "Pretty much as," Sangston, p. 120.
289-290 "About 50 of the prisoners," Sangston, p. 120.

CHAPTER 26. Optimism and the General Amnesty

Fletcher Pratt, *Stanton, Lincoln's Secretary of War* (New York, 1953); Gideon Welles, *The Diary of Gideon Welles* (Boston, 1911).
Page
292-293 "There is hardly" and "King of Steubenville," Pratt, p. 24.
293 "Where did that" and "If that giraffe," Pratt, p. 62.
293 "Painful imbecility," Pratt, p. 126.
294 "Were in perfect agreement," Pratt, p. 130.
294 "Stanton the Divine," Welles, I, 68.
294 "Almost universal satisfaction," New York *Herald*, Jan. 14, 1862.
294 "The Secesh call him," Louisville *Democrat*, Jan. 25, 1862.

Page

294 "Has given the best," Wood to Lincoln, Jan. 15, 1862, Lincoln Papers.

294-295 Stanton's business methods, Pratt, p. 142.

295 "Fort Henry is ours," Halleck to McClellan, Feb. 7, 1861, Lincoln Papers.

295 Joy over Fort Donelson, New York *Herald*, Feb. 18, 1862.

296 "The marvelous change," New York *Tribune*, Feb. 18, 1862.

296 "The other day all was," New York *Tribune*, Feb. 18, 1862.

296 Stanton's reply, New York *Tribune*, Feb. 20, 1862.

296-297 Feeling that war would end in April, New York *Tribune*, Feb. 5, 1862; New York *Journal of Commerce*, Feb. 13, 1862; Everett to Seward, Feb. 18, 1862, Lincoln Papers.

297-298 Executive Order No. 1, *Official Record*, Ser. 2, II, 221.

298 "That the reign of lawless," New York *Tribune*, Feb. 17, 1862.

298 "Neither the Secretary," New York *Herald*, Feb. 19, 1862.

CHAPTER 27. Lincoln the Humanitarian

James Randall, *Constitutional Problems Under Lincoln* (New York, 1926); John Nicolay and John Hay, *Complete Works of Abraham Lincoln* (New York, 1894); S. G. Fisher, "Suspension of the Writ of Habeas Corpus During the War of the Rebellion," *Political Science Quarterly*, III, 1888.

Page

299 "Words, oral, written," *Charge to the Grand Jury—Treason*, 30 Fed. Case 1035.

299 "In the midst of," Randall, p. 83.

301 "Unless the necessity," Nicolay and Hay, IV, 372.

301 Question of Maryland Legislature, Lincoln to Scott, April 25, 1861, Lincoln Papers.

301 "Mitigated so far," *Official Record*, Ser. 2, I, 276.

301 "Supply decent lodgings," *Official Record*, Ser. 2, I, 677.

301 "They might go," *Official Record*, Ser. 2, II, 1020.

301 "Permit me to lay," Wall to Lincoln, undated included in August 10, 1861 letters, Lincoln Papers.

301 "Mr. Lincoln doesn't believe," New York *Times*, Oct. 30, 1861.

301 "Lincoln used this power," Fisher, p. 457.

302-303 *Ex parte Milligan*, 71 U.S. 2.

INDEX

NOTES

AT THE BEGINNING of the notes on each chapter I have included full citations of books and articles referenced in that chapter. In order to avoid constant footnotes throughout the book, these notes include, in addition to the page, a short statement of the general subject or the first few words of the quotation prior to giving the citation.

There are three sources which affect a number of chapters and are therefore not included separately under the general list of references for each chapter. They are specifically identified wherever they are quoted or referenced, of course. These three are:

1. The newspapers of the day.
2. U.S. *War of the Rebellion: Official Records of the Union and Confederate Armies*. Most of the material is included in Series 2, Vol. I and II. This is cited as *Official Record* throughout.
3. The Lincoln Papers in the Library of Congress.

CHAPTER 1. Insurrection in Baltimore

George Brown, *Baltimore and the Nineteenth of April, 1861* (Baltimore, 1887); George Radcliffe, "Governor Thomas H. Hicks of Maryland and the Civil War," *Johns Hopkins University Studies in Historical and Political Science* (Baltimore, 1902); George Nason, *Minute Men of '61* (Boston, 1910).

Page

2 "Damn black Republicans," Baltimore *Sun*, Sept. 6, 1861.
5 Mayor Brown incident, Brown, p. 50.
6 "Week of terror," this phrase was used frequently. See Baltimore *American*, Aug. 9, 1861; Baltimore *Clipper*, Aug. 23, 1861.
7 Marshal Kane's "reputation," Baltimore *Sun*, Sept. 7, 1861.
9-10 Wallis speech, Baltimore *Sun*, April 20, 1861.
10-11 Governor Hicks' speech, Baltimore *Sun*, April 20, 1861.
11 Brown telegram to Lincoln, *Official Record*, Ser. 2, I, 564.